CONFESSIONS
OF A
GUIDE DOG

The Blonde Leading the Blind

CONFESSIONS
OF A
GUIDE DOG

The Blonde Leading the Blind

To Michelle—

MARK CARLSON AND MUSKET

iUniverse, Inc.
Bloomington

Confessions of a Guide Dog
The Blonde Leading the Blind

iUniverse books may be ordered through booksellers or by contacting:

iUniverse
1663 Liberty Drive
Bloomington, IN 47403
www.iuniverse.com
1-800-Authors (1-800-288-4677)

ISBN: 978-1-4620-5811-2 (sc)
ISBN: 978-1-4620-5813-6 (hc)
ISBN: 978-1-4620-5812-9 (ebk)

Printed in the United States of America

iUniverse rev. date: 11/09/2011

DEDICATION

This book is dedicated to the people who breed, raise and train assistance animals to work with persons with disabilities. Their work and selflessness have given thousands of people more freedom, confidence and respect. With these wonderful animal partners they are able to grow and succeed beyond their limitations.
To these people and those who give donations to assure this noble work is carried on the author wishes to convey his eternal gratitude.

And most of all

To my mother, Margit Ingeborg Carlson 1921 – 2011
who encouraged my dreams and gave me a love of history, reading and learning.

And to my father, Eric Roland Carlson 1917 – 1995
My role model, my friend and teacher, who always wanted to write a book but never got around to it. This is his book too.

And most of all, to my loving and supportive wife Jane, who saw the eagle in me long before he grew wings and learned to fly.

And last, but not least, to Musket
The single most wonderful thing to come into our lives.

ACKNOWLGEMENTS

This book would not have been possible without the support, assistance and efforts of many people whom have given freely of their time and encouragement. To all who provided ideas, stories, anecdotes, suggestions and critique, we are most grateful. Special thanks to Virginia and Dan Vogel, Katerina Petersson, Virginia Piper, Ruthie Dean, Keith Tomlinson, Dina Dimaggio, Sharon McCabe, David Carlson, the staff at the Braille Institute, Beverly Warner, Dr. Joan Esnayra, all our friends at the San Diego Air and Space Museum, Karen Gamble and the other wonderful people at the California Department of Rehabilitation, Laura Bretton, Jack Doxey, Wayne Holley, Susan Waynelovich, Lila Defensor, Air Group One of the CAF, Dr. Elizabeth Gray, Melissa Toh, Menaya Bradley, and the rest of thc staff at Carmel Mountain Veterinary Hospital, Nancy Martin-, Liz Chase, editor of Bark Magazine, Ross Davis, Barbara Woodbury, Rear Admiral James D. 'Jig Dog' Ramage, USN (Ret), Captain W.S. 'Griff' Griffin, USN (Ret), Lt. Ed Davidson, USAAF (Ret), astronauts Gene Cernan, Neil Armstrong and Alan Bean, Judy Horning, Susan Meissner, Sandra Bishop, B.J. Taylor, and the hundreds of Musketmaniacs and friends we love and cherish.

And to Linda Stull, who truly believed in this book, its author and 'the sweetest dog in the world.' Linda took many of the photos and added to the content and spirit in many ways. We offer her our sincere thanks.

CONTENTS

INTRODUCTION - By Musket and Mark xi

PROLOGUE - Dog Day Afternoon xxi

CHAPTER ONE - Up Denial Without a Paddle 1

CHAPTER TWO - Musket 18

CHAPTER THREE - The Three Musketeers 42

CHAPTER FOUR - Marching with my Musket 65

CHAPTER FIVE - Blind/Low Vision Mobility Specialist 76

CHAPTER SIX - Adoggable 100

CHAPTER SEVEN - No Dogs Allowed... Wanna Bet? 120

CHAPTER EIGHT - A Dog's Life 159

CHAPTER NINE - Flying the Furry Skies 192

CHAPTER TEN - My Furry Co-pilot 226

CHAPTER ELEVEN - Musketmaniacs 247

CHAPTER TWELVE - Where is she going with that thermometer? 267

CHAPTER THIRTEEN - The 401K-9 Plan 287

Introduction

BY MUSKET

First of all, I'm not sure I agree with the title. To call it 'Confessions of a Guide Dog' seems to imply I have something to confess.

Well I don't. It's not that kind of book. I'm not going to air all my dirty laundry or expose any skeletons in the closet. Well . . . I will confess how food-driven I really am. I love food!

I love my mommy and daddy, but if there's a treat anywhere in the vicinity, I can't focus on anything else. My attention is totally aimed at the treat and nothing on earth but Daddy's stern command can deter me. It's like the Postal Service Motto.

'Neither pulling on my leash nor calling me nor pretending you have nothing in your hand will stay this beggar from the swift consumption of his intended morsel.'

How's that for a confession?

But what actually triggered a book about Musket? Sorry bad pun. Get used to them, Daddy does it a lot. It all came about because everywhere I went with Daddy and Mommy, amazing things happened. We met lots of people, travelled all over the country, had adventures and made a difference in the lives of men, women and children everywhere. I don't know why or how. I'm really just a Guide dog, trained to take care of my handler and keep him safe. I'm no different than any of the other hundreds of thousands of Guide and Assistance animals all over the world.

But darn it, incredible things happened, and as the years went on, Daddy began to realize they were pretty unique. Even other seasoned Guide dog handlers commented on me and how amazing I was.

Daddy started thinking to himself a lot and that got both me and Mommy worried. He's not only blind but a guy, and a thinking guy is a bad combination. Want proof? Remember those stupid hats with hands that clapped? Or putting a fake Rolls-Royce hood ornament on a VW Beetle? Or the T-shirts that looked like a tuxedo? All guy ideas.

Then one day he said, "I think I should write a book about Musket."

It could have been a lot worse. Daddy once thought of getting a black Labrador, painting white spots on it and saying he was a 'negative Dalmatian.' Oy.

First he thought of silly titles like 'Pooch Tales' and 'Zen and the Art of Begging.' Then he came up with 'Confessions of a Guide Dog.' Everybody thought it was great.

It should be called 'The Remarkable and Amazing Life Experiences of the Most Wonderful, Lovable, Cute, Adorable, Intelligent, Loyal, Sweet, Perfect and Humble Guide Dog in the World.'

I suggested that one to Daddy. He didn't stop laughing for a week. He said it wouldn't fit on the cover.

Okay cut out 'Humble.'

Well anyway, 'Confessions of a Guide Dog' it is. Then I suggested a subtitle, 'The Blonde Leading the Blind.' He liked that.

Daddy knew no one would buy a book just by him. But with my name on the cover it'd be a bestseller. Daddy's a pretty good writer and what better subject than me?

He narrates what happens to us, and I add my comments. Sometimes they're sort of confessions, others are clarification, and sometimes they're 'spin control.'

I'm supposed to be the 'co-author' but he's really the one who did all the writing. Not that I didn't try.

Remember those 1950s Disney films of cute and lovable animals (seals, monkeys, dogs, cats, wombats) getting into trouble and causing total mayhem while catching the crooks?

I didn't catch any crooks but boy did I cause mayhem.

I actually got up on the chair in his garage office one night when he went into the kitchen for a snack, and planted my front paws on the keyboard. And I accidentally deleted about a week's work. When he came out I was back on my bed looking innocent. Well it didn't matter. He's blind, remember? He immediately freaked out. After a minute of hysteria he turned to me. "Musket," he asked me in a fake syrupy voice, "any idea who erased two whole chapters?"

Busted.

"Seems like a certain Guide dog might need a trip back to school for some re-training," he said with a dark gleam in his eyes.

I know he was kidding.

I'm sure he was. I think.

Now I'm coming clean and going to tell the truth, the whole truth and nothing but the . . . um, maybe that's too much. I once heard Mark Twain said, 'Truth is a very valuable thing. I think we should be a little economical with it.' Makes sense to me.

I'll tell the truth.

When it suits me.

When it doesn't you'll have to just take my word for it. After all, I'm so cute.

Have fun reading our book. I think it's pretty good.

Love, Musket

The Tale Wagging the Dog

BY MARK CARLSON

My little buddy musket. This book is a love story with far more than the usual two players. Musket is loved by people all over the country.

Me, well not quite that many. I'm hardly even noticed when he's around.

Nevertheless the remarkable events in this book couldn't have happened without me. In order for Musket to touch the lives of hundreds of people, to make them laugh and smile, I had to go blind.

That's all. Of course I never planned it that way, but sometimes things just have a way of working out.

Musket is a male yellow Labrador Retriever. People have said he is very beautiful with an absolutely irresistible face. His eyes are a deep chocolate brown; he has soft fur the color of vanilla ice cream with velvety caramel ears. He looks delicious. He has been my Guide Dog for over nine years. And in that time a lot of incredible things have happened. The people we've met and places we've traveled, the lives we've touched are a story we wanted to tell.

We wrote this book together. I did the typing, but he was looking over my shoulder, inserting his comments, feelings, rebuttals and sneaking treats off the desk. He really believed I didn't know he was doing it.

"Dang. I was so quiet, too."

It'll help the reader to know Musket's 'voice.' I think he sounds like Art Carney's Ed Norton from the *Honeymooners*. "Hey, Ralphie boy."

"Groan. How embarrassing."

Kermit the Frog?

"A muppet isn't an improvement."

Okay, one of our friends said she thought Musket sounded like David Niven, sort of debonair with a hint of an English accent.

"Ah, jolly good. That's much better. Let's carry on, shall we?"

Getting back to reality, as of this writing Musket is eleven years old. Late middle age in dog years.

Physically he's not a puppy anymore. But in spirit, Musket is as youthful as any puppy you might see scampering sideways with his tail wagging, wanting attention.

As for my age I'm just barely past my forties and that's as much as I'll admit.

"'Reality' he calls it. *My* age he blabs all over but he can be Jack Benny."

Musket and I live, work and travel together. We're a team. A dynamic duo. A daddy and his boy. Damon and Pythias. Abbott and Costello.

"Damon and who? At least he didn't say we were Beavis and Butthead.

He should have said the Skipper and Gilligan. He calls me his little buddy."

Yeah. After all, the Skipper was the boss.

🐕 "Wait a second. I'm the brains of the outfit. He picks up my poop. That's all the proof you need.

Forget the Skipper and Gilligan. How about Mr. Peabody and Sherman? The dog was the smart one, remember?"

Humility isn't one of Musket's strong points. We'll leave it to the reader to decide.

Lord Musket's Coat of Arms

🐕 "We're going to tell our story, beginning with when we first met at Guide Dogs for the Blind. Then Daddy will back up to his early life, 1960-2002 B.M. (Before Me). It must have been boring.

Then I'll come in and save the day. So just hang in there."

I should add Musket, as the reader might already have guessed, is not a typical Guide dog. He's good at his job but his relationship with family, friends and the people he meets every day are definitely not typical, or even common for Guide dogs.

He's very food-driven and has a fetish for belly rubs. We all indulge him beyond what might be normal because our love for him is more than enough reason.

"Yep. That works for me."

This book is meant to make the reader laugh and cry, shake their head at the absurdities and smile at the victories. The one thing we don't want it to be is preachy. I may occasionally step onto the soapbox for a second or two, but only to illustrate a point.

"Yeah like they'll believe that."

We hope it will inform, enlighten, and above all, be enjoyable.

Let's get to the heart of the matter.

What's it like to be blind? Some people want to ask, but are too polite or worried I'll be offended.

But it's no big deal. I don't mind talking about it. If I did, this book would never have been written.

I'm more sensitive about my bald spot, which my darling wife Jane takes great pleasure in describing to me, than I am about my lack of sight.

It's part of who I am, like being tall or artistic or hating peanut butter.

"I love peanut butter! Oh, sorry. I was supposed to be letting Daddy talk."

Blindness can be from birth, caused by sickness or injury or age.

In my case it's a hereditary disorder known as Retinitis Pigmentosa, or RP. It causes a clouding over of the retina at the back of the eyeball, and closes off my ability to see clearly, resulting in tunnel vision, night blindness, loss of contrast and color perception. I'm legally blind, not total. Total is no sight at all.

Bluntly put, my sight is lousy. I can see shapes, movement, light and dark. I could face a person and see their silhouette but not be able to discern details.

At night it's totally black to me.

But that's not all. For the price of the RP I was also given another disability. Yes, you heard me right. Two for the price of one. The type of RP I had was called Usher's Syndrome II which affected my hearing, so I wear two hearing aids.

If you really want to split hairs, I have one more disability, a sort of bonus. I'm a guy.

That's a lot harder to deal with than the first two.

Some people tell me I don't 'look blind.' I always smile at that. I probably don't sound deaf either.

Let's get one thing cleared up, that being the issue of Political Correctness.

I don't care what someone calls me. Blind, visually impaired, hearing impaired, hard of hearing, or whatever. It's not important. The only reason I use the term 'visually impaired' is because that is the currently acceptable term. For this week, at any rate. PC has gotten way out of hand.

🐕 "Yeah, I'm a dog, not a Canine American. And Daddy's going bald, he's not follically challenged. And he's—"

I think they got the point, Musket.

Being blind has some drawbacks most people might never imagine.

Managing in public, shopping, doing errands or working are simple if handled properly.

The most annoying thing about being blind is misplacing something and not being able to find it.

And God knows I can't drop a small object and have it land by my feet.

No. It has to end up under a boulder.

Beneath 50 feet of water. Guarded by rabid alligators and personal injury lawyers.

In the next county.

I try not to move fast or reach for something quickly, because I know darned well something delicate and expensive will be in the way and I'll knock it on the floor.

In my own house I'm constantly bumping my shoulders into walls and doorways. That's because my shoulders are wider than my visual field.

I use my other senses a lot, particularly touch. Identifying objects by feel is learned, not instinctive. Putting away the dishes is easy, but getting my CDs in order is nearly impossible.

Sight, hearing, touch, taste, smell. Those are the usual suspects of sense. But above all the most important sense to have is humor.

Gotta have it to survive in the world today, especially if you have a disability.

This is our story.

"And we're sticking to it."

Let's get started. Musket, will you do the honors?

"Sherman, set the Wayback Machine to April 2002, in San Rafael California. That's where it really began."

Sure, Mr. Peabody. Wow, that is one smart dog.

Prologue

DOG DAY AFTERNOON

It was a warm, sunny morning, just after 10:00 on Wednesday April 24, 2002 in the common room of the dormitory of Guide Dogs for the Blind. The scent of blooming azaleas wafted in from the patio.

Inside, the room held a few couches and overstuffed chairs. The sixteen first-time students waited, white canes clutched in tense fingers.

Every one displayed the same emotions: Excitement. Anxiety. Panic. I'm sure it was written on my face, though I tried to be nonchalant. I thought only about the dog I would be meeting in a few hours. 'My Dog.' Would it be a male or female, would it be a black or yellow Labrador? Or a Golden retriever?

The senior instructor came into the room and said, "You'll be meeting the dogs this afternoon."

'The Dogs.' Note the capitals.

The idea of 'The Dogs' was almost mystical, even sacred. It was like knowing a group of VIPs were coming to visit. Not celebrities like rock or movie stars, but war heroes or astronauts, who'd done something great and noble.

He continued. "Right now we're putting a sheepskin mat, a tie-down, leash, harness, and bowls in your rooms. The harness will already be fitted for your dog."

Wow. I was becoming even more tense.

"Each of you will be taken to a room where you'll get to meet your dog and sit with it. Bring only the leash. After you're feeling comfortable, take your dog to your room and sit down with it. Let it get used to you. Tell it to lie down on the mat. The command is 'Go to bed.'"

I was trying to absorb this. It was like being a newbie in an advanced computer programming class.

"Don't worry if you don't bond with the dog right away," he said gently. "It can take months for a good bond to develop. But it will happen. Now I'll tell each of you what you're going to get."

There was a small fly in the ointment. Both my hearing aids were giving me trouble. One was in for repair and the other unreliable. I would have to manage with limited hearing until the repaired one arrived by mail. I had to listen very carefully to hear every word.

He turned to me. I was like a kid waiting for Santa Claus.

"Mark, you'll be receiving a male Yellow Labrador named Mutthead." Some words were garbled in the translation.

I almost choked. "Mutthead?"

He laughed, knowing I was having trouble hearing. "No, *Musket*."

In that incredible moment I was in love, even though I hadn't met him. Musket! What a name! I couldn't believe it. Musket. It was as if the dog Gods had chosen it just for me. When I still had some sight I had been a Civil War re-enactor. It was a heaven-sent name.

For the first time that day I smiled from ear to ear, half-deaf or not.

The instructor told my roommate Andy he was getting a female Golden named Loran. That was a cool name for a Guide dog. Loran is a navigation system.

Jennifer, another student, learned she was going to have a female Golden named Floria.

And so it went until we all had been told. We went to our rooms to wait.

On the floor next to my bed were a three-foot square sheepskin mat and a tie-down cable. The dogs were to be tethered to the wall bolt at night. This wasn't meant to be cruel. It helped the dog establish his space, his safe zone. He learned to know where to go when entering the room.

The clock ticked away each second in a slow, relentless cadence like Chinese water torture.

I know it was digital. But I swear I felt every blink of the LEDs.

I called Jane to tell her what I'd learned.

"I don't care for the name," she told me. "But he's going to be your dog."

Just after lunch a knock at my door made me jump. It was Ben, another of the instructors. "Ready?" he asked.

I leapt to my feet. "Oh yeah." All down the hall, which felt like the Last Mile, I was a genuine chatterbox. "What's he like? Do you think he'll like me? What if it doesn't work out?"

Ben was chuckling. He'd heard it all before. "Just relax, Mark. We know what we're doing."

We arrived in the common room, and I sat on a large couch, wringing the leash as if it were saturated with water. But it was just my sweaty palms.

Ben came back. "Here's Musket."

He was excited, wagging his heavy tail and panting. He came close and I touched Musket for the first time. His fur was as soft as velvet. I had tears in my eyes. He sniffed my hand and looked right at me. And then . . .

He turned away. Then he started sniffing around, totally absorbed in the scents of the room.

Musket acted as though he couldn't have cared less if I was there.

Ben, seeing my look of panic said, "Give him time. He doesn't know you yet. Take him to your room and sit down on the floor with him."

I clipped the leash to Musket's collar ring and we stood. "Okay little buddy," I said, my voice trembling with emotion. "Let's go."

Using my cane we walked down the hall to my room. Musket still showed excitement, but not directed at me. He was probably just happy to be out of the kennel.

Sitting on the floor by my bed I was distracted by the sound of Andy playing with Loran. They'd hit it off right away. I was worried. I expected fireworks, love at first sight. Something. But Musket just sat there, looking around. Maybe it wasn't meant to be. I sank into despair.

Then someone down the hall yelled "Dinner!" An amazing thing happened.

I had the leash wrapped around my wrist. In the blink of an eye Musket jumped *over* the bed, pulling me off my butt and halfway onto the floor on the other side.

I suddenly realized he was one strong, motivated and food-driven pooch.

He looked back at me as if wondering why I wasn't following him. I grinned, knowing then it was going to be okay.

I commanded him, 'No! Stay.' My wrist was sore. Small wonder. He'd almost broken it.

Musket, hearing the firm tone in my voice, obeyed. I put his harness on.

I then realized life with him wasn't going to be boring.

"Okay now I'll tell my side of the story. I was born along with three other puppies in the breeding kennels at Guide Dogs for the Blind on August 27, 2000. My parents were Mitch and Iris. Mom was great, Plenty of nipples for all of us. But even then I was the greedy one.

Mom had to cut me off because I was always at her. Some things never change. I was named by the breeders at the school. All the puppies born in a particular month were given names with the same first letter. I have a sister named Miami. I don't know why they chose 'Musket' but I think it was a cool name. When I was a few weeks old they decided I would be best as a working dog, not breeding stock so they . . . wow, I can't even talk about it without shuddering. Well, they neutered me. Never asked me what I thought about it, just 'snip snip' and that was it. 'Sorry pup, your future doesn't include humping other dogs. Maybe in your next life.' Birth control in one easy lesson.

Then I was given to Mommy Carrie, a nice lady from Sacramento who raised me. She took me everywhere with her, taught me basic obedience, and helped me become acclimated to lots of different public environments. She took me on buses, trains, into stores, restaurants, offices and everywhere. I'll tell you more about her later.

Musket while he was with Carrie. She too had a sense of humor

When I was about nine months old, she brought me back to Guide Dogs where I was tested and given a very thorough medical exam. I was deemed in good shape so I started guide work training. The instructors taught me to work with the harness, learn the commands, to steer my handler around obstacles and keep him safe. After I completed the training I was tested. Of course I passed with flying colors, then back to the kennels. Months went by waiting to be given to a student. Soon many of my kennel mates had gone away. They all got new mommies or daddies. I was wondering what was wrong with me. Wasn't I a good guide? Didn't I ace the test? Wasn't I cute enough? Who was going to take me home? Every meal I ate was the same, and it all tasted bland. Maybe I was destined to stay there forever and sleep on concrete.

One day a trainer took me into the dormitory. There I met this man.

He wasn't any different from anybody else I'd met in the last year. He was just another face, another human smell. They all smell different. Sometimes the scent is sharp, especially if they're excited. And this man smelled that way. He was nice and rubbed me behind my ear. But I didn't know who he was. I was waiting for someone to come and take me back to the kennels and the cold concrete. Just another day at Guide Dogs.

We went to dinner together, but again I thought it was another part of the training. I guess I shouldn't have jumped over the bed, but he didn't seem to be mad, just amused. He called me 'little buddy' and played with me, which was nice.

The hours passed and no one came to take me back.

Later that afternoon he filled a bowl with food and put it in front of me. Then the light went on in my head. That was my bowl. Mine.

This was him. This was my new daddy! I had a daddy and I was going to have a home. I ate my food and it tasted wonderful. That night I slept on a warm soft mat next to my daddy for the first time. My new life had begun.

Chapter One

UP DENIAL WITHOUT A PADDLE

Well here's the part Musket warned about. My short autobiography.

Well, relatively short. It's not *War and Peace*. But it will help the reader to learn a bit about my life.

Ahem.

I was born in a log cabin . . . no, I'd better play it straight. Sorry.

My parents, Margit and Eric Carlson, were typical white, middle-class Protestant Democrats. Can't get any more bland than that. No wonder I like vanilla ice cream.

Dad was born in Jamestown New York in 1917, attending Tri-State College for his degree in electrical engineering. He also had RP, and his sight kept him out of the military, so during the Second World War he joined the Civilian Conservation Corps, building roads and bridges.

Mom was born in Sweden in 1921 and came to the U.S. in 1947.

They married in 1949. My older brother David was born in 1952 and I came along eight years later.

Dad, an engineer at GTE Sylvania, was transferred from Buffalo to Sunnyvale, a town 40 miles south of San Francisco in 1962. Mom was a wonderful cook. She was short, plump, rosy-cheeked and strong-willed as hell. Life wasn't bad for a kid with a healthy appetite. I have vivid memories of Swedish meatballs, Swedish Christmas decorations, Swedish pastries and Swedish friends coming over for *Kaffe*.

My dad, a gentle and intelligent man who looked like the actor Raymond Massey, was legally blind but never let it stop him for a second. He was a good carpenter, machinist, electrician and ham radio enthusiast. He read using a small handheld magnifier, and never even used a cane. He was a great role model and I was proud of him.

The Carlson family, circa 1965. David is trying to look like astronaut Alan Shepard. Mark is the precocious one in front

I imagine some of my friends thought having a blind dad was difficult, since we couldn't play catch or go on fishing trips. But I didn't feel cheated. That's the way it was and he was a great father.

At the age of eight the first signs of RP emerged in me when I needed hearing aids. It was just one of those little things which can define a child's personality. I was a sensitive kid and truth be told, I was a sissy, really.

Mom's niece Katerina, whom we called 'Chick' because of her radiant blonde hair and sunny smile often visited us. Chick was a very beautiful Swedish woman who came into our house like a movie star. David and I both had a crush on her, but I think she liked me best.

Mom brought out my love of history and reading. I read *Gone with the Wind* when I was ten years old.

David and I weren't close growing up. He thought I was a pesky kid brother. Well, sure I was. It was my job.

He liked photography and music. He'd mastered the piano, saxophone, clarinet and guitar by the time he graduated from high school. Darn near a prodigy. He was the 'golden child,' and I had a lot to live up to.

My hobbies were drawing and reading. I was the local kid artist, winning awards in school and community contests.

Mom and Dad encouraged our interests and dreams.

I've often wondered why they supported our interests in such visual arts when there was every indication we would eventually be blind. Perhaps they hoped David and I would be millionaires early in life.

I think it was a form of denial. And I caught the denial bug.

We had a dog, a black toy poodle named Puff, so named because as a puppy he looked like a puff of black smoke. He liked to lick Mom's shoes, so when she put them on you heard a squelching sound. Ick. But he was a great family dog.

Puff sometimes had competition from me as I found lost dogs in our neighborhood and dragged them home on a rope, telling Mom, "He followed me home, can we keep him?" I was an early advocate of dog rescue, I suppose.

Puff lived for 17 years and died when I was 23. With tears in my eyes I buried him in his favorite spot in the back yard, with a big obsidian rock as a headstone. Rather appropriate, I think.

Wherever we traveled, I read the map. Mom, who drove, trusted my navigation. We never got lost because I had a great sense of direction.

It still comes in handy today. We traveled to Yosemite National Park in the Sierras many times. I think Yosemite is the most beautiful place in the world and will always remember the spectacular vistas of towering granite peaks looming with Olympian splendor above the lush green meadows of the valley.

When we camped in the valley during the summer, Mom cooked on a Coleman stove on the tailgate of our red Rambler station wagon.

FYI, a Rambler was *not* high on the teenager approval list of cool cars for a family to own. It was way down at the bottom with Metropolitans and VW Beetles.

The four of us slept in a green canvas wall tent so heavy it would stop an artillery round. No Gore-Tex in those days. Evenings in Yosemite Valley gave me one of my most enduring memories.

The Firefall. A huge bonfire of railroad ties was built at the top of Glacier Point, and after nightfall it was pushed over the precipice with thick poles.

A blazing stream cascaded down the black cliff like an orange veil sprinkled with glowing yellow diamonds. They don't do it anymore but I was lucky to have seen it.

By the time I was at Patrick Henry Junior High in 1972 I was wearing glasses. To make matters worse, Mom was a cook in the school cafeteria. I might as well have had a 'kick me' sign permanently sewn onto my clothes.

My personality and interests had solidified. Perhaps congealed would be a better word. Shy and introverted, I never called attention to myself.

I liked art, history, science, astronomy, reading and girls, but not sports.

My favorite place to hang out was the library. A nerd? You bet. All I was missing was the plastic pocket protector. To me, Led Zeppelin was an airship, not a rock group.

But I survived my school years, graduating from Marion A. Peterson High School in 1978.

Monty Montgomery was my best friend through high school and ever since. We were both into classic horror movies, comic books, science fiction, Mel Brooks and Monty Python. He understood my problems seeing in the dark and often guided me in movie theaters.

Monty was witness to one of my less stellar moments. I broke my ankle walking off a cliff at a beach.

I couldn't blame that one on my sight. I just wasn't looking where I was going.

It was a nude beach. There were more important things to look at than 20-foot drop-offs.

The fire department had to lift me to safety in a basket. Cool but embarrassing.

To this day Monty ribs me about it. What are old friends for?

I could see well enough except for my narrowing visual field and night blindness.

I tried to join the Marine Corps in 1981, but my hearing kept me a permanent civilian.

I was disappointed, since it seemed to mean I wasn't a whole man. But those were the cards life dealt me.

In 1984 I decided to move to San Diego. Living at home wasn't getting me anywhere, and I needed to take a serious step away from the nest. Even at 23 I wasn't sure what to do with my life and my parents were getting frustrated with my lack of direction.

David was already an engineer at Hewlett-Packard and married with a son. His sight was failing, following the pattern which would eventually claim his vision and mine.

I arrived in San Diego and found an apartment in Clairemont. My lack of focus on a career still made stability difficult, so I went through a succession of roommates and jobs until 1988, when . . .

A funny thing happened to me on the way to Gettysburg

I joined a local Civil War reenactment unit. G Company of the Sixth U.S. Infantry Regiment. Since the Marines couldn't use me, maybe Abe Lincoln could.

I was hooked. We did events and battles all over Southern California and I had a ball. It wasn't cheap, but it was my true passion for the next several years.

Mark as a Union soldier in 1989

There were a few snags. By then my night vision was lousy. Everyone in the regiment looked out for me. They were wonderful friends and I truly felt a part of something special.

I did participate in battles. There was no danger. Safety was always paramount. I knew my limitations.

I owned a reproduction 1863 Springfield Rifled musket. The first of two muskets, actually, though I didn't know it at the time.

Reenacting brought me out of my nerdy shyness, and in time I was as extroverted as Charlie Sheen. Well, maybe not that much.

I liked public speaking and at events where I didn't feel safe on the battlefield, I narrated to the crowd. Try and imagine a wanna-be stand-up comic narrating a Civil War battle. I liked making people laugh in addition to describing tactics.

"The only danger when the infantry charges into battle after the cavalry is watching where they step."

One of my friends in the regiment finally got me on a career path by encouraging me to go to a local design college and learn how to take a talent for drawing and turn it into a marketable skill. I took graphic design and computer graphics, earning my certificates in 1991.

A New Life

Back at home, David was married to his second wife Carol, and already legally blind. He still worked at HP and used early versions of the assistive computer technology I would soon learn about. He had his first Guide dog, a Golden retriever named Galahad. I didn't really know much about Guide dogs, but I was intrigued by Galahad. He was a very loyal, intelligent animal.

I didn't consider eventually getting a Guide dog. I was still in denial. My RP hadn't been more than an annoyance to me and I coped with it.

In 1992 I began working for a company in Mission Valley that published three national magazines.

Gun magazines. *Guns, American Handgunner* and *Shooting Industry*. Testosterone city.

I loved that job, really sinking my teeth into production graphics. I felt good holding a published magazine with my own artwork in it.

It was while working there that my life changed again.

I had an apartment in Normal Heights overlooking Mission Valley and rode the bus to work.

On a cool late-winter day in 1992 I met Jane Vogel. She too worked in Mission Valley and took the bus.

Well I sort of met her. She noticed me long before I saw her. As usual I had my head buried in a Tom Clancy novel.

And one glorious day I looked over the top of the book and saw her. Looking at me. She was probably thinking, 'It's about time, you putz.'

It wasn't love at first sight but for sure there was some electricity. She was nearly as tall as my 5'11' and full-figured with short dark-brown hair, and a perfect smile.

Her skin was as clear as cameo around wide expressive brown eyes. Really built, too. I've always been attracted to busty women, and she sure got my attention.

Since she's going to read this, suffice to say Jane was a dream and it didn't take long for me to fall head over heels in love. She recognized my disabilities, and to her credit and my everlasting gratitude, loved me anyway.

Jane lived near the airport in a very tastefully decorated apartment. She really had it together. Intelligent, competent and practical women impressed me. But I was and still am, a guy. In other words, hopeless.

She came from Hicksville Long Island.

A real New Yorker, she was part of a close-knit family, one of three sisters and a brother.

They really enjoyed Broadway plays and knew the songs of everything from *West Side Story* to *Cats*. The most I've ever wanted to try was to play the role of Charlie Cowell the anvil salesman in *Music Man*. Or Javert in *Les Miserables*. Never mind I couldn't sing any better than a tone-deaf giraffe with emphysema. In my fertile imagination I sang like Michael Crawford.

In a futile attempt to civilize me Jane took me to *Phantom*, the *Lion King, Beauty and the Beast*, and Lord of the Dance. But let's be honest, I was still a Monty Python fan. A lost cause as far as Jane was concerned.

Her parents, Dan and Virginia moved to San Diego after Dan retired as a master machinist.

They were cordial and friendly, but Jane later told me they had reservations about her dating a man who would likely be blind in a few years. They thought she would have to take care of me.

I took a page from my father's book and determined I would be independent and show them they were wrong.

Dan was a real joker who liked bad puns and war stories. He'd served in the Seventh Army in North Africa and Italy during the war. His family had heard his stories hundreds of times, so he liked having a new audience.

A sweet and quiet woman, Virginia was a real lady with east coast manners.

Virginia and Dan Vogel

Their first and only son was named for his father. Darcy, as he was known was a very ambitious and intelligent, hard-working man with superb taste and ability. Sue and Kathy were next. They were as different from one another as night and day. Then came my baby, Jane. No pun intended.

Darcy doted on his little sister, and she was devoted to him. Jane's maternal grandmother Nana had been a wonderful Queens housewife with a talent for hospitality to make family get-togethers perfect. I truly believe Jane inherited all of Nana's best qualities. Do I think I got the best of Dan and Virginia's daughters? I do.

Darcy had done well in life. He'd been a lieutenant in the Navy and served on the aircraft carrier *USS Oriskany*. His hobby was to buy a house, totally remodel it and resell it at a profit. The man was a genius.

When I met him in 1992 he was dying of liver disease.

Jane knew the end was coming and I did what I could to soften the inevitable.

Getting Hitched

About this time my own father, long retired, fell off a ladder while cleaning the gutters and sustained a brain injury. I flew home to see him. Dad lingered on for more than a year, but never really came back to us. Once in a while, certain aspects of his personality and abilities showed themselves, but there was no use in kidding ourselves. Eric Roland Carlson, a kind, gentle devoted and amazingly able man was gone forever.

In a way I felt life had cheated him. He'd never lamented the loss of his sight or hearing. He had an inquisitive and wise mind. And in the end, that's what his accident took from him.

In December 1993 Jane's brother died. She was truly crushed by the loss, and I don't think she or her parents ever really got over it.

We married in April 1995. My best friend Mike, one of my buddies from the regiment was Best Man, and my brother was an usher.

Yes, a blind usher.

As long as I live I'll never forget the sight of my bride-to-be coming down the aisle on Dan's arm. I don't know if it was the lighting or the candles but she glowed with misty radiance. I soon realized the misty part was in my eyes, but the glow was real.

The most beautiful thing I'd ever seen, before or since.

The new Mr. and Mrs. Carlson

We bought a place in the new community of Carmel Mountain Ranch near Escondido. It was a nice two-story attached three-bedroom two-bath condo with a small yard and two-car garage.

The front bedrooms became a TV den and Jane's office.

I got the garage.

I resisted the idea at first, but since we only had one car it made sense. With tall bookcases and carpet to define my office, it was well-lit, comfortable and totally mine. I decorated it my way.

That is with lots of guy stuff. Military memorabilia, signed astronaut photos, books on history, seven decades of *National Geographic Magazine*, and my huge video collection of war movies, classic TV comedy, old films, and documentaries.

At last count I had about 400 tapes. DVDs took a while to get a grip on me but I was slowly being dragged kicking and screaming into the 21st Century.

Life as a married couple had its ups and downs as everyone who has done it knows. I was a rank amateur, but Jane, ever practical and devoted made it work.

I was working for a graphics company in Kearny Mesa, and Jane was at a credit union when my father died in May, exactly a month after the wedding. We flew up for the memorial services.

Dad was laid to rest in a cemetery overlooking San Francisco Bay. I finally told Dad that I loved him and would try to be as good a man as he.

I'm still trying, Dad.

David and I grew closer, finding common ground in history, reading and even being blind.

Jane had been working in collections for most of her adult life and it got to her at times. It was very tedious and spirit-sapping.

I loved my work. I at least got to see the tangible results of my labors in magazines and advertisements. I think Jane envied that. I encouraged her to find a creative outlet.

She started with rubber stamping, then found her real passion, scrapbooking. She did very beautiful work. Her talent blossomed with each new project. I sincerely supported her hobby, even when the number of rubber stamps in her office grew to a point where she couldn't count them anymore.

That's the mark of a true stamper. If you can count them, you don't have enough.

In late 1995 I was laid off from the job in Kearny Mesa.

I went through a few contractor jobs, trying to find that perfect niche.

For the first time, my increasing blindness was a factor.

1998 found me working for a company in Poway which made electronic membrane switches and screen printed circuits. It was exceedingly precise work. I got the job because I had the experience. And I hid my bad eyesight from the owner.

I figured once I got in, my skills would help him overlook that I kept bumping into walls. Brilliant strategy.

He kept me on for a year, but on a fateful day in 1999 had to let me go. I was costing him too much money in mistakes.

For the very first time in my life I had to face reality. My graphics career was over.

I was already using a cane to get around safely. That came about one day while shopping with Jane, and I bumped into a kid coming around the end of an aisle. I apologized and moved on.

Behind me I heard Jane say to the parent, "I'm sorry. He's visually impaired."

That hit me like a punch to the stomach. Jane had been apologizing for my occasional accidents for who knows how long. It wasn't fair to her.

I had been in a serious state of denial. At the same age, both my father and brother were already almost totally blind. Deep down I thought it would never happen to me.

But there I was, up Denial River without a paddle.

Still had my sense of humor, though.

The RP had taken its sweet time in making a difference in my lifestyle but it had finally done so with a vengeance.

The problem wasn't so much how I looked out at the world but my outlook on the world. And my outlook was worse than my sight.

How's that for an epiphany?

Finding the Paddle

My cane was a tool to navigate with, and also a flag. Anyone seeing it would realize I wasn't blind drunk, just blind.

I went to my doctor and asked the critical question: "Doc, am I blind?"

(Insert drum roll soundbite here)

The retinal specialist said I was considered legally blind.

(Insert cymbal soundbite here)

There it was. No more denial.

And so we come to the last part of our pre-Musket life. I went on state disability. I was only going to use SSDI funding as a way of paying the bills while I redirected my career path. Jane was depending on me.

The Braille Institute in La Jolla was a great organization that provided training to the blind. I started attending classes there in late 2000. Orientation and Mobility, or O & M polished my cane skills. I also learned computer skills.

There I met Craig Schneider who also had RP. But in his case it wasn't hereditary, and not expected. One morning he woke up blind. That's it. No warning at all.

Craig had a Guide dog, a Golden Retriever named Luster.

He told me about an advanced blind program in Los Angeles.

The California Department of Rehabilitation (DOR) helped persons with disabilities with educational and vocational assistance.

I think someone's trying to get my attention.

🐈 "Hi, Musket here. Just in case you were wondering, this is when I came into the world.

Okay, I'll let Daddy get on with his story.

I'll be back really soon, and I promise it'll get better."

Wow, I thought *I* was the conceited one. Karen Gamble became my DOR counselor and helped to set up the plan which paid for me to attend the Davidson Program for Independence (DPI) in LA. It wasn't cheap, close to $16,000. DPI was a residential program with students staying the week and returning home on weekends.

DPI could take anywhere from eight to twelve months to complete a student's goals. I was in a hurry, and learned how to read Braille, to use a cane in nearly every environment, independent living skills and most importantly, about new assistive computer technology. I was already a competent computer user so I learned fast.

One of my fellow students was Jennifer Peters. A nice, willowy grandmother. I behaved around her.

Two people really deserve special mention here. Virginia Piper was an O & M instructor. She was an excellent teacher, helping me to be confident with the cane. I could walk safely in any suburban, urban or rural environment, relying on my other senses. She saved my life, and I don't say that lightly. She always walked behind me while I took a wrong turn and found myself unable to figure out where I was. Then I heard her sweet-as-pie voice, lightly garnished with sarcasm and just a pinch of professional concern. “What have we here?”

How could I not succeed with support like that?

I’m sure everybody knows blind people develop good hearing, smell, touch, and so on.

In my case it didn’t do squat for my hearing. But I learned to maximize my sense of smell and touch.

Listening at an intersection, the sounds told me which way traffic was moving, either parallel or perpendicular to my route of travel. I could hear the difference between ‘all clear’ and ‘all quiet’ before crossing a residential street.

Virginia Piper

The other gem at DPI was Ruthie Dean. Totally blind, Ruthie taught Braille. It can take a long time to become proficient at reading and writing Braille. Ruthie taught thousands of young and old blind persons to communicate with Braille.

Braille was tricky to learn but also fun. I don’t use it for everything but it was helpful for organizing and filing.

Many major publications are produced in Braille, even *Playboy*. No, not the pictures. If a blind guy says he reads *Playboy* for the articles, you can believe him.

Ruthie could read whole pages of Braille in seconds. I'm not making this up, she was that fast. Eat your heart out, Evelyn Wood.

My Braille reading speed? *Gone with the Wind* would require a few more lifetimes than I'm entitled to.

I will always consider myself lucky to have known Virginia and Ruthie.

I didn't achieve any of my successes by myself. I owe every single one of them to other people. In other words, what I lacked in brilliance I more than made up for in luck. Fate and coincidence had a lot to do with it.

Four months later I graduated. It was time to find work and earn some money.

But doing what? Ah, there's the rub. Astronaut was probably out. So was brain surgeon. I considered running for President but I was born with a congenital defect. A conscience.

I set my sights a bit higher and looked for honest work. How is that for cynicism?

DOR paid for the technology I would need to find work and maintain a career. One of these devices was called a CCTV, for Closed-circuit television, or a video magnifier. Basically a TV camera on a swing arm, it displayed a magnified image on a screen of any printed page. It allowed someone with low vision to read newspapers, books or whatever. My dad used an early model so I was familiar with it.

And that's how I met Beverly Warner, a distributor for Clarity, a company which made CCTVs. Portable, easy to use and versatile, the Clarity was perfect for me.

Beverly took a shine to me. She was a sweet, elderly lady with a lot of spirit. She asked me if I'd like to be her assistant. She wanted me to do demonstrations of the Clarity.

I would earn a commission for each one I sold. CCTVs could run around $2,500 so a commission wasn't to be sneezed at.

Was it a real job? Maybe, but I'd be carrying the CCTV and a monitor around on the bus. Not too practical but I gave it a try.

Jane and I had discussed getting a Guide dog while I was at DPI. David, Ruthie Dean and Craig Schneider had dogs from Guide Dogs for the Blind. But it was Chick who had the most positive influence on our decision. She told me she really believed I would not only be more independent but even succeed with a dog as my guide.

With their encouragement, I decided to take the plunge.

I applied to Guide Dogs for the Blind in August 2001.

A few months later I did a Clarity presentation at a small agency for the disabled called Independence San Diego.

They had need of some assistive technology and wanted demonstrations.

That was one of the most fateful days of my life.

I must have impressed them, because Roberto Frias, the Assistant Program Manager asked if I'd be interested in a job as the Assistive Technology Specialist.

It was a heady moment. On the plus side, it was great to be offered a job like that. On the other side was the question: Was I qualified?

Jane was 100% behind me. I went for it.

Roberto was one of the most even-tempered, nicest men I've ever met. He was also very short but that might be because he used a wheelchair.

At the interview I told him about my application to Guide Dogs. I hoped to go in the spring.

He said with a smile, "That's fine. We're going to hire you. Get settled in, and you go and get the dog. You won't lose your job."

On January 2, 2002 I began a new career in the best environment for someone with a disability in San Diego.

It was one of those critical moments in my life. For the next seven years I was ISD's Assistive Technology (AT) Advocate. But I had to take a trip first.

🐕 "Now we're getting to the good part."

Life hasn't been the same since. Thank God.

CHAPTER TWO

MUSKET

The Guide Dog application was reviewed by the training staff, who considered my needs, vision, general health and home environment. The dogs were expensive and special, and GDB had to ensure a student would not only benefit from the dog's assistance, but would take good care of it.

Phone interviews, letters of reference, medical history, and a home visit were important steps in the application process. The field representative asked some pretty direct questions. "Do you have a good area to relieve the dog?" "What is your daily schedule like?" "How often do you travel?" "Do you ever get angry with children or dogs?"

All good questions and I answered them honestly. From Puff I knew how to take care of a dog, but I said I'd follow Guide Dogs' recommendations.

In order to qualify for a Guide dog, the applicant must be skilled with a cane. This seems either oxymoronic or sensible depending on what end of the cane you were on.

Thanks to Virginia Piper I was qualified. The letter arrived just before Christmas. David, a seasoned Guide dog handler had told me spring was the best time to be in San Rafael. I chose the April-May 2002 class.

The plane tickets arrived with my instructions. I was already becoming simultaneously impressed and anxious.

The reader might be wondering how I paid for this. I had a full-time job, but didn't make enough to pay for a $50,000 dog. Guide Dogs for the

Blind are completely free. It's all paid for by private donations and grants. The students didn't have to pay for a thing, from plane fare to meals.

A running joke at GDB was someone could arrive totally broke and leave with money. Just dig in the sofa cushions. Blind people were always dropping money.

Jane, ever the perfectionist prepared my clothes, personal items and other things to the Nth Degree.

"Now this outfit is for cold days, and you can wear either this or that shirt with these pants. Hang them up right after taking them from the dryer. For the Sunday days off, you should have either shorts and a t-shirt or corduroy pants and a polo shirt." On it went.

She made sure I knew how to wash each type of garment so I couldn't accidentally ruin a nice shirt with bleach.

It was an old story. Make a mistake just once, and you're damned for life. She never forgot the pink socks.

Jane then laid down some rules. "When you bring the dog home, I don't want him on the furniture, or to beg at the table. No food scraps, and he'll have to stay in his bed. He's *your* dog."

Learning the Ropes

My Southwest Airlines flight from San Diego landed in San Francisco just before noon on Sunday April 21, 2002, a warm sunny California day.

Stepping into the vast carpeted terminal, I heard a man hailing me. I turned towards the voice.

"Are you Mark Carlson?" He asked me.

"Yes, I am."

The man, who sounded about thirty and pleasant, shook my hand. "I'm Ben. I'm going to be one of your instructors."

"Glad to meet you Ben," I said.

He told me there were three other flights coming in and he needed to meet them. "Would you mind waiting here?"

I didn't mind at all. Finding a centrally located seat in the terminal, Ben told me the next flight was coming from Bakersfield with Jennifer in about fifteen minutes.

Something in my mind clicked. "Would that be Jennifer Peters?"

"Yes, how'd you know?"

I smiled. "We were at the Davidson Program for the Blind a year ago. Small world."

A short time later, Jennifer and I were reunited. She was glad we'd be in the same class.

In about an hour all the students arriving by air had been assembled. We were taken to the white Guide Dogs bus. I was already impressed by their efficiency. They did everything exactly right.

The drive north from SF Airport took us through the city and over the Golden Gate Bridge to begin an adventure.

San Rafael in Marin County was a quiet community of small-town character with turn-of-the-century Victorian homes and quaint shops.

Guide Dogs for the Blind was north of downtown on a small campus of green lawns and neat modern buildings.

As we stepped off the bus I inhaled the springtime air, clean and fragrant with the scent of pine trees and flowers. Traffic on Los Ranchitos Road was muted, so we might as well have been in the country.

The dream of Lois Matthew and Don Donaldson, Guide Dogs was begun in May of 1942 in Los Gatos, California, a wine community near my hometown of Sunnyvale. They wanted to train dogs to guide blind people, particularly blinded soldiers from the war. The first man to receive a Guide dog was Sergeant Leonard Foulk, a Marine blinded in combat in the Aleutian Islands. In 1947 the school moved to San Rafael.

Since then more than ten thousand men and women have been given freedom and independence from the wonderful animals born, raised and trained at Guide Dogs.

Efficiency Personified

I'd heard a lot about the school from David, so it wasn't totally unknown to me.

I would be in Class #624 scheduled to graduate on May 18. Twenty-eight days was the state-mandated training period to receive a Guide dog.

There were to be twenty-one students in the class, sixteen newbies like me and five re-trains. Some of the older ones were on their third or fourth dog.

I was anxious about managing just one. We were paired off. My roommate, Andy hailed from a town in Northern California. We hit it off pretty well, another indication that GDB knew what it was doing. They partnered roommates based on mutual interests. And gender, I suppose. No male-female roomies.

After unpacking I got the lay of the land. The room was rectangular with beds at each end and a small fenced patio on one side.

We each had a closet and small desk with a phone.

On either side of the central bathroom door was a sink for each of us. Beneath the sink was a tiled basin, where the dog's dishes were to be washed and filled with water.

Everything imaginable was provided. The bed linen was washed for us, but we were responsible for our own laundry. I could handle that, despite Jane's dire predictions of me coming home with pink underwear and bleached polo shirts.

Down the long main hall were the dining and common rooms, with comfortable couches, chairs and a fireplace. Picture a nice ski lodge in the Sierras and you'd have the dormitory. The sound of twenty students with white canes headed down the tiled, paneled hall was like a convention of woodpeckers.

Guide Dogs for the Blind dining room

We met the staff. The instructors knew everything about each of us, the kitchen staff knew who was diabetic and had special dietary needs, the nurse knew all our medications, and the administrators had arranged for our families to be given our room phone numbers. If the U.S. Government was run like this, we'd be rulers of the planet.

The instructors were as different from one another as could be. The senior instructor, Mark, was about 30, thin with black hair and a razor wit. He was also very serious about his work. Ben was quiet, easygoing and mellow.

Dina DiMaggio was the wild one. Rapier-thin, with a black ponytail and more energy than a nuclear reactor, she proudly said she was the great-niece of Joe DiMaggio. Dina was a whirlwind and every day I was astonished at her vivacity and spirit.

Have you ever tried to catch about fifty baby chicks loose on a football field? That's what keeping up with Dina was like.

The first two days of training taught us the basic commands and using the harness. This was 'Juno' training. Apparently the first dog trained at GDB was named Juno. They rolled up a large towel and put a collar and leash on it. Then the instructor pulled it around as if it were the dog. We gave the commands while getting a feel for what the dogs would be doing.

We hadn't yet met any but I knew somewhere on campus was my dog.

The pre-dog training also allowed the instructors to gauge a student's needs, walking speed, personality and other factors. They already had a pretty good idea what a student would need based on their preferences.

I hoped for a Yellow Labrador, strong, easygoing and lovable.

Physical attributes were considered. I was a tall, solidly-built guy with a long stride and fast pace, so they wouldn't team me with a small, hyperactive dog. It would be strong and a fast learner.

After we had all learned the skill of working with the harness, Mark, Ben and Dina interviewed each of us. I reiterated the same preferences I'd had on my application. By then they'd decided what dog I was to be given. But it was still a secret to me.

It made sense but I'm sure they had a sense of the dramatic as well.

Then came Dog Day.

🐕 "And life hasn't been the same for either of us since."

Musket looking regal for his first picture

My New Eyes

The day began at 6:00 a.m. when my alarm went off. I reached down and found Musket there, and he rolled on his side. I thought he might have wanted a belly rub.

🐕 "I had to start training him right away."

After he had eaten, we went to the dining hall for breakfast. That was an interesting experience. Twenty-one excited dogs and their energized handlers tried to find the most workable way to get the dogs to stay by their chairs. Musket was no different, but I got my first inkling of his attitude towards food. More on that later. A lot more.

Musket and I worked together for the first time that morning. It was a very emotional and exhilarating moment for both of us. It was just a walk around the campus, so we could learn each other's pace and habits. It felt wonderful to know the freedom of total trust in his ability to guide me.

He did very well. I remembered the commands, mostly because I had spent the previous two days practicing them in the halls.

🐕 "When we went out that first day together, I was the proudest Guide dog you ever saw. My head was up, my tail wagged and I did my job perfectly. I wanted to say to the other dogs, 'This is my new daddy!'"

I learned Musket had a tendency to take turns slowly, but he made up for it with his strong pace. In a short time we were working as a team. I never stopped smiling.

🐕 "Neither did I. Daddy was consistent and did everything the same way every time. That's how I learned."

Software and Hardware

Guide dogs are already fully trained by the time they are given to a student. It was the new handler's job to learn to work with the dog, to become a team. Just a note here, I usually use the term 'handler' to mean someone who works with an Assistance dog. 'Owner' applies to a pet.

The best metaphor I can think of is a computer with all the software installed. The handler had to learn how to use it.

"A computer? Is that the best you can come up with? What am I, MusketSoft 1.0?"

The harness handle was stiff and loosely attached by links to the straps, one across the chest and the other under the belly. They weren't tight but snug, so the dog's actions could be easily felt by the handler. The leash could be extended during relieving and shortened for guiding.

To put it simply, the harness told the handler what the dog was doing and the leash signaled the dog to what the handler wanted.

They were both held in the grip of the left hand, the leash hooked under the forefinger so it could be quickly taken in the right hand if needed.

The common commands were Forward, Left, Right and Halt. Others were Stay, Sit, Up, Down, Steady, and Hop-up.

Most were self-explanatory, but for Hop-up. It meant 'pick up the pace.' No not the salsa. When a dog was lagging, the command 'Hop-up' would get them going with a flick of the leash.

The leash, attached to the chain collar, was used to redirect the dog if he was distracted or needed to be corrected. Corrections were not to punish, but to refocus the dog's attention on his job.

Let's say Musket and I were walking by an outdoor restaurant where he saw food on the sidewalk, and tried to get it. I took the leash in my right hand and said in a firm voice "No. Forward," while giving the leash a gentle tug.

If he behaved and got back on track, I said "Good boy." If not, I repeated the command more firmly until he did. That's usually all it took.

Guide dogs were never punished or told 'Bad dog." The key was to provide positive reinforcement. They liked to hear they were a good dog and responded to it.

The dogs were given lots of praise and love. I realized early on he liked working. When I held out the harness he slipped his head into it right away. Most dogs didn't do that.

🐕 "Do I like being a Guide dog? Yeah! I'm proud to be a working dog.

Those first days were a learning experience for both of us. Daddy had a good strong voice and he used the leash properly. He sometimes had to correct me, but never hurt me.

He learned to trust my guiding. I never steered him wrong. Well, okay, once or twice, but let's not get into that."

The buses took us to the Guide Dog Lounge after breakfast and again after lunch. The lounge was a comfortable building on 4th Street in downtown San Rafael. It had two rooms with computers and games, and a patio.

The instructors took us out four at a time on the 'basic route' every day for weeks. A few blocks east, then south, back west a few more blocks, north for one block and back to the Lounge.

It took about twenty minutes and brought us through business and residential areas and across busy intersections. The instructors followed close behind to assist, but Musket and I rarely needed it. He was one sharp dog.

Mark and Musket on their first day together. Lower right:
The Guide Dog Lounge

Crossing intersections was no big deal. We learned to 'push' the traffic by hitting the signal button. That way we could make the light change. Some intersections had audible signals for us blind folks, and they were really nice. The 'chirp' sound was for crossing streets running north-south, and the 'cuckoo' sound was for east-west roads.

Ironically, the hardest time to cross an intersection was while there was no traffic at all.

🐕 "Doesn't make sense, does it?"

When cars were moving we could hear them. But when no cars were nearby, such as early in the morning, we had no way to know. I've often stood for several minutes literally waiting for a car to go by so I could tell when it was safe to cross.

I could determine my location by the smell of a jasmine bush or the rattle of an auto repair shop. The smell of Italian food marked one spot while the raucous music of a pool hall was another landmark.

All my skills were put to use when I worked with Musket on the streets of San Rafael.

Dina the Distractor

More advanced training took us to San Francisco, the Muir Woods, and rolling country roads and wide pastures in Marin County.

Jennifer did very well with Floria. And one day an incredible thing happened.

Jennifer and Floria

We were walking on the shoulder of a road curving through rolling countryside. There was no traffic.

Jennifer and her Golden walked at a brisk pace and then began jogging. Actually running! I heard her laughing with joy. She later told me it was one of the most exhilarating experiences of her life. She felt so free. That's what her Guide dog gave her.

Fisherman's Wharf provided me with one of my first Musket stories. Musket and I were waiting on the sidewalk by the bus when a man came up to me.

He said, "That's a beautiful dog."

"Thank you," I replied.

"Can I ask you something?"

"Sure."

"What happens if the dog goes blind?"

Oh, what to say? The comic in me begged to reply, "We get him a guide cat."

I answered honestly. "He'll be retired and given to someone as a pet."

"Oh, that makes sense. Well I hope he works well for you."

He walked off, curiosity satisfied.

"It was close. Daddy was dying to use that line."

Dina DiMaggio took us to a very busy mall on Market Street to use escalators and elevators. Escalators were something to be careful about. A dog's claws could get caught in the teeth of the stairs as they slid under the sill.

We were taught to hold the leash taut, and just before reaching the end, say 'Up! with a small tug. The dog jumped over the sill.

Elevators were simple. I told Musket, "Find the elevator." He went right to the door, led me in and did an immediate 'about face' so we were facing forward.

Guide dogs are trained to find doorways, stairs and exits. Musket did well with stairs. I never tripped on stairs with him guiding.

"I could do elevators and escalators easy. I knew Daddy would protect my little paws. Stairs were a cinch. We always went up the right side and I stopped at every landing."

As for revolving doors, Never. They're the stupidest things ever invented, especially the powered ones. Someone with a disability is in real danger in those things and Guide dogs didn't know what to do. Try and go into one with your eyes closed sometime.

"Daddy's right. I backed away from those things. They scared me."

Distractions were something a Guide dog handler had to get a good feel for. Anything which made a dog turn away from its job, or place the team in danger was not tolerated.

Dina was a real firecracker. A true free spirit, Dina loved to distract the dogs on their walks.

As part of her job, that is.

At random places on the route she jumped from a doorway and said "Hi, Musket!" and petted him vigorously.

My job was to get him under control immediately. If he turned to Dina, whom he adored, I took the leash and said firmly, "No. Forward, Musket."

If all went well we moved on.

If that didn't work, a more firm command was used. I gave the leash a quick jerk. Not hard, just sharp.

A corrcction was not a punishment; but a quick and gentle way to redirect the dog's attention.

I never mistreated Musket and don't know any Guide dog handlers who have.

"Daddy took good care of me. And I took care of him. A sort of symbiotic mutual love and respect."

Dina was relentless. In the common room during a lecture, the dogs were on the floor at our feet. Suddenly there was yelling, whistling with two or three big dogs charging through the room behind the running Dina.

"Dina was my sweetheart. I knew she liked me. I didn't mind being distracted. I know Dina had a thing for me."

Musket was a bird dog breed but he wasn't no huntin' dog.

We went to a lake by the Marin Civic Center, a magnificent building designed by Frank Lloyd Wright. It looked like Starfleet Headquarters. The lake was bordered by winding walkways and home to hundreds of ducks, geese and coots.

More distraction training. As if Dina wasn't enough. We walked along the paths close to the waterfowl which presumably, our bird dogs would try to catch.

Some tried. But Musket, my dog of many guises, couldn't have cared less. I imagine if the birds had been on a platter with dressing and gravy it would have been another matter.

I was praised for keeping him focused and under control.

🐕 "Sure, Daddy got the credit. I chased ducks when I was being raised by Mommy Carrie. I never liked feathers in my teeth."

The day I realized Musket was a damned good Guide dog was when an instructor tried to run us over with a car.

No, he wasn't fed up with my bad jokes. We were told one day in the third week Peter O'Reilly, a senior instructor and one of the nicest guys I've ever met was going to try and run us over with a real car.

At some point on our normal route downtown he would come out of a driveway right in front of us.

Oh-kay . . .

David never mentioned any student road kill so I presumed it would be safe.

It was over in two seconds. Musket and I were walking along, minding our own business when all of a sudden there was Peter in a huge roaring 18-wheeler truck, tires screeching and air horn blaring.

🐕 "Um, that's not the way I remember it."

Okay, it was a small minivan. But it *sounded* big.

Musket did exactly as he was trained. He stopped short and the harness handle pushed against my hand. I stopped, and Peter called out, "Good work!"

To this day I wonder what he'd have said if I hadn't managed to stop. "You might want to work on that when you get out of the hospital, Mark."

Seriously Peter wasn't close. But I could still feel the heat of the engine on my face. Musket got a real nice 'Good boy!' and petting for that.

"What's the big deal? I did as I was trained. But it made Daddy happy. And when he was happy, I got lots of love and belly rubs."

In One End and Our the Other

I suppose this might be a good time to get on the topic of food.

"My favorite subject. Go ahead, Daddy."

The school provided a dry food called Eukanuba. We took the bowls to a food bin in the early morning and again in the afternoon. The dogs ate about four cups a day depending on their size. Musket was about as food-driven as they come. He watched me bring that bowl to his mat with hungry eyes and wolfed it down. I mean *fast*. An industrial vacuum cleaner would take longer. I had to count my fingers afterward.

"He did not. I never ate a finger. Sure I had a healthy appetite. I was a working dog, remember?"

I called Musket my 'muzzle-loader,' a term familiar to black powder shooters.

"Like I said it was a cool name."

At specific times each day the dogs were taken to the 'relieving circle' where the buses picked up and dropped off. On the large concrete ring with an evergreen grove in the center, I removed his harness, extended the leash and gave the command "Do your business." I wonder who thought of that.

The dogs had carefully-regulated meal times, so the relieving schedule was usually on the mark. Not for Musket. He took his sweet time.

He was not a 'shoot 'n' scoot' dog. Concrete wasn't very appealing to a grass aficionado like Musket. Sometimes he just wouldn't go and I was out there for twenty minutes, walking in circles.

"Sure I preferred grass. And I took my time, sniffing. Whose walk was it, anyway?

When humans peed outside, they hid in the bushes. I couldn't blame them. If I looked like that I'd hide too."

It took me a year to get Musket on a predictable schedule.

"Daddy has it backwards. It took me a year to get *him* on *my* schedule."

Now we come to the one thing most new students feared like nothing else. Picking up the poop. Icky as it was, it had to be done.

We were advised to set a good example for the community.

How did we find it? The handler pulled the bag on their hand and felt the dog's back.

We judged about where it was and picked it up, turned the bag inside out, tied it off and threw it in the trash. Not a big deal, but a lot of new students were squeamish about it.

I was one of them but I got over it pretty quick.

A lot of sighted owners are also reluctant to pick it up, to judge by the poop we've had to skip over.

"I don't like finding other dogs' poop on the sidewalk. I have to make sure Daddy doesn't step in it."

At night Musket was tied down at his mat. The tie-down was a cable about three feet long, clipped to a ringbolt. He had room to move about and get comfortable.

Only once did I hear of a dog having trouble with the tie-down. One evening we were in our rooms relaxing when we heard canine shrieking from down the hall.

In a second the senior instructor burst out of his quarters and shot down the hall. I mean fast.

In a minute all was quiet. One of the other students had a German Shepherd. The dog was a little high-strung as most Shepherds are, and gotten itself tangled in the tie-down. It just frightened the poor dog.

"He was scared. The instructors took really good care of us. I felt safe on tie-down."

The last week of training included lectures on grooming, basic health care, and services the school provided to graduates. They also took pictures for our ID cards. To Jane's chagrin, I had grown a beard. Yes, a beard. What men won't do when away from their wives for a month.

I thought it made me look like a distinguished academician.

Jane thought I looked like a homeless wino.

"Well, he did."

The beard came off.

By then we were doing well with our dogs. But then we reached the final exam, a test of our Orientation and Mobility skills with a dog. The bus took us into the residential section of San Rafael.

Onc at a time in different locations, each student was dumped and told to find their own way back to the lounge.

Surprise.

It wasn't quite like that.

San Rafael is a very logically laid-out town. The streets were either numbered or lettered. 'A' Street ran north-south; First Street was east-west, and so on. With a little forethought and asking someone for the intersection it wasn't hard to find the way back. In about an hour we had all made it.

"It was a cinch. I knew just where we were but I let Daddy give the commands so it would increase his confidence."

Had we been totally on our own? I doubt it. I'm sure instructors were nearby, just in case someone got into a jam.

The last week of training we were witness to a special event. A man named Michael Hingson was given an award from a United Kingdom

Guide dog association. Michael graduated from GDB some years before with his Golden, Roselle.

What earned Michael the honor was what Roselle did on September 11, 2001.

Michael was on the 78th Floor of Tower One of the World Trade Center when it was struck by the airliner flown by terrorists.

Roselle, well trained and under good control, guided Michael safely down smoking stairwells crowded with frightened people, out of the burning tower.

As amazing as it was to hear the saga of a GDB Alumnus, we all thought the same thing: 'Would I have survived?'

Today I can think. 'Yes, Musket would have done the same thing.

🐕 "Sure I would have. I got the best training and I knew I could trust Daddy."

That's how good GDB trained their dogs.

As graduation approached, the school took care of the last details. We were taken to the Veterinary Department for a last checkup and information on each dog's medical history. Graduate services explained what we were entitled to and how to use the services offered.

We were given papers to give to our own vets, full grooming kits and a week's supply of food.

🐕 "Is that all? What if I wanted a midnight snack?"

The dogs were provided with lifetime veterinary care and follow-up training visits at home.

🐕 "They gave me a tag for my collar, the Guide Dogs I.D. I also had a tattoo. It wasn't anything cool like a pirate ship or skull. It was just my I.D. code. And it was on the inside of my right ear. At least if it had been a pirate ship I could have had an earring too."

Musket with his new Daddy. Note the short-lived beard

Again I was impressed by the efficiency of the institution.

The last few days were a whirlwind. I was given the name of Musket's puppy raiser, a woman in Sacramento named Carrie Baker. She had been in, of all things, veterinary school while raising Musket. As a puppy he'd been in classes with her, playing at her feet and melting the hearts of all the female students.

She along with all the other raisers were invited to the graduation. At the ceremony I would be introduced and Carrie would then bring out Musket and formally present him to me. Then I was to make a speech.

At least that's what was *supposed* to happen.

Dog Got my Tongue?

On May 18, a beautiful warm Saturday, I was dressed in my grad clothes, carefully chosen by Jane, and anxious as I've ever been. Jane and her parents, and my mother and David were coming. And for the first time they'd meet Musket.

Ben poked his head into my room. "Mark, your family is here."

I stood and so did Musket, who sensed something was up.

Walking down the packed halls towards the common room, I heard Jane's voice.

I would never have guessed what happened next.

Musket's 'New Mommy' and Jane's 'New Baby' found one another.

He knew exactly who his new mommy was. A lot quicker than he'd recognized his new daddy.

Even before I was able to give her a hug Musket was jumping up, tail beating the wall in a frenzied staccato, licking her face.

He was in love.

And so was Jane. I couldn't believe the transformation.

"Who are you and what have you done with my wife?" I asked, wonder in my voice.

Remember Jane said Musket was to be 'my dog?'

Well that went right out the window and into San Francisco Bay.

"He's so beautiful!" she said, almost crying with joy. "Honey he's perfect!"

I finally got my hug, but Musket to this day has always had to get into any embrace between Jane and me.

"Daddy brought me out of the room. The other dogs were moving around with their handlers and I could tell Daddy was excited. And it just happened. I saw my mommy. I knew it was her right away and I ran up to kiss her. I was so happy to be with her. Daddy seemed to be amused about something, but I never found out why."

In the common room Jane's parents, Dan and Virginia stood to meet the newest member of the family.

Musket won them both over in two seconds.

Dan was an avid photographer, and very talented. In 1939 he'd taken beautiful pictures of the New York World's Fair good enough for *National Geographic*.

When he met Musket he knelt on the floor, camera in hand, saying "Musket, look at Pop-pop, look at me."

Wonder of wonders.

Virginia, ever ladylike and proper, tried her best to resist, but it was no use. When Musket gave her kisses on her cheek, she was hooked. "Who's my Musket? Is Musket Nanny's good boy?"

"Nanny and Pop-pop were the coolest grandparents. They just doted on me, giving me treats and thought I was the best thing in the world. Who could blame them?"

Finally we found Carrie. Actually it was Musket who did.

I was taking Jane to my room and we passed the small common room. Then Musket, in a manner I was fast learning to recognize, literally twisted away from my grip.

I'm glad Dina didn't see it. I'd have flunked big time.

He jumped to give his Mommy Carrie a kiss. She was a lovely slender woman in her forties with medium-length dark brown hair and big brown eyes.

"Hi, you must be Mark," she said when Musket's tongue wasn't giving her a bath. She gave both Jane and I a warm hug.

"I am. I'm really glad to meet you."

"I guess we have a lot to talk about."

"I guess. He's very happy to see you."

It was true. I've learned over the years that Musket never forgot a friend. No matter where, when, or how much time had passed, he remembered every single person he met. His memory for people was phenomenal.

"Mommy Carrie! She was my first mommy and I lived with her for nine months while she went to vet school. She's the only vet I ever loved.

Mommy Carrie had been married before she raised me, and was going to have two baby boys. But they both died when they were born and her husband said he didn't want to be married to a woman who couldn't have children. So he left her. Mommy Carrie was hurting badly. Her friends reminded her she'd always wanted to raise a Guide dog and maybe it was the time.

Carrie brought me home when I was about five weeks old.

We went everywhere together. She even took me into the shower with her for my bath. We had a lot of fun with her other dog. Shana was a real pretty Golden retriever, and like a sister to me. I think all the love Mommy Carrie was going to give to her babies she gave to me. And that's why I'm such a lover boy."

My mother and David arrived. Born in Sweden, Mom kept many of her cultural traditions alive.

I introduced them. "Musket this is your Farmor." Farmor was a Swedish short name meaning 'Father's mother.'

She bent over and petted him. "You're so beautiful, yes, you are, sweetheart."

She was saying it in Swedish.

"I didn't understand what Farmor was saying but it was nice anyway. I gave her kisses too."

David, already on his third dog, was nonchalant as he shook my hand. "So kiddo, you did it."

"Yep," I said, equally deadpan.

"I was wondering if you could do it," he said with a hint of brotherly teasing.

"You did. How hard could it be?"

Musket and Jeremiah, David's Golden, were only moderately interested in each other.

I'm sure Jeremiah was jealous because Musket was so good-looking.

"I'm sure Hugh Jackman gets the same reaction."

The ceremony was at Noon on the graduation patio. Rows of white chairs were arranged on the large lawn under the shade of the big oak and pine trees. The sun was high but a breeze kept the air cool.

The students, without their dogs, were in a row of chairs on the patio.

I would be the first one up.
Hoo-ray.

🐕 "I was with Carrie in a big room with all the other dogs. They were as excited as I was. But for a little while I had Carrie all to myself. She took me to the door and we waited."

After some speeches by the instructors and the school director, the graduates were on.

I had an idea what to say. I was pretty good at outlining a speech in my mind and winging it. I did it all the time for work.

Now let's get something straight. I was not the shy, quiet type. I was outgoing, wisecracking and talkative.

That being said, what happened that day is beyond the belief of everyone who knew me.

Ben was on the microphone. "Our first graduate is Mark Carlson, from San Diego. Mark is receiving a male yellow Labrador named Musket, raised by Carrie Baker of Sacramento."

Dina led me to the microphone. I could hear applause, and my family cheered.

🐕 "I saw Daddy go to the front of the patio with Dina. Something was up."

Then Carrie came out with Musket. He was excited, and when he saw me, started to jump up. I said in a firm whisper "No. Down." I knew Dina was watching. And probably grinning.

Ben offered me the mike. And to the amazement of my family and my everlasting shame, I said in a choking voice, "I don't have anything to say. Just thank you."

Carrie kissed my cheek and rose to the occasion. I think the emotion I was feeling must have been written all over my face. She made a speech about raising Musket and how proud she was that he was going to guide me.

As it turned out, I was the only one of all twenty-one students who didn't make a short speech.

🐕 "My new daddy was holding my leash while we watched Loran, Floria and the other dogs given to their new mommies and daddies. For some reason Daddy seemed upset with himself. I licked his hand and he smiled. "Thanks, little buddy," he said. I liked that name."

David commented on my unusual silence. "Dog got your tongue, Bro?"

"Smartass."

He understood, since he'd been through it before. He still kids me about it.

And then it was over. Musket was mine.

More than nine years have passed since that day, and I can't even imagine my life without him.

🐕 "And I feel the same way. I have a wonderful mommy. Oh, and a good daddy."

By the way, I threw out the pink underwear before I packed.

Chapter Three

The Three Musketeers

We drove home in a rented van, Jane at the wheel and her mother next to her. Dad and I sat in the back seat.

Even though I was going home after a month, I distinctly got the feeling I just barely won the privilege of riding on the seat and not in the back, where Musket spent the trip.

For a day and a half it was all about him.

🐕 "Daddy's exaggerating. I heard Mommy ask why there was no underwear in his suitcase. I don't think Daddy heard her. I was excited to be going to my new home. Every time we stopped, Daddy took me for a little walk. Pop-pop took pictures of me peeing. That took some getting used to."

When we reached the house I showed Musket around. He scampered from room to room.

🐕 "Smells, scents, aromas, fragrances, odors. I found them in every room. Dogs see with their noses and my new home was beautiful.

No other dogs. That was a good thing. Oh, goody! Carpeting for me to rub my face on! It sure beat cold concrete."

A set of matched Longaberger ceramic bowls were in place under the kitchen desk. Only the best for Jane's baby.

🐕 "Mommy put two bowls on the floor for me. They were big, but Daddy didn't fill them. At first he gave me about four itty-bitty little cups of food, barely enough to live on. I'd have to work on him through Mommy. She could see my big soulful eyes even if he couldn't."

Musket's bed was in the master bedroom upstairs, a plush plaid flannel pillow with, I swear I'm not making this up, his name embroidered on the front.

She poofed it up before he got into it. "Here you go, Musket," she said, her eyes shining.

🐕 "I lay down in my bed and Mommy petted me. I was so happy."

Deep down in the bedrock I felt a subtle and relentless shifting of the familial tectonic plates which defined my status in my own home.

The Three Musketeers

Of course Jane was happy to have me back, but Musket was the star of the hour.

Jane's increasing love for Musket made her early resolve wilt like a wax flower in a microwave. And the first to go was the 'tie-down' rule.

The school recommended the dog be tied down for a couple of hours a day and all night for the first few weeks to help him feel comfortable in his place. 'Go to bed,' was the command, and when Musket climbed in, he was praised and petted.

Jane didn't like the tie-down yet understood how it helped the transition. But before long she started asking me if Musket could stay off tie-down for a night, just so she could feel he wasn't a prisoner.

🐕 "I was framed, Mommy! Get me a lawyer!"

Musket at Halloween

In time I gave in, and Musket slept in his bed without restraint. A few weeks later he made a break for it. One night he crept over and lay on the floor next to the bed.

I'll give you one guess whose side.

"Well what do you expect? Daddy snored like a chainsaw."

In an amazingly short time Jane and Musket had forged a bond based on love and affection rather than trust and duty.

The way Musket reacted when he saw his mommy after being out all day or even an hour had to be seen to be believed. Once his harness came off he was all over her, slobbering her with kisses.

"I got so happy when I saw her I couldn't think straight. Daddy thought it was funny but I was totally sincere. I'd die without Mommy's love. She held me close to her soft and warm chest, kissing me and telling me how much she missed me. I was the happiest dog in the whole world."

The center of Jane's world

He became the joy of her life. With no children of our own, Musket filled the role of an adopted son, but without asking for the car keys, running up a cell phone bill, or getting into trouble with the police.

When Jane relaxed on her overstuffed chaise lounge watching TV or reading, Musket liked to climb up and lie between her feet. It was quite a stretch for her since he was no Yorkshire Terrier but they were as happy as a mommy and baby could be.

Jane sometimes sang to Musket. She had a rich melodious voice, like Anne Murray. She loved to sing 'You are my sunshine' to Musket, ending with "Please don't take my Musket away."

"Mommy sang to me and I felt the love in the sound. She sang a lot better than Daddy. His singing made me want to lie down and put my paws over my ears.

She made up short ditties for Musket.

"What's new Bugaboo? Whoa wah-whoa ho-ho, What's new Bugaboo? Whoa wah-whoa ho-ho . . .

Bugaboo, Bugaboo, I love you, yes, I doooooo . . ."

"I'm sure Tom Jones wouldn't mind."

She came down the stairs singing "Gimme an 'M!' Gimme a 'U!' Gimme an 'S!'" By then Musket was in a frenzy, spinning and panting like crazy.

Jane continued, in a more excited voice. "Gimme a 'K!' Gimme an 'E!" Gimme a 'T!'"

She reached the base of the stairs to Musket who was almost berserk with excitement.

Then without missing a beat, Jane said "Gimme a kiss!"

"Oh, that was fun! Mommy really got me going. I gave her a good kiss."

On holidays Musket and I went to the Hallmark store where we made friends with Sandy, a wonderful saleslady. She always welcomed us and asked, "So a Mother's Day card for Musket's mommy?"

"Yes," I answered for him.

She took us to the right section. Then she asked Musket, "What kind of card do you want, Musket?"

🐕 "I want something that tells Mommy how much I love her."

That was easily done. She often found the right card in two or three tries. I paid for it.

🐕 "Yeah, for some reason I never seem to have my wallet on me."

Sure. I believe that. We got cards for her birthday from each of us, for our anniversary, the date of which I have memorized, for Easter, Valentine's Day, Christmas, and National Rubber Stamping Day.

There really is one. It was funny when the saleslady read the cards out loud to me. Some of them were pretty passionate. I'm sure it raised a few eyebrows.

🐕 "I don't know why Daddy got squeamish about it. The lady was reading them for me."

Then we went over to Trader Joe's and bought flowers. They have the best fresh flowers there. Jane always thanked Musket for his thoughtfulness. And me, too.

Zen and the Art of Belly Rubs

Musket twitched in his sleep. After about ten or fifteen minutes he had minor spasms, barking or whimpering. Jane only had to say, "Musket, Mommy loves you," and he settled down.

🐕 "I felt better knowing Mommy was there to protect me."

Musket was allowed to get on our bed while we were dressing. That was another rule Jane conveniently forgot.

Jane loved to play 'Where's my Musket?' I pulled the covers over him. He was completely out and didn't care.

I said loudly, "Honey I can't find Musket."

She said her line. "Where's my Musket?"

Soon the covers quivered and a big lump moved to the edge. His sleepy head emerged.

"There he is!"

His tail was wagging under the blanket.

Sure it was silly but cute as hell. Like I said he was her baby.

🐕 "I liked to do it for Mommy. But calling me a 'lump' was a bit insulting."

Musket loved belly rubs. And he wasn't shy about it. When I stepped out of the shower or went from one room to another, there he was, in the way, 'paws up.' Jane said he looked as if he were drying his nails. Very cute and impossible to resist. He loved to have his belly rubbed by pretty much everybody. Believe me he wasn't picky.

🐕 "It was my way of making the world a happier place. I think a belly rub made everybody happy. Just an FYI, I tend to shed just a bit, so it's not a good idea to wear dark clothes when rubbing my belly."

I've often wondered about that little quirk when dogs have their belly rubbed. Dogs have a particular spot which made their hind leg kick. Musket, maybe you can clear that up?

🐕 "I'd be happy to. Only people we love can find that special spot. When they hit it, we show our pleasure by trying to scratch at the spot while they rub it. Their fingers are like a really ticklish flea. It's totally involuntary but wow, it feels soooooooo goooood!"

Sort of a 'Tickle me Elmo button, huh?

🐕 "Whatever, it feels good."

Musket also loved getting his butt scratched. He slid in between someone's legs and stopped like a furry car in a car wash.

His tail wagged while his now-captive friend used all ten fingers to vigorously massage his rump. Boy, did he love that.

"Yeah, almost, more, more, a little more, that's the spot! Ahhhhh."

Musket used people as Kleenex. He rubbed his face and nose against our pants to wipe his nose, but made it seem as if he wanted to show how much he loved us.

"It feels like lovin' but it'snot."

Wagging the Flag

It's been said some people wear their heart on their sleeve.

Dogs wear theirs on their butt.

A dog's tail isn't a prehensile tool, as for monkeys, or balance for cats. Some dogs don't even have tails. So what good are they? What purpose do they serve?

A very important one. It's a flag, an indicator of the dog's mood and intention.

When they're scared or guilty it's tucked between their legs; if they're sad, it droops. Excited dog tails twitch. And it wags when the dog is happy.

I don't know what the tail of an aggressive or mean dog does. I'm too busy avoiding the teeth.

Believe me if people had tails, there would be a lot less bar fights, domestic violence and war.

But on the other hand, or should I say 'end' is Musket's tail.

It's called an 'Otter' tail, very heavy and thick at the base, tapering to a point. He wagged it the way enthusiastic fans wave the flag at the Olympic Games. I've had an idea to tie a fan on it for hot days.

"Sure, make me do all the work."

He knocked over lamps, vases and bric-a-brac, making bric-a-broke. He was Mr. Oblivious, a furry wrecking ball.

"I never did that. Did I?"

Musket's tail was one of his most interesting features. I don't think he knew it was even there. I liked to grab his tail and show it to him. "Hey Musket, go get the tail! Get the tail!" He turned and looked as if to say 'Hey where'd that come from?' Sometimes I could get him to take it in his mouth and spin around a few times. Nine times was the record. The crowd roared.

"He's a funny guy. Of course I knew I had a tail but the darned thing had a mind of its own."

When his Mommy came into a room his tail knew it before he did. He was sound asleep. Then a couple of inches went Twitch, twitch.

"Where's my Musket?" Jane asked.

Half his tail went active, rapidly patting the floor. Whapwhapwhap.

"Is that my Musket?"

And then the sound of a pile driver was heard. Wham, wham, wham.

He hadn't even moved. Just the tail.

Then he leapt up and slobbered Jane with loving kisses.

His tail was his antenna, ready to transmit his feelings about everything from meeting a new friend to waiting to go for a walk.

"Follow my butt, Daddy."

Doggy Daze

Musket could tell time better than me. Almost exactly eight hours after being let out at night he woke up, ready to start the day.

The day started at around 4:30. He began by giving Jane a lick on her sleeping face.

"Good morning, Mommy!"

It drove her nuts. Grunting, she reached over to wake me.

"Why can't he wake you instead?"

"Because he loves his mommy. I'm just the butler."

I went down the stairs with Musket at my heels. That prompted one of my first rules. He was so eager to get downstairs he frequently rode the back of my legs all the way. After a couple of near accidents, I made him wait at the top of the stairs.

🐕 "Well hurry up, slowpoke. I gotta pee."

I heard his tail banging against the banister in anticipation.

🐕 "It was like that ketchup commercial, only harder. 'An-tic-cip-ay-tion . . . he's making me way-ayt.'"

At the front door I called him.

If I live to be a hundred I'll never figure out how he could control all four feet running down the stairs. It sounded like a truckload of bowling balls. His tail banged along the banister like a playing card in a bicycle's spokes. He charged out the door and disappeared.

Sometimes he tried to trick me. He went out, did an 'about face' on the doormat and came in.

🐕 "Daddy wasn't fooled. 'Nice try, Musket. You go right back out there and do your business. Now.'"

When he came back inside his tail propelled him like a helicopter rotor.

If I closed the door and went into the kitchen it didn't stop him. I heard a 'thump' and 'BANG!' as the door was pushed open. A police battering ram would have been quieter.

When I closed it completely I heard a 'bump' and then another one. It was hard not to giggle.

🐕 "Daddy. The door is shut. I don't have opposable thumbs. Open it!"

While I filled his bowls that tail beat the hell out of the wall.

When I lowered the bowl to the floor his head followed it down, thrusting his nose into the mound of wet kibble. A mere eleven seconds later not a speck of food remained.

I once offered to let him chow down in the bin where we kept the kibble. I opened the lid and said "Go ahead, little buddy."

He just stared at it. I think his mental circuits overloaded.

🐕 "I didn't know he really meant it. The food was just sitting there, mounds and acres and tons of it. And I couldn't move."

I knew when Jane was coming down the stairs because Musket's tail beat the wall, he panted like a racehorse after the Kentucky Derby and ran in circles with excitement.

"Mommy's here," I said unnecessarily.

Jane said "Where's my Musket? Does Mommy get kisses?" Then she bent over and he slobbered her face with wet puppy love. See a pattern here?

Then he got his treat.

While he was inhaling it I got my morning kiss and ready to leave for work.

Then came what we called the 'spiel.'

She sat down with him and said, "Musket you be a good Guide dog. Take good care of Daddy. Anybody touches your harness you bite their butt. Anybody offers you any food you say 'No thank you my daddy fed me,' and tonight when you get home you give Mommy lots and lots and lots of kisses. Can I have a kiss now?"

He was probably thinking about that 'no thanks my daddy fed me' bit. He never, ever said it. Believe me, I've listened carefully.

🐕 "Well . . . I kept forgetting."

I kept his harness on the newel post at the bottom of the stairs.

"Okay, Musket let's get you racked up," I said.

He put his head in the harness, then I reached under to connect the belly strap. The leash was clipped to the ring on his collar.

🐕 "Okay, Daddy. Let's run through the check list. Treats?"

Check.

🐕 “Poop bags?”

Check.

🐕 “Treats?”

Again, check.

🐕 “Water bottle and collapsible bowl?”

Check.

🐕 “Lots of treats?”

Sigh. I’ll get some more.

🐕 “Mommy has been kissed. Okay we’re good to go.”

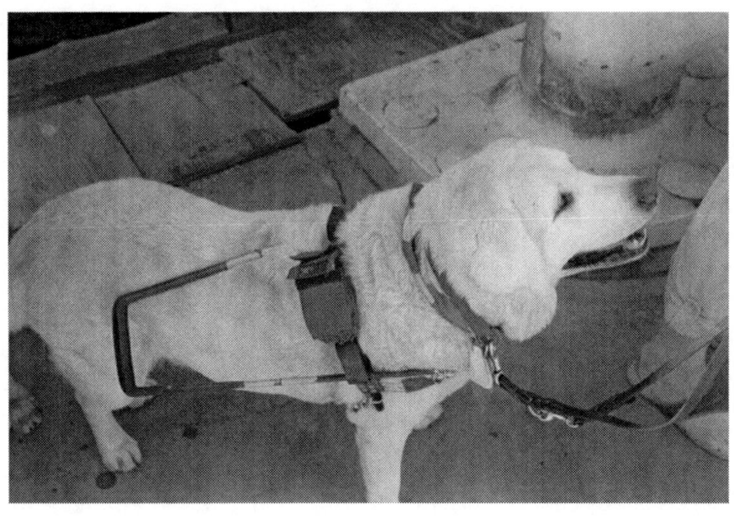

Musket in his work clothes

The beginning of Musket's work day began at the front walk to the sidewalk. We walked to the bus stop every day.

Then about three years after Musket joined us a couple of things changed. Jane started caring for her parents every day and my office moved to Mission Valley. That meant an earlier departure, so Jane dropped us at the bus on her way to her parents. Jane was really practical about shopping and errands. She knew how to get the most out of a tank of gas.

And she was a wizard with coupons. She could buy $400 worth of groceries for $200. Amazing.

Musket usually grabbed a few more minutes' sleep in the back seat of our Hyundai Santa Fe SUV.

The license plate frame declared 'I Love My Dog' and magnetic paw prints scampered up the back. A bumper sticker proudly proclaimed 'My Labrador is smarter than your honor student.'

Wait, there's more. The license plate was 'I♥Musket.'

Sometimes people who thought Jane was a black powder shooter.

Were we crazy? But it gets better. Our answering machine message was 'You've reached the home of Jane, Mark and Musket, the Three Musketeers. One for all, and all for . . . Musket! Please leave your name . . .' and so on.

"No one but Nanny ever left a message just for me."

At the bus stop Jane called Musket forward and kissed him.

I got one AFTER Musket.

"Mommy had her priorities, so did I."

In the next chapter I'll write about working with Musket.

The Little Engine that Begged

Food was as much a part of Musket's life as breathing. More, in fact. I'm sure he'd survive if he gave up breathing.

"Funny man."

When Jane was working a regular full-time job the schedule was predictable, but after she started caring for her parents, we had to wing it.

If she got home first dinner was often waiting when we arrived. Typically she had a good, hot and tasty meal ready. Jane's great cooking never disappointed me, as my waistline will attest.

Musket was right there, unwilling to miss a thing. When food was being made, moved or consumed, he watched like a hungry wolf.

🐕 "'Mommy's in the kitchen with din-ner,

Mommy's in the kitchen I know-oh-oh-oh . . .

Mommy's in the kitchen with din-ner, strummin' on the old ban-jo.'

Sorry, got carried away."

If we got home first I made dinner. I fry up a mean hamburger.

🐕 "Mean he called it. Yeah, mean like in 'nasty.'"

I did know my way around our kitchen.

Even blind, I managed well. But I'm a guy, too. Therefore nothing I did made any sense whatsoever to Jane.

Jane tried to cope with it but I was hopeless. And probably not trainable.

🐕 "Maybe we should send him back to school Mommy."

Don't tempt her, Musket. I had to put things where I could find them. With my lousy peripheral vision it was lost as soon as I blinked.

Sometimes I even lost track of the walls.

When I moved around in the house I might get disoriented, thinking I was facing one way when in fact I was pointed somewhere else.

Bonk! Oh, there's a wall.

Then I heard Jane's resigned sigh. "That wall hasn't moved, Honey. It's right where it's always been."

🐕 "I laughed every time Mommy said that. She was so funny."

Yeah, a real hoot.

On a related note, I was hopeless at remembering things she told me.

"I told you last week we were going to . . ." and so on.

Hubby readers can relate. It's true I didn't hear very well.

But in my defense, Jane could change the subject in the middle of a syllable. I'll give you an example:

"Honey tonight we're going to the Smith's for dinner wear the clothes I ironed for you need to bring that bottle of wine in the refrigerator has to be cleaned this weekend can you weed the garden before I have my friends over for tea on Saturday you need to be out of the house."

🐈 "All I got out of that was the word 'dinner.' Daddy hasn't a chance."

If you were counting she put seven subjects into that one sentence.

1. Smith's for dinner.
2. Wear the clothes I ironed.
3. Bring the wine.
4. Clean the refrigerator.
5. Weed the garden.
6. I'm having friends for tea on Saturday.
7. I want you out of the house.

Read it again and you'll see all of them. But just try hearing it once.

Was it too much to ask for a pause? Try taking a breath between sentences.

🐈 "I think I'm with Daddy on this one. I was confused too."

Now that's loyalty.

When I heard Jane drive into the garage I said, "Mommy's home, Musket."

I stood by the screen door to the garage, holding it until Jane shut off the engine.

Musket shot out like a missile.

Jane opened the car door and the usual ritual began. He stood and slobbered her while his tail wagged furiously.

"Mommy missed you!"

Anticipating Musket's greeting helped get her through the day.

At the precise instant we sat down to eat, we heard the sound of the Little Engine That Begged.

He panted like a steam locomotive in preparation for his life's work. Eating.

🐕 "It was a labor of love and I had to psych myself for it."

Remember those 'rules?'

Jane had said 'He's not going to beg at the table or be given food scraps.'

That rule lasted, according to my talking watch, six seconds. They were falling like a row of dominoes.

🐕 "I wonder why it took so long."

He gave her 'The Look.' Even though I couldn't see it I knew what it looked like. His gorgeous cocoa-brown eyes bored into hers, the caramel ears cocked as he twitched his expressive eyebrows. She caved in before the steam stopped rising from the plate.

🐕 "Look into my eyes, you are growing weaker . . . yes, you will succumb to my begging."

Musket started doing what we called 'Watching a tennis match.' His head went back and forth, left and right. Jane said he never blinked.

🐕 "I didn't want to miss anything."

Those rules were dead and buried. To add to her disgrace, another hard rule fell in flames.

While I cleaned off the table Jane said, "Give Mommy kisses." He climbed up to her lap and gave the table the 'once-over' first.

She let Musket lick her plate on the table. That was too much. It could lead to problems later. I hadn't totally gone soft.

It was pretty rare for me to put my foot down but I did.

I know she still does it when I'm not around.

🐈 "I checked the table for anything they might have missed."

Over the years Musket fine-tuned his 'begging look' by learning what earned the most response. If he heard an 'Oh, he's so cute!' he knew he'd hit pay dirt.

I suspect he even sucked in his cheeks and stomach to appear malnourished.

🐈 "Dang. I think Daddy's on to me. Sure I tried to look cute but I never, repeat never sucked in my belly. I *am* undernourished. Really. He only fed me two measly cups of food a day. I used to get four but then I started gaining weight and couldn't fit into my harness. I think he tightened it to fool me."

Jane often bought bagels. Hot, fresh, Sesame, Onion, and our favorite, Cinnamon Raisin. And there was Musket. We began to call them 'Begels.'

🐈 "Cute."

Musket had a healthy appetite for pretty much anything. He liked vegetables and meat. We were careful what we gave him, and only in very small bits. When we were eating something he couldn't have, we could only say, "I'm sorry, Musket. You can't have any of this. It's not good for you."

🐈 "*You're* sorry? How do you think I feel?"

It wasn't easy to say no, but we loved him too much to risk it."

🐈 "Oh, that's okay then. NOT!"

He had a good long-term memory for commands, routes, places and people. But his short-term memory for food was virtually nonexistent.

Even before the morsel reached his stomach he forgot about it.

🐕 "That was then, this is now."

And willpower? Not our dog. Sometimes I dropped things. And 'things' could mean food. Musket set a rule too. It was called the 'one-nanosecond rule.'

A nanosecond is one-billionth of a second. For non-astrophysicists, light travels one meter in a nanosecond. When food was on the floor Musket made the speed of light look lazy.

Yes, Musket I'll make sure I get it right.

🐕 "We'll see."

Ahem. 'Any food item dropped on the floor and not retrieved before the elapsed time of one nanosecond is automatically his.'

🐕 "He is trainable."

If I had some gravy or meat juice on my fingers I let him lick it off. He was a great napkin.

I often wondered why does he have a tongue? He just inhales food. Can anybody eat a strip of chicken jerky in less than ten minutes?

Musket can swallow a whole strip like a wood-chipper set to maximum.

The food was down his gullet so fast his tongue was never involved.

🐕 "No wonder everything tastes the same."

I tried to find ways to slow him, short of tying his mouth shut. We bought a couple of bones at the pet store. They were clean hollow beef bones and I put a strip of jerky inside. The trick was to jam it in deep to make him work for it. The bone was good for his teeth. He usually got it out in under a minute. If I got lucky he was at that bone for an hour. I'm sure he swore at me the whole time.

🐕 "I didn't swear, Daddy. I just glared at you. But I never gave up."

But Musket did surprise us. We had dinner at the Hunter Steakhouse in Oceanside. The waiter was fawning over Musket and asked the chef to come out. The chef, also a dog lover, asked if we would like to take home some Prime Rib bones for Musket.

Of course we agreed. Musket liked bones, and a good Prime Rib bone with a little meat on it should be a real treat for him.

Guess what he did?

Nothing. Just sniffed the bones and walked away. I'll never figure it out.

🐕 "He served it with white wine. Hello?"

While writing this book I was on a Star Trek binge. I'm a purist in addition to being old enough to remember the original series. Never mind William Shatner's wooden ham acting. That show had style. I memorized tons of useless dialogue and trivia. And one day I had a thought. Imagine this in Shatner's eloquent voice, accompanied by Alexander Courage's evocative theme music.

Food . . .
The *only* frontier
These are the forages of the Guide dog Musket
His lifelong mission, to explore strange new scents,
To seek out new morsels and new bits of food,
To boldly eat where no Guide dog has eaten before!

🐕 "Does anybody have a phaser?"

Climbing Mt. Musket

After dinner I either went out to my office to work and exercise or upstairs to watch TV with Jane. We turned the front room into a TV room with a comfy couch.

Musket had one of his beds in the corner. But of course he hardly used it. He preferred to lie either in the doorway or at my feet so I had to climb over his furry butt. I felt like Sir Edmund Hillary conquering Mt. Musket.

🐕 "He might go and get something to eat without me knowing about it."

When I was in my office Jane was usually in hers, paying bills or doing a craft project.

Once in a while, usually on weekends she asked me to take Musket for a while. He could get a bit clingy at times. She called him furry Saran Wrap.

🐕 "Clingy? Me?"

While I worked at my computer Musket slept on his mat. But he couldn't sleep for long so he came over and made his presence known by a soft whine.

🐕 "I don't whine."

That was his 'pay attention to me I need love' signal.

I turned around and bent down. If he gave me a kiss I gave him a few pieces of kibble.

🐕 "Okay, maybe a little whine. Just a bit."

Musket may have been a hard-working and dedicated Guide dog, but when he wanted to be lazy he could qualify for the Couch Potato Olympics. I once put some kibble in front of his mouth while he slept.

Any normal dog would lift his head and eat. Not my dog.

The mouth opened, the tongue scooped the food in, chewed and swallowed.

All without moving his head.

🐕 "That would waste precious energy."

The Troll Under the Bed

I let him out about 9:00. Jane was almost always asleep. If he was upstairs I had to whisper loudly. It isn't easy. Try it sometime. Jane was a very light sleeper. A ladybug fart would wake her.

Finally Mr. Lazy Butt rose, gave himself a shake and arrived at the top of the stairs.

Then he stopped. I knew he was standing up there looking down at me.

Sigh. "Come on," I had to say nearly every night. "I'm not standing here for my health."

Then he finally came down the stairs like a comatose drunk. I opened the door and he dragged himself out to kill the plants.

"Go forth and spray," I told him. Or "Leak now or forever hold your pee."

"Sheesh. Yawn."

After he did his business I told him to go upstairs.

Did he listen to me and go upstairs? Nope. He stood on the bottom landing and watched me like a hawk. You've heard about that feeling of being watched? I knew just what it felt like.

"Daddy made his lunch at night. Why would I go upstairs?"

Bedtime for me was later than for Jane. She was a morning person. I'm not as much of a late-nighter as I used to be, but I was usually ready for bed by 10:00. Musket was snoring on the floor.

Remember the old fairy tale about the troll under the bridge? Where the traveler had to pay the troll in order to pass? Well that troll, in our house was named Musket and he lived under Jane's side of the bed.

"Troll? Me? Grunt."

His head was under the bed while the rest of him was out on the floor. If Jane needed to get up during the night, there he was, blocking the way and demanding the toll.

🐕 "Ye who wishes to pass must pay first. My belly needs rubbing, fair lady."

He somehow managed, even in sleep to roll over and present his belly to her. But he didn't move out of the way.

Her line was usually "Don't bother moving, Musket. I don't mind climbing over you."

He never seemed to recognize sarcasm.

🐕 "As long as you're up, can you get me a treat?"

Snuggling with Daddy

When Musket was sleeping on the bed and I came upstairs, I heard him before I stepped into the room. A long, drawn-out, exasperated 'Dang, Daddy's here. I have to get off the bed now' sigh.

🐕 "Daddy never took the hint and slept on the floor."

When he did get up, it was like watching a glacier move. I mean s-l-o-w. His front end slid off the bed to the floor and moved away.

His butt was still asleep.

Then it too poured onto the floor until only his back paws clung tenaciously to the bed. He looked like a furry bridge.

"I was comfortable. Now his side of the bed is warm and I have to get on the hard floor. You bet I took my time."

CHAPTER FOUR

MARCHING WITH MY MUSKET

In the first week after we came home from Guide Dogs, Musket and I took walks so he would get used to his new surroundings.

The route to the bus stop, stores, bank, and vet became second nature to him and soon he became well known in the neighborhood.

This is a good opportunity to explain what a Guide dog really does. Some people asked how Musket knew where to go. He actually didn't. That was my job, not his.

"It's not like he could just say, 'Let's go to the bank, Musket.'

It was my job to get us there safely. I watched out for obstacles, moving cars, curbs, anything that could be a danger to Daddy and me.

If I saw something big on the sidewalk, I stopped. Daddy used his foot or hand to identify it and then commanded me to go around it. When we were moving again, he told me 'Good boy.' I loved hearing I did a good job."

Cane or Canine

I recently did something amusing when I was using my cane. Musket wasn't feeling good so I gave him the day off. Standing on a curb waiting to cross the street, I made sure it was clear. Then I said, 'Forward.'

To my cane.

Tell me I'm not a seasoned Guide dog handler.

🐕 "Now that's funny."

Some blind persons prefer the cane to a dog. I did pretty well with the stick. But with my fast pace I often didn't have enough warning to avoid an obstacle. Canes don't have brains and they break. It's a matter of preference. I like dogs.

🐕 "Canes are okay but I got nervous when Daddy used his to go get the mail. Daddy could trip on a painted line."

Sometimes when I used the cane people asked me where Musket was. I said, "This is him. He just lost a lot of weight."

🐕 "I can't understand why Daddy hasn't made it at the Improv. He's so funny. NOT!"

A bond had to develop between Musket and myself, a total trust in each other. It didn't take long for him to show me how good a Guide dog he was. Walking through a supermarket parking lot one night, we found ourselves in an area with dozens of shopping carts haphazardly scattered around us. I guess some teenagers did it to show how cool they were.

Anyway, we were surrounded by them. It was a real obstacle course.

But did it faze Musket?

🐕 "Puh-leeze. Daddy followed me through and he never bumped a single cart. When we got out he gave me a big hug and a treat. He said he was really proud of me."

It felt like following a snake, weaving in and out, past and around the overturned carts. Just incredible.

One late winter evening during our first year together we stopped at a curb in our neighborhood. When I was sure it was safe, I said, "Forward."

He didn't move. I repeated the command with a flick of the leash. Still nothing. I even gave the harness handle a little push. He wouldn't budge.

I decided to find out what was stopping him. I reached out and felt nothing. No parked car, no garbage can. I reached a bit farther. My fingers touched a strip of plastic tape. It finally dawned on me we were standing at the edge of a construction pit. The tape wouldn't have stopped me if I'd moved off the curb. I had no idea how deep the pit was, but that wasn't important. Musket had saved my butt.

🐕 "I sure did. And he gave me a lot of praise for doing my job."

After those two incidents I learned to trust him fully. He was never wrong.

When we were walking to the bus stop, every day was different, even though we followed the same route. It was surprising how many obstacles and dangers we encountered in our own neighborhood. Cars parked too far out on the driveway, uncoiled garden hoses, plumbing trucks with long pipe, bikes, you name it, Musket and I have found it. We even found a long-dead Christmas tree lying on the sidewalk in February.

One night, arriving at home after a long walk, I told him, "It must be boring to guide me, Musket. Nothing ever happens."

🐕 "Not as long as I did my job right."

Even though Musket was very good at being a guide, there were a few mishaps, but nothing serious. Musket is trying to censor me, but I'm going to tell the truth.

🐕 "Sigh. If you must. I won't forget this."

Jane and I visited a Japanese Tea Garden in San Jose a few years ago. We both love the quiet fragrant beauty of the orderly garden environment.

Musket was guiding me along a raised zigzag wooden boardwalk over rock gardens. He cut an inside corner and I stepped into the open space. I fell about three feet and my face ended up on a level with one sheepish Guide dog.

He gave me a few guilty kisses.

🐕 "Okay, I goofed. Let's move on."

"Seafood, anyone?" Musket at the Koi pond in the Tea Garden

More recently we were walking to a bus at a transit center. The bus was parked about a foot from the curb with the door open. Musket just jumped up into the bus and I missed the step.

I went tumbling. Again I wasn't hurt. The leash was still in my hand as the driver tried to help me stand. I felt Musket's gaze on me.

🐕 "Daddy was okay. He was laughing and threatening to send me back to the school. He was joking. I think."

Well, in Musket's defense he also did some very selfless things I still can't believe.

We were going through an area in Mission Valley with no sidewalk. For at least two hundred yards the roadside was rough gravel.

I didn't want to risk walking out in the traffic so we stayed on the gravel. I knew it had to be uncomfortable for him. We reached the end and I moved him to some grass and let him rest.

On the way back he again had to lead me through the gravel.

Unknown to me, he had earlier developed a foot infection which caused him a lot of pain. And yet my loyal Guide dog did his job. I never forgot that.

Tricks and Treats

Musket was an excellent Guide dog and earned praise. I fell into the habit of giving him a treat when we reached the bus stop or work or home.

He very quickly got used to it. When we reached our destination he immediately turned to me. 'Okay Daddy, pay up.'

"Daddy didn't have to pay me. But it was our routine. I got tired walking and needed a bit of energy to survive."

It was a delicate balance. At school he ate in the morning before a workout and in the afternoon before the last workout. He burned off the food.

But at home he wasn't working off the second bowl and slept on it. That made his weight bloom. I wasn't about to take his weight gain lightly.

"I said he liked bad puns. That was one of them."

I changed to a healthy reduced fat Eukanuba and cut down on the amount per meal. On walks he got bits of chicken jerky. If he got me somewhere safely, he got a treat. C.O.D.

"UPS. United Pooch Service."

That's how I learned Musket could count. If I put three treats in my pocket and in the course of a walk he only received two, he knew there was one left. And he was persistent until he was paid in full, even to the point of pushing his nose against my pocket.

🐕 "I didn't have to be Einstein. How hard could it be to subtract two from three?"

Sometimes I casually put my hand in the 'pocketful of miracles.' People laughed when they watched Musket cock his head. "Aw, isn't that cute?"

🐕 "It wasn't cute. It was survival."

Some Guide dog handlers have harness signs reading 'Please don't pet me,' or 'Working dog, please don't pet.'

🐕 "That wasn't Daddy's style. He wanted people to meet me. He made a sign like you used to see in car windows which cautioned 'Baby on Board.' His sign said 'Blind Guy on Board.' A lot of people thought it was funny. I thought I should have a sign like they have on taxis. 'On Duty.'"

That sign was probably my first attempt to break down the barriers of public anonymity. I wanted to show Musket off. I kept the sign until if finally fell apart. By then everybody knew us.

Musket's memory for places we've been or routes we traveled was phenomenal. I called it his 'route memory.' No matter how myriad and twisted a course we took to enter a building, Musket always got us out with no trouble. He was really good in dark crowded restaurants.

When we checked into a hotel somewhere the first thing I did was find the nearest lawn, and taught Musket the route. He only needed to be shown once.

🐕 "Finding my way in was a lot harder than finding my way to the nearest lawn."

Once when walking past a row of shops on a downtown sidewalk, Musket suddenly stopped at a doorway.

I had to determine what made him stop. Finally I realized we were in front of a sandwich shop we'd been in once before.

Five years ago.

🐕 "Just in case Daddy was hungry."

When we entered a shopping center he wasn't sure where I wanted to go. It might have been the supermarket, the bank, office supply or any of a dozen other destinations. He slowed at every doorway.

🐕 "That was my job. Of course I might linger a bit longer at the food stores. Just in case."

Recently we were on a sidewalk we hadn't walked in at least a year. He stopped. I reached out with my foot and felt a thick crack in the concrete. I had once tripped on it. He remembered it perfectly.

Some Guide dogs develop 'behaviors' which require corrections or retraining. My brother's second dog, Geppetto started showing a tendency to 'hug' the building side of a sidewalk.

In other words he was staying as far from the curb as possible.

That was okay up to a point. But it wasn't correct behavior and could have been dangerous with open doors, moving cars, sidewalk cafes and such. David tried to correct this but it soon became apparent the dog needed retraining and was returned to the school.

🐕 "You won't do that to me, will you Daddy? I'll be good, I promise."

Musket did develop some quirks I wanted either to stop or control. For instance, when he smelled another dog's scent or needed to pee he just stepped off the sidewalk and began sniffing.

I managed to discourage that behavior but I also didn't want him to have to hold it in. I trained him to warn me by slowing down and signaling he needed to go. Then I stopped and said "Okay, little buddy. Go for it."

🐕 "And boy did I appreciate that."

I could feel his gait through the harness. He walked pretty fast, with little variation. He quivered when another dog was nearby and I felt it. If he started limping I checked his paws for slivers or gravel.

When a car horn honked or we heard a loud noise Musket snapped his head around to see what it was. It was probably reflex but he was also being alert for danger.

"That was partly training and partly instinct. And sometimes it was Mommy honking the horn when she drove by."

Dirty Weather and Dirty Deeds

Wintertime in San Diego wasn't freezing but compared to the summer heat it did get chilly. Musket had his winter coat and didn't mind the cold at all.

"Are you blind? I'm barefoot!"

We got caught in our first rainstorm in November of 2002, coming up Ted Williams Parkway from the bus stop. The wind was blowing in our faces, the air pregnant with moisture. I wanted to get home before it started.

We didn't make it. The skies opened up like an air tanker unloading on a brush fire.

We had about a quarter mile to go, and we were getting drenched. Musket took it in stride. His ears were plastered back and his thick coat became sodden.

Me? I was laughing like a hyena. It was just so funny. I knew we'd be drowned by the time we got home but what was the harm?

On we trudged forcing our way into the icy black teeth of the raging torrent.

"There goes Daddy being a writer again."

When we reached the house, the rain stopped. Of course.

Jane ran to get some towels and started drying her baby, cooing to him. "Poor Musket, are you cold? Did Daddy make you walk in the rain? Let Mommy dry you off and put you in a nice warm bed."

Sigh. I, on the other hand had to dry myself off.

"Hi Honey, I'm home."

"Well think about it, Daddy. You can dry off in ten minutes. I take hours. Mommy was worried I'd catch a cold."

I bought a raincoat for Musket in case we got caught in the rain again. One fell apart in a week, and the next made him look like a yellow plastic monk.

Fortunately the Great Flood was rare in San Diego.

"The last raincoat he bought me was just right. It was blue with Velcro straps. I thought it made me look pretty cool."

On the other end of the thermometer, San Diego weather was warm at the best of times, but in late summer it could really be blazing hot. Musket handled the hot sidewalks pretty well but I knew dogs could have their paws burned on heated blacktop.

"Daddy rinsed my feet with cold water on hot days. I gave him kisses when he did."

I was worried about him walking on the hot pavement. We bought some doggy shoes online. This requires a bit of word imagery. They were like sneakers, oval-shaped with long laces to tie around the ankles. The first and only time we put them on he gave us a look of pure humiliated loathing. Even with my lousy vision I could see how he looked. Like a clown. Despite our love for Musket it was the funniest thing we'd ever seen. If we had a video camera handy it would be on Youtube.

I asked Jane, "What did we ever do for entertainment before he came along?"

"I don't remember," she said, trying not to laugh.

"One time is all it took to convince Mommy and Daddy the shoes were a mistake. They flopped and I had to pick my feet up really high to walk. Then the laces worked loose and in a few moments they were dragging. I never forgot those awful things. And if Daddy ever brings them out of the closet again I quit.

On hot days Jane often picked us up from the bus. She didn't want his little feet to be burned.

"It's too hot for Musket," was her usual defense.

I agreed. He wore a fur coat, after all.

🐕 "I sure didn't have a problem with the ride home with Mommy."

When we stepped off the bus and didn't start home he knew something was up. "Is Mommy coming? Are you going to give Mommy kisses?" Yes, I was shameless. I knew his kisses were the high point of Jane's day.

She pulled over and his tail wagged so hard it created a breeze.

I pulled open the back door and he jumped in and started plastering her face. Frequently Jane had to clean her sunglasses.

Meanwhile I climbed in, unnoticed. Finally he was done. Jane's face was wet and happy.

"Good Musket," I told him.

I was lucky to get a handshake.

But there were exceptions to this. If Jane did the 'dirty deed,' committed a ghastly and unforgivable crime, it was a completely different story.

🐕 "She's been with another dog!"

I wondered how she could hold up her head in public. She should have a scarlet 'D' on her chest.

Musket jumped into the car to kiss her and stopped. His tongue retracted and his nose began to twitch in an accusing manner.

🐕 "Mommy, how could you?"

Jane knew what she'd done. "But Musket, it was just a cute little puppy. I only held him for a moment."

She was speaking into deaf ears.

Mr. Jealous Butt continued to probe with his nose, his eyes displaying deep betrayal.

I tried to reunite the sparring lovers and called him forward. "Come here Musket. Mommy loves you more than any puppy. Give Mommy kisses."

Finally he did and peace was restored.

🐈 "Okay Mommy, we're good."

CHAPTER FIVE

BLIND/LOW VISION MOBILITY SPECIALIST

Independence of San Diego, a non-profit Independent Living Center or ILC was dedicated to helping persons with disabilities in San Diego County to become more independent.

ISD established the first office near downtown in 1976.

I worked for ISD from 2002 to 2009. I got paid to work there, but Musket played a very pivotal and wide-ranging role. I'm still amazed at what he brought to the job.

A disability is defined as a condition which limits an essential life function. Reading, walking, eating, working or communicating are essential life functions.

There is a distinct difference between a disability and a handicap.

Having severe arthritis and using a wheelchair is a disability. Not being able to get into a bathroom stall is a handicap.

The Independent Living or IL Philosophy contradicted the long-established idea that someone with a disability was sick or had something wrong with them. A disability was something to be fixed or cured, or worse, ignored and shunned.

In contrast, the IL Philosophy taught someone with a disability was a person first. They had the right to go as far as they wanted, with no barriers, either intentional or otherwise to stop them. And that's where an ILC came in.

When the Americans with Disabilities Act was passed in 1991, individuals with disabilities were finally able to take control of their own lives.

ISD and the other 300-plus ILCs across the country helped people reach their goals in housing, access, education, daily living, mobility, communication or vocational training for employment. We provided information, advocacy and resources a person needed to become more independent.

In other words a person with a disability could stay in a nursing facility and be dependent on others for care or they could grow to the best of their abilities, earn their own living and become productive taxpayers. More than half the staff at ISD had disabilities.

Unfortunately individuals with disabilities had a bad image in the eyes of the general public. I never say 'normal people.' Normal is a setting on the dryer.

Someone in a wheelchair was often considered a burden, someone to be ignored.

And that's not the American way.

People deserve the freedom to decide for themselves what they want and have a fair chance to succeed.

My title was Assistive Technology (AT) Advocate. I was Inspector Gadget. I determined what consumers needed to reach their vocational, educational or daily living goals. I, as part of the IL Team, worked to find the technical tool, the gadget which would work for them.

My office computer had software to enlarge everything on the screen, and it vocalized menus, text, e-mails and documents. Next to the computer was a video magnifier for reading letters and books. I had the same equipment in my home office.

I also used a small hand-held video magnifier. It was as useful to me as my voice-activated cell phone. AT made it possible to do my job.

AT was virtually anything that provided the link between a person's disability and what they wanted to do.

Another path to independence may be an Assistance animal. See how neatly I tucked that in?

"Ah. I thought he'd forgotten this book was about me."

Musket and I arrived at ISD a week after graduation. My co-workers knew he was coming. It was like a visit from a popular president.

Other than the occasional service or Guide dog owned by one of our consumers, Musket was the first permanent canine ISD employee.

He didn't get a salary but he immediately filled a role I hadn't foreseen.

Mascot? Yes, that was expected. But he soon gained a job title. Blind/Low Vision Mobility Specialist.

Because he was so mellow and affectionate it wasn't long before my co-workers were coming in to say hi to Musket. I swear I'm not making this up. Some even got on the floor and snuggled. The staff was a pretty laid-back group, but their reaction to Musket amazed me.

He was furry Prozac without the side effects.

The women became Musketmaniacs. I had to set some rules. I wouldn't let them give him treats without my knowledge, or take him out of my office.

But like Jane's rules, they were soon ground to dust.

"My first day at the office was fun. I met a lot of wonderful people who seemed to think I was something special. Daddy will write more about them later.

He used a cane around the office so I stayed in his office under the desk on my sleeping mat. I had a bowl for water and a few toys. When anyone came in to see Daddy I ran over and offered a toy to them."

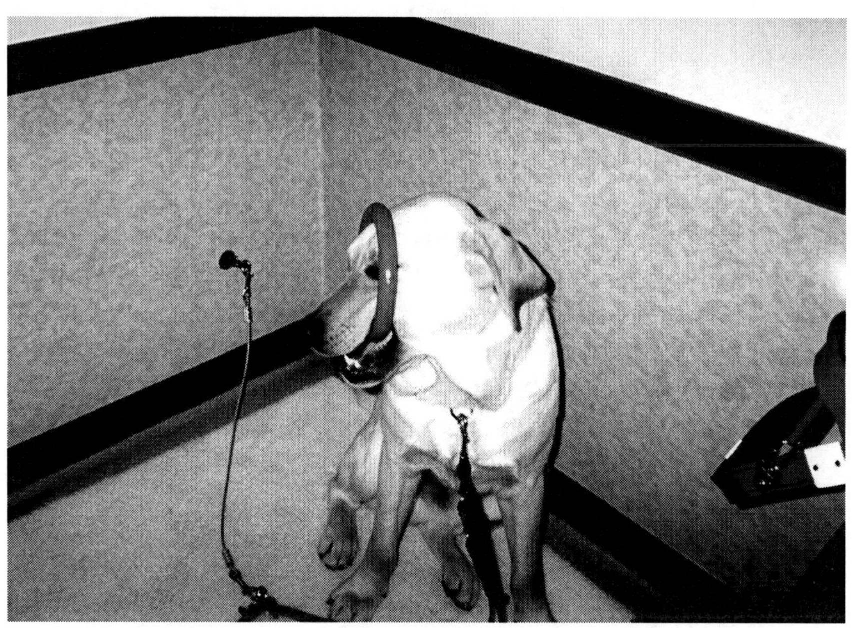

Musket trying to get the hang of playing with a rubber ring

Stress Relief Counselor

The building was about thirty years old, long and narrow on two floors. The ground floor held the parking garage and our wheelchair sales and repair shop. Up a pair of temperamental elevators were the offices of ISD. The central reception area was the domain of Jean Farrington, a strong-willed and sharp-witted black woman. She ruled with an iron fist in a velvet glove. Off to the right were the executive offices, and to the left was a long carpeted hall with offices on either side. Mine was at the far end, next Roberto's.

My 'L' shaped desk was tucked into the left corner. It allowed me to sit in the center and face my consumers without having a desk between us. I was surrounded by AT devices and displays on the walls. Several framed paintings I'd done in my earlier life added a personal touch. I couldn't see them but I knew they were there. Musket's mat was under the CCTV behind my chair. I had to be careful not to kick over his water bowl.

"It wasn't easy trying to sleep with him rolling back and forth, making calls and reading stuff. But I managed."

I already had an inkling of Musket's ability to make others smile, but little did I realize how important he would become in my work.

The consumers who came to the center generally had two things in common. Disabilities, which are a trial in themselves. But a fair number had a lot of hard breaks in life. They were out of work, living at the poverty level, and dependent on aid for food and shelter. They were marginalized, mistreated, and fell through the cracks of county, state and government programs.

So it was no wonder some were at their wit's end, frustrated and without hope. We helped to give those people a direction, a goal to reach for. We didn't baby-sit, but helped them along.

So when a consumer came into my office, needing help and on the verge of tears, there was Musket.

He easily sensed when people needed comfort. He went to total strangers with his tail wagging and a toy in his mouth. He licked their faces. For the first time since coming into my office, they smiled, and even laughed. I mean it, every single time.

Musket just seemed to understand when someone was upset or scared.

"I knew when people were sad and I didn't want them to be. I liked making them feel better."

If I had a dollar for every time Musket made a consumer smile or laugh I wouldn't have to work.

Old women, single moms, veterans, people with speech impairments, blind, deaf, children with learning disabilities, all loved Musket's attention.

In time I learned to use it. When a new consumer came in for an appointment I went to the reception area and introduced myself. Then I asked, "Are you allergic to or afraid of dogs?"

Most told me they loved dogs.

And so it began. Musket saw me enter with a new friend for him and out came the toy. He loved to play. The consumer asked his name, petted him and felt truly welcome. It made working with them much easier and more productive.

Little by little Musket became a fixture, even to the point of co-workers asking to borrow him to calm or comfort an upset consumer.

🐕 "Daddy outsourced me, but I didn't mind at all. It was fun."

Several consumers made a habit of coming in, not for services but to see Musket.

"I'm going to be in your area tomorrow," they'd tell me on the phone. "Will Musket be in?"

I'll check with Mr. Musket and get back to you.

🐕 "I asked for my own office but Daddy's boss didn't think he could swing it."

I had a woman interning with me for a few months in 2004. Rita had cerebral palsy, used a power chair and had severe physical and speech limitations, but her mind was sharp and quick. She laughed at my jokes. How could I not like her? Rita and I worked together on various projects towards her degree in Recreational Therapy at SDSU.

Musket loved Rita. He always stood up and gave her kisses and made her laugh.

🐕 "Rita was cool. I liked it when she came to see me. I mean Daddy. It was hard to reach her face, and her hands weren't very strong but she smiled and her eyes twinkled when she saw me."

With Musket's help we made a real difference in some peoples' lives.

I had a consumer named Debbie, who was about 50. She also had RP Usher's Syndrome II. In her case the hearing was worse.

She had come to me for information on low vision technology. During our first meeting I asked if she'd ever considered getting a Guide dog.

She told me she was afraid of big dogs.

"Well I have a very friendly and gentle dog. Would you like to meet him?"

Debbie demurred, but then her natural curiosity won out and she agreed. I kept my hand on Musket's collar.

"Debbie this is Musket. Musket this is Debbie."

I swear, she absolutely melted and got on the floor with him. In seconds she was hugging him, laughing as he kissed his new friend. Debbie was a very ebullient lady, and on that memorable day, became a dog lover.

"She was really nice. I could tell she was afraid at first but I fixed that. She's been my friend ever since."

Debbie applied to Guide Dogs and was accepted in the summer of 2004. Coincidentally my brother David was in the same class, getting his fourth dog, Beemer. Unfortunately it didn't work out because her hearing was too impaired for her to work with the instructors on the workouts.

Debbie was crushed, but didn't give up. She learned of another school in Michigan, Leader Dogs, which was more experienced in working with blind and hearing impaired students.

In the spring of the following year, Debbie brought home Chloe, an impish, playful and high-spirited black Labrador.

When she introduced Chloe to Musket they became fast friends.

"Chloe was cute and fun, but way too spirited for me. I like mellow women."

Debbie and Chloe worked well together, and for the first time in her adult life as a blind woman, felt secure in walking the streets of downtown San Diego, even at night. She was one of the success stories and Musket really made the difference.

Another woman who gained more independence and self-respect from meeting Musket was Danielle. She suffered from a degenerative nerve disorder which caused her to appear drunk. Her speech was slurred and many people verbally attacked her for being drunk in public. Over time she grew more and more reclusive, afraid to go out into the community. Then she read an article about myself and Musket in the San Diego paper, and she was encouraged by how working with an Assistance dog had given me confidence and independence.

Danielle contacted me at work, and after hearing her story, I asked if she might like to talk to the reporter who'd done the story on me.

She agreed and I arranged the meeting.

A few weeks later an article was in the paper, telling the story of a wonderful and brave lady forced to endure public ridicule and scorn because of her affliction. It gave her confidence and made a great difference in how she stood up to uninformed and judgmental people.

Above all it renewed her self-respect.

"I liked Danielle. She was really pretty. She needed to know it wasn't her fault the way people acted around her. It was their problem, not hers."

She decided a dog could help her with some of her physical problems. In time she too applied for an Assistance dog. Musket had again made a difference in someone's life.

Reaching Out (For Food)

Musket and I visited many organizations, companies, agencies, state and county offices, support groups and legislative meetings around San Diego County. And everywhere we went people wanted to meet him. In time he became an ambassador, setting an example for other Assistance animal handlers.

"I knew it was important to do my job for Daddy. He was also using me to show everybody what a Guide dog does. So I was on my best behavior . . . most of the time."

I preferred the general public not assume since I was disabled I was unemployed.

On the bus to the office in the morning, I was occasionally asked by other riders, "Where are you headed?"

"Work," I replied.

I could feel the raised eyebrows. "Oh, you have a job? How nice."

Sigh. It was a never-ending climb.

I had strong feelings about promoting disabilities in the workforce. The current rate of unemployment for disabled individuals hovered around 70%, a real disgrace. It was due to a host of factors, not the least of which was society's attitudinal barriers.

Since so many individuals with disabilities were not working, they were perceived as being lazy or unwilling to work.

The image of a man with dark glasses holding a sign with 'BLIND' on it selling pencils from a cup still pervades the mainstream media.

It's true some were just not capable of work. But with the right tools and support there would be a lot more people in wheelchairs, with hearing aids or Guide dogs in the workforce.

I long for the day when a disabled person working is the rule rather than the exception.

Okay I'm stepping off the soapbox now.

"I've always been around people like Daddy, Rita, Debbie or my friends at the office. I'm used to people with disabilities and to me they're people."

Musket's role as my guide brought a lot more public awareness of what it meant to be independent and live according to my own abilities and goals.

He gave me that freedom. I went everywhere with him.

We've been on TV, in the newspaper, and written about in several trade newsletters. I don't claim any credit for this. I'm no Tom Hanks. And most of the contacts we've established in our work were triggered by Musket's wagging tail.

"Daddy's exaggerating. He did a lot of work and was really good at public speaking. He knew how to promote a good image for people with disabilities. I'm a conversation piece. He liked to call me a 'coffee table book that sheds.' Funny, Daddy. Real funny."

I joined Toastmasters International in 2006 to improve my speaking skills and because I was a wanna-be stand-up comic. Musket of course accompanied me. He was always welcomed by the other members.

One of the commands for a Guide dog was 'Come.' The signal was a hand clapped to the thigh, or both hands clapped.

When we had a meeting at work and some announcement resulted in applause from the staff, I heard "Here's Musket!" And there he was, next to me.

"Did you want me, Daddy? I was sleeping."

We did a lot of presentations to support groups and organizations about the center's services and AT. After hundreds of them I had a pretty good feel for how an audience would respond.

The presentations were pretty routine so I tailored them to the audience. For seniors I kept the computer references to a minimum. For teenagers I inserted more electronic gadgets.

Before long Musket was asleep on the floor. He'd heard it all before.

"Oh, you can say that again. Daddy joked about me snoring through his talk. What was I supposed to do, applaud?"

I began by telling the audience about myself.

"My name is Mark Carlson. I have three disabilities. I'm legally blind, hearing impaired, and I'm a guy."

The response I received told me how receptive the audience was. If I heard nothing, it was a tough crowd.

But if I heard laughs, we were good to go. Either way, Musket soon played his role.

I went on to say that being blind and nearly deaf was a cinch next to being a guy. I attended Guy support groups to discuss power tools and drink beer.

The jokes had the effect of helping the audience relax and realize I wasn't going to be boring or uncomfortable to listen to.

Disabilities were a hard sell. They either caused guilt or pity. Humor was one of the best ways to help sell an unpopular subject.

I brought in the star of the show by saying, "Musket is a sort of assistive device, in a very loose sense," I said. "A Vision and Mobility Aid, if you will."

🐕 "Zzzzzz . . ."

Whether he slept an hour or five minutes, he had to stretch when he got up.

He yawned, got to his feet, extended his forepaws, and raised his butt. The tail wagged.

I swear he grew about 40% longer when he did it. He was like a furry Slinky.

"I'd like you to meet my most important assistive device. My Guide dog, Musket."

Timing was everything. I clapped my hands once. He woke up.

"Take a bow, Musket."

Then he did the stretch and the audience roared.

🐕 "Hmph. All these years I thought Daddy wanted me to show what a Guide dog did. Not audition for 'Stupid Pet Tricks' on David Letterman."

I also called him 'low-tech AT.' "If he poops and I gotta pick it up, that's low-tech."

🐕 "At least he got that part right."

1,200 Grubby Hands

My favorite outreaches were to schools. Usually a co-worker or Rita went along so we could work as a team. We knew we'd be talking to about 600 kids, ten at a time, from Kindergarten to the Sixth Grade over two long days. AT was a cool subject by itself but it was no contest. Musket fascinated children. They were captivated by him, even the ones who had dogs at home.

Musket took it all in stride, up to a point. After being poked, prodded, petted and hugged by a few hundred kids, he was pretty worn out. Having his belly rubbed by 1,200 hands must have been torture.

"It wasn't easy. The school shows were really important. We taught a lot of children about people like Daddy and Rita. But Daddy's right. I got tired after hundreds of kids petted me. I didn't know where they'd had their grubby little hands.

But sometimes a little girl half my size came to put her arms around my neck and hugged me. That was nice."

I answered their questions about being blind, how Musket did his job and the most important one, "Does he sleep all the time?"

"No only when he's working." The adults laughed.

"Those kids had it all wrong. It wasn't how much I slept but how long I was awake. Too long."

I also taught kids how to approach an Assistance dog in public.

"What do you do if you see a working dog and you want to meet it?" I asked them.

As one might imagine I heard answers from 'Run away' to 'Don't let the owner see you.'

Believe it or not even a lot of adults didn't know.

The answer: Always Ask First.

If the dog was working, whether guiding someone who's blind or assisting someone in a wheelchair, it had a job to do. And distractions, as I mentioned were not a good idea.

Especially when they're crossing the street.

"That's not a good time to ask for my autograph."

I told the kids, "If the handler is comfortable with it then they'll say it's okay to pet the dog."

One of my great thrills was when Musket and I were in a store and I heard, "Mommy you're not supposed to pet him. He's working! You have to ask!"

Smart kid. I felt like giving Musket a High Five when I heard that.

Musket doesn't do high fives but he was pretty good at shaking hands. I mean paw.

It was a simple trick and any good dog owner won't be impressed. But I liked to do it with style. I snapped my fingers and said "Gimme paw."

🐕 "I liked doing it. Little kids laughed like crazy when I gave them my paw. The only problem was they wanted me to do it again. And again. And again. Sigh."

A few weeks later we received a packet of letters from the kids. Jane read them to me. They thanked us and said they liked Musket the best. And a few future artists included drawings of him. I still have them and cherish every one.

The Biggest Test

Often we talked to college or business organizations and they asked questions about Assistance dogs. I helped them with their concerns, the most common of which was 'how do we know if it's really an Assistance dog?'

I'll write more about this later, because it's an important subject. One lady asked me about other species of animals. Cats, rabbits, horses, even monkeys are often trained as Assistance animals.

"Are we expected to allow someone with a rabbit into the store?" She asked me.

I explained that if the animal's handler states they have a disability and the rabbit helps them, don't sweat it, it's not like it's dangerous.

Then my humor circuit kicked in, and I recited in a gruff John Cleese voice, "Oh, that's no ordinary rabbit. That's the most foul, cruel and bad-tempered rodent y'ever set eyes on!"

Of course it got a laugh, especially from the Monty Python fans.

🐕 "Even I think that was funny. I never met a mean rabbit. Just tasty ones."

A regular event at the LAX Marriott was called CSUN, for Cal-State University Northridge. It was an AT convention, mostly concerned with blind and low vision technology, learning and communication aids, and reading systems.

Disneyland for a blind guy. And butt-sniffing heaven for Musket. Thousands of people attended CSUN every year and a lot of them had Guide dogs.

Dogs, dogs, dogs everywhere. No matter how good a Guide dog was, or how well the handler could react to distractions, CSUN was a true test.

Dina would have shaken her head and walked away, overwhelmed.

The aisles in the large convention halls were about 10 feet wide, with booths and displays packed with hundreds of people standing, walking and talking. Many wheelchair users had service dogs.

The poor dogs were pulling, turning and getting tangled up in each others' harnesses.

What a show. Musket tried to work, but he wasn't too focused to miss a cute black Labrador from Arizona, or a friendly Golden from Hollywood.

Here is 10 seconds of dialogue within earshot:

"Pardon me."

"Oops, is that my dog?"

"May I get by, please?"

"Can I help you?"

"What does your company do?"

"Sorry, that was my fault."

"No, come back here. Good girl."

"Was that your dog or mine?"

"Oops I goosed you with my cane."

"What school is yours from?"

"No. Stop that.

"Did I hurt you?"

"I'm walkin' here."

"Oh, it's been so long! How are you?"

"Oh, sure. He was checking out the new gadgets and I was on the floor, getting stepped on and trying to keep him safe. He's going to have to bring a lot more treats next year."

Virginia Piper always came to the CSUN with several of her students from DPI.

We met for lunch at Denny's and talked about our lives and the good times when she was trying to get me killed.

No, seriously, Virginia was proud of what I've done.

And she was pretty fond of Musket too. In fact, I owe my success with Musket to Virginia. I know she'll read this so from the bottom of my heart, Miss Virginia, thank you.

🐕 "Me too, Miss Virginia. Thank you for keeping my daddy alive. And for slipping me those fries the last time we went to lunch."

The AT Expo was another annual event focusing mainly on mobility and durable medical equipment.

The most memorable moment was when a little girl perhaps five years old with Cerebral Palsy came over in her tiny wheelchair. Her mother was with her and asked, "Can she meet your dog?"

"Sure she can," I said, dropping his harness and kneeling beside Musket.

The little girl reached out a shaking hand. Musket sniffed it, probably hoping for food. Then he moved closer and without missing a beat, started giving her slurpy kisses. She giggled, and then laughed. She was in love. She kept laughing as he kissed her. Her mother said, tears in her eyes. "He's wonderful."

"Yes, he is," I agreed, deeply moved. A small crowd had gathered, smiling and taking pictures.

"Can I ask you something?"

"Sure."

"How can I get an Assistance dog for her?"

I smiled. "I'll be glad to help you. I have lots of contacts with Assistance animal schools and I can give you some referrals." I gave her my card.

"She's really young, but do you think a dog could help her?"

"Let me see what schools work with children when I get back to San Diego."

Musket was finally done washing the tyke's face, and I gave her a treat to give him. He took it, earning more laughs.

Her mother thanked me and they moved on. I was still wiping my eyes and gave Musket a kiss on his head. What an amazing dog.

🐕 "She was sweet. I liked her. She had ice cream on her face so I washed it off. I'm glad I made her happy."

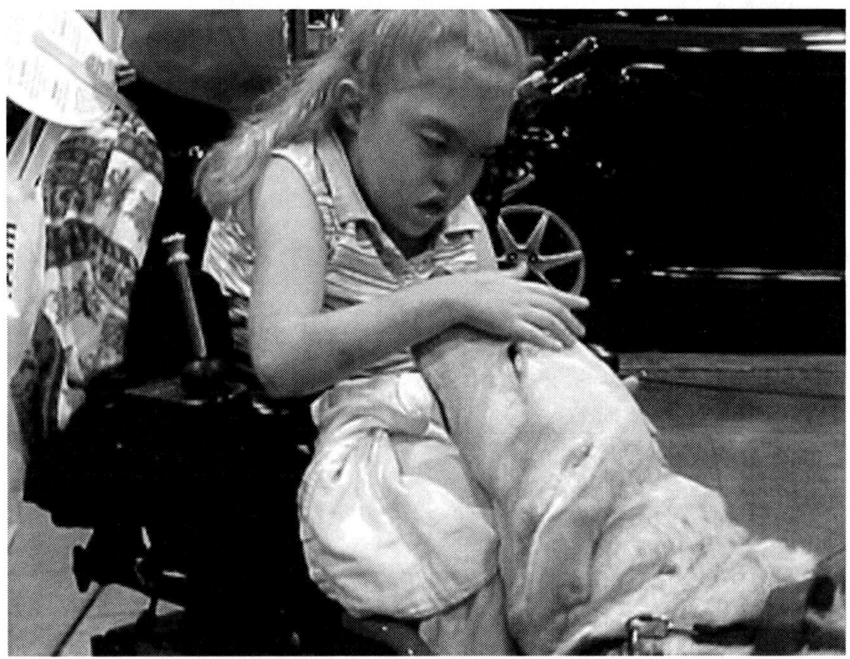

Musket with his little friend at the AT Expo
Photo courtesy Roberto Frias

ISD often participated in rallies and marches to promote disability rights or protest service cuts. I wasn't crazy about doing the marches but it did bring me back to the 1960s. No, I'm not old enough to have been in the anti-war movement. But I remember watching them on TV.

The media often covered the event and the first thing I did was call Jane and tell her what channel we'd be on, because the media always seemed to get Musket on TV. Nanny and Pop-pop wanted to see their little furry celebrity. Only once did he embarrass me. He had to poop. And that's when the cameras showed up.

That's my boy.

🐕 "Hi Mom!"

Sleeping at the Office

Musket loved to sleep. Most Labradors sleep about 18 hours a day on average.

Musket was above average.

He slept pretty much all the time at work. Some of my co-workers berated me for overworking him.

Musket was oblivious, snoring like a sailor sleeping off a hangover.

"Poor thing, he's tired."

"Oh, sure," I snorted. "He's had a hard day. Let's see, I work eight hours a day. He works about two hours a day and sleeps here and on the bus. He gets belly rubs and treats from everyone."

Don't tell me about a dog's life.

🐕 "Hey, it's very stressful being a Guide dog. I need to recharge my batteries."

A hard day at the office

Beg-O-Matic 2000™

Like a lot of small companies we had potlucks and birthday parties. It was a chance to let our hair down and have fun. I never left Musket alone in my office for long, so I brought him with me. There was always plenty of food and the place was full of Musket's fans.

I started out with Musket but I arrived with . . .

'My friends, your attention please! I am proud to present to you a wonder, a contrivance, and a labor-saving device the likes of which the western world has never seen.

You'll never have to eat again! This little baby does it all for you!

It sniffs, it chews, and it swallows and begs for more! Yes you heard me right. Four incredible features in this one package. Look at the sleek streamlined design, intended to convey images of hunger, malnutrition and neglect.

But wait, there's more. Note the carefully crafted soulful brown eyes, the slightly damp twitching nose and most importantly, the restless tail. And it can all be yours for the price of a tiny morsel.

Just think! You'll never again have to endure the drudgery of cooking, serving or even using a fork. Chewing your own food is a thing of the past, my friends.

And here it is, the one and only, Musket Beg-O-Matic 2000™!'

'And that's not all. With your purchase of the Beg-O-Matic, you get the handy pocket Musket™ LickMaster Pro!

Operators are standing by. 1-800-FEEDMEE, or visit our website at www.beggarboy.com.'

"I think Daddy's making fun of me. So I beg. Is that a crime? Humph. By the way, are you going to eat that?"

The agency did some self-promotion through brochures, videos and local TV coverage. More than half the people who worked at ISD had some type of disability. Wheelchairs and walkers were as much a part of the workday as phone calls and time sheets.

A few years ago Musket and I were photographed in the community along with other staff members. The photos conveyed persons with disabilities as productive, working members of society.

Personally I think they conveyed how cute Musket was, but at least they showed his best side, as a working dog.

He was an excellent way to present what people can do when given the chance, not forced to deal with society's apathy and misunderstanding.

Sorry, I was supposed to be off the soapbox.

"Yeah, you better get off or lose weight. It's cracking."

I'm almost done. I'm not going to pretend I'm speaking for all persons with disabilities but enough of my fellows have expressed the same opinions.

We don't expect preferential treatment, but don't want life to be harder either.

We don't like to be ignored as if we were invisible. That's worse than pointing at us.

🐕 "If you folks want to skip this part, just look for my next comment. Otherwise, put the book down and get a snack. I'd love one too. Chances are Daddy will wind down in an hour or so."

We don't want pity, just respect. After all, we're human beings first. I for one never wanted pity. I was relatively able and independent. I knew my limitations and asked for help when I needed it.

A lot of people aren't sure whether to assist a person with a disability.

Actually it's a bit of a minefield. Some don't want any help, and some expect it. Best course is to let the person know assistance is available if they wish.

Go online and look for 'The Ten Commandments of Communicating with Someone with a Disability.' Great stuff.

🐕 "Is he done now? This book is about me, remember?"

Back to Musket. He was also used by the AT Network, a state-funded information source which provided assistance with AT resources.

The Network's website used Musket on one of its resource pages. I didn't even know about it till much later but it really didn't surprise me. Musket had a lot of fans.

🐕 "Now that Daddy has said all that, I'll add my two bits of kibble. He's right. People like him and my other friends at work did a lot of good to make life better for people with disabilities. It was funny how many people thought because Daddy was blind or Rita had Cerebral Palsy they didn't work. I saw Daddy and his friends working every day. And I saw plenty of people with no disabilities at all who didn't work.

I'm proud of Daddy. I met a lot of really nice and interesting people. Some of them had guide or Assistance dogs too. Not as cute as me, but you can't have everything."

Homeward Hound

At the end of the workday Musket was pretty sleep-drugged and I had to get him going again. I pretended his leash was a starter cord like you'd find on an old lawnmower. "Vrooommm," I said. Then he got the hint.

🐕 "Yeah I got it. Sheesh."

But usually when I turned off my computer and put my ball cap on, he was up, tail wagging. He knew the sound of Windows shutting down. Smart boy.

"Wanna go home to Mommy?"

His sudden alert scampering and panting was all the answer I needed. The harness went on, I got into my backpack and off we went.

A minute later I came back because I forgot his treats.

🐕 "You don't want to do that, Daddy."

When Jane came to pick us up at the office things were different. Very different.

When he heard her voice he was off like a shot. I never even tried to stop him. I liked my arm just where it was, attached to my shoulder.

His mommy was the only thing on his mind. He jumped and scampered in circles while giving her kisses.

My co-workers often said Musket was like a different dog.

🐕 "I'm the same dog, but Mommy makes me happy."

We rode as many as four different buses a day in our commute, plus the San Diego Trolley.

Much of riding the bus was taken by waiting at the bus stops. While writing this I recalled an amusing incident from a few years ago. We were at the downtown bus stop, waiting for the express. Several other regular riders were around me and Musket was sitting at my feet.

I heard someone say, "Hey that's the fourth time that patrol car has passed here."

I didn't pay any attention. But a minute later I heard a car pull over and the doors open. Then a voice. "Sir, may we talk to you over here?" I felt a gentle but strong hand on my arm.

"What?" I asked, totally taken by surprise. "Who are you?"

As one of the other riders told me, the cop then looked down and saw Musket sitting next to me. He then said, "Oh, I'm sorry sir. Have a nice day." And the car drove off, presumably with two embarrassed police officers inside.

It was amusing in retrospect. I guess I resembled someone they were looking for.

"A bank robber with a Guide dog. I can see it now. "Stick 'em up. Give the money to the dog."

My little buddy had saved me from a life of running from the law.

A few of the other riders laughed and patted Musket.

Most of the drivers knew me so I rarely had to show my monthly pass. They waved us in. "Welcome aboard, Musket."

"Some of the drivers were friends of mine, and I wagged my tail when I saw them."

Seniors and disabled riders had priority for the front seats. But I usually took whatever seat was open as long as there was room for Musket on the floor.

Once I was settled in, Musket began his routine.

"First I sniffed the floor, to make sure it wasn't another dog's territory and to find any dropped food. I had to be quick because Daddy always reached down to find out if I was doing just that.

Then I crawled under the seat."

When he went under the seat, it often caused comments from other riders.

"Oh, look at him. He knows just where to go."

Or, "What a good dog you have."

Sometimes I wasn't sure about Musket's common sense. He tended to try to get under the seats *before* he was lying flat on the floor. He never made it and I had to remind him.

"Uh, Musket you did it again. Lie down first, and then crawl under."

🐕 "I got confused especially in the morning. At least Daddy had coffee."

The route was very familiar, so even if I fell asleep in the morning, I woke up just before our stop. When we were on a new route, I asked the driver to announce the stop for me.

Once in a while we encountered another guide or Assistance dog. My first indication was Musket suddenly raising his head. Just to be sure there wouldn't be any conflicts I told him to stay. Sometimes the other handler didn't want contact with another dog.

🐕 "Not even me?"

They often asked, "Is there another dog here?"

"Yes," I said.

"What school?" was the most common question.

"Guide Dogs, San Rafael."

Most replied, "Same here. What year?"

And a new relationship was born.

🐕 "Relationship, he calls it. You know how hard it is for two dogs to sniff each other from five feet away?"

Musket had a lot of friends on the express bus. He led me up the stairs and onto his 'balcony.'

"Hey Musket!"

"There's Musket. Hi, doggy."

"How was your day, Musket?"

"You're looking good, Musket."

The only thing missing was rose petals in his path.

🐕 "Daddy let them pet me as I walked by. He once said it was like being in a Roman Triumphal Parade. Hail Caesar Musketus."

Notice anything? Yep. I was there too. But for me? Nada.

Musket was a local celebrity, especially after the articles in the paper and the TV coverage. If I was thin-skinned I'd be jealous. Sometimes it really was all about him.

"Well duh."

I really didn't mind. I had friends on the bus too, but Musket always came first.

Since he was lying on the floor of the bus and had no view of the world passing by, it amazed me how he always knew when we approached our stop. The drivers called out the stops. Once he heard 'Stony Creek Drive,' he probably knew Highland Ranch Road was next. He climbed from under the seat and started getting antsy.

"It wasn't rocket science. Daddy always pulled the cord to signal the stop too. That's what I listened for."

In any case he was ready when the bus came to a stop and we stepped onto the sidewalk. A quick sniff and pee if he needed it and then we headed for home, tired and hungry.

"Yeah. Hungry. Hungry for a kiss from Mommy."

When we finally reached home I took Musket's harness off. Then I heard Jane.

No, it wasn't "Hi Honey how was your day?"

"I was so happy when we got home.

Sometimes she was upstairs and I heard 'Where's my Musket?' And I charged up the stairs to give her kisses."

With my Civil War re-enactor background I could say with confidence the sound of Musket running upstairs resembled the all-out charge of a brigade of mounted cavalry. Then I heard a stifled laugh as he started kissing her.

"And boy, do I need a break. Someone rub my belly."

Chapter Six

ADOGGABLE

Jane's parents lived in Rancho Bernardo exactly 3.9 miles from our home. I knew because it was a standing joke in the first years we were married. I wasn't sure how comfortable I would be having my In-laws that close but Mom and Dad were tops in my book.

Dad had a skill at carpentry and working with his hands. He made beautiful things from wood, including a hanging pot rack for Jane's 40th Birthday.

He was meticulous, careful and never made a mistake, a holdover from his career as a master machinist. A talented gardener he had a neat yard with a koi pond.

Mom was a wonderful lady, warm-hearted and old-fashioned. She believed in sending thank you notes for birthday presents or when invited for dinner. For St. Patrick's Day she made the only Corned Beef and Cabbage I ever liked.

Their house was on a hillside overlooking the valley. It was cool and dark, but never quiet. The TV was always on. Mom did her needlework or reading while Dad laughed at *M*A*S*H* reruns

When Musket came home with us he found a quicker route to acceptance with Mom and Dad than I did. In no time at all he was a favorite and welcomed like the charmer he was.

🐕 "Nanny and Pop-pop were the best grandparents I could ever have."

Jane and I went over to their house at least once a week. In time it became a joke that Musket got so much more attention from Mom and Dad than their own daughter and son-in-law.

Even standing in the living room, they hardly notice us. I once suggested we send Musket in and see how long it took for Mom and Dad to notice we hadn't come in yet.

About five minutes, I recall.

But as long as Musket made them happy we could suffer a little anonymity.

"I loved going to Nanny and Pop-pop's. They were crazy about me. Long before we pulled into their driveway I sat up in the back seat. Mommy said 'Where are we, Musket?'

Treat heaven! I could smell love and warmth in their house.

Pop-pop liked to spoil me. He got me water, took me for walks and gave me treat after treat after treat."

Musket saying hello to Pop-Pop

If Jane and I went to the movies or on a bus tour, it was often better for him to remain behind. He would be miserable in the theatre. We took a day bus tour to the Tournament of Roses Parade in 2006. For the first time in 50 years it rained on the parade. Lucky us.

Musket would have been drenched with no way to dry off.

We left him with Mom and Dad, who were only too happy to babysit him for the day.

It had a few drawbacks, however. Musket was going from an environment where two people catered to his every whim and told him how wonderful he was to one where he had to work and be obedient.

I'm sure he preferred the former.

🐕 "Now why in the world would Daddy think that?"

In one day Dad had given him a full bag of treats, two bowls of water and taken him for several walks.

Musket was definitely tired. But very satisfied.

🐕 "Daddy can say that again. Looking starved and neglected for a whole day wasn't easy."

When Jane was on the phone with Mom or Dad, I often heard her responding to Mom's question about Musket, "He's perfection on paws. He's lying right here."

My usual line was "I'm fine too, thanks for asking."

That always got a laugh from Dad.

🐕 "I think Daddy was trying to tell them something."

Jane even put the phone to Musket's ear so his Nanny could talk to him or in some cases, nag him. If Musket pulled some boner during the day, like humping another dog or begging too much, his Nanny learned of it.

Jane always said "He's listening, Mom."

I know he really wasn't. I don't listen to nagging either.

🐕 "When Mommy put me on the phone I knew it was Nanny, but I also knew I did something wrong. She wanted me to be her perfect little gentleman dog, her furry ambassador."

When San Diego experienced a rare thunderstorm, Mom was on the phone, asking if Musket was scared. "He doesn't like the thunder. Are you taking care of my baby? Tell him his Nanny loves him."

Spoiling Musket was their favorite pastime. And it worked. He was spoiled to the point of not even listening to Jane. I had a bit more influence but I didn't enforce it too strongly.

When I told Musket to 'Sit' or 'Stay,' Dad grumbled I was being mean to him.

🐕 "You tell him, Pop-pop. Don't let Daddy abuse me."

He watched Dad like a hawk, waiting for another treat.

Let's clear something up for the reader who hasn't figured it out.

Mom and Dad had absolutely no willpower when Musket looked at them.

Zero. Nada, Zilch.

Did Musket understand this and try not to take advantage of it?

🐕 "Puh-leeze. Give me a break. I milked it for everything I could get."

I didn't mind too much, since it made them happy but I had a job getting him focused on listening to me afterwards.

Family Tries

Dad was very strong-willed and self-possessed. He had worked three jobs while they raised their son and three daughters, instilling in them a sense of the value of money and virtue of hard work. In some cases it stuck. Jane had all of her parents' best qualities. Kathy, her next-oldest sister was an operating room technician for a Hollywood cosmetic surgeon.

Divorced and very much image-conscious, Kathy tried her best through health foods, exercise and cosmetic surgeries to hold off the ravages of time. She was a lot of fun to have around most of the time. When it came to medical issues, Kathy was the unquestioned expert. Jane often said, "She has the hands of an angel," A pet owner, Kathy liked Musket. Her cat, Martini, came along when she visited Mom and Dad. I think Kathy was a little jealous of the attention Musket received and tried to insert Martini into the same 'most favored grandchild' status.

She once had a Basenji named Micah. Dad wasn't about to call Micah a grandson. Micah was a cute, affectionate, clean and fun dog. His only failing was he wasn't Musket.

"I never met Micah. I know Martini, or at least I saw his tail a few times. When I came over he ran behind the TV. I think he was afraid of me but I never tried to hurt him."

Jane's oldest sister, Sue lived in Vermont with her husband. She was what I would call an 'Earth Mother,' a hard-working, fun, and warm-hearted woman. All three daughters were very different, but Jane and Sue had a lot in common. Sue talents as a seamstress was in making cute and useful things like placemats, potholders, pillows, quilts, napkins, you name it. They were of better quality than any I ever found in stores.

She was very allergic to animal fur, so when she came to visit, she stayed with Mom and Dad. I made sure Musket was given a bath and groomed to minimize her discomfort.

"Aunt Sue gave me the best belly rubs. When I saw her I just rolled on my side. Then she gave me a great rub, saying 'Bellybellybellybelly.' I was in puppy heaven when Sue visited. Aunt Kathy played with me like a big plush toy."

They were a very close-knit family, and rallied together in times of sorrow and need. As Mom and Dad aged their independence diminished. Dad was having trouble remembering things, while Mom had difficulty walking. The two vibrant, active people I had grown to love and respect slowly lost more and more of their freedom to Alzheimer's and joint deterioration.

Mom did her best, but hip and foot problems further limited her ability to take care of Dad.

It didn't help she'd never learned to drive. Dad had always done most of the shopping, paying the bills and making decisions.

The loss of his role as head of the household took its toll on his behavior.

Jane spent more time before and after work with her parents to help out.

Sue flew from Vermont a couple times a year and Kathy wasn't far away.

In 2007 three things happened in quick succession. Mom fell and broke her hip, then Dad accidentally knocked her down with the car, and Jane lost her job.

She took Dad's license away when he didn't pass the next test. It was hard for him but the matter soon lost its intensity as his memory deteriorated.

"Mommy started driving Nanny and Pop-pop around. Sometimes I rode with Pop-pop in the back seat. I didn't mind him losing his license."

The Ambassadog

Mom spent three months at the Casa de las Campanas, a rehabilitation facility, recovering from hip replacement surgery. She was doing well for a while, learning to walk again but it was apparent her walking days were numbered. She also had several serious infections and a minor stroke that scared hell out of us.

"We went to visit Nanny at the hospital. I was allowed to climb on the bed and kiss her. Daddy made sure I didn't hurt her with my feet."

Jane went to see her every day with Dad, spending several hours there. She soon learned the morning and afternoon TV schedules by heart.

It was the beginning of one of the hardest periods in Jane's life, being the primary caregiver first for Dad, and then both Dad and Mom. She had a sense of family responsibility I truly admire.

"My mommy took care of everybody she loved. Including Daddy and me. She was wonderful but it worried me when she got so tired and stressed. Then it was my job to give her even more love and kisses. And Daddy's job too. Right Daddy?"

Right little buddy.

Jane had a special gift for meeting people and making them feel good. She'd be an incredible talk-show host or therapist.

Like her grandmother, Jane had the ability to meet someone, and in ten minutes know most of the important aspects of their lives, their birthdays and the names of their children.

Come to think of it, she'd be a terrifying IRS auditor. Anyway, walking down the halls of the Casa she said hello to elderly women and men from her previous visits and met new ones. She was particularly sensitive to finding lonely little old ladies whose families never visited.

Musket sometimes accompanied Jane on her 'rounds' on weekends and some evenings to visit Mom. As an Assistance dog he had access to such places, even if he wasn't, strictly speaking, Jane's dog.

But no one at the Casa minded. Musket was a hit with the staff and patients. Musket remembered everybody. He was often the reason for the first meeting.

"Oh she's so pretty," they'd say, or "What a lovely dog."

"Whoa. Let's get something straight right now. I'm handsome, not pretty. I don't understand why everybody thinks I'm a girl dog. What do I have, boobs? I know I pee like a girl but that's because they cut my nuts off. And who watched how I pee?"

Jane said, "Do you want to meet him? His name is Musket."

Jane felt a deep compassion for lonely old people. Musket just liked to make people happy. "Give kisses," Jane told Musket. And he did, making the old people smile.

Down the hallways, in the recreation rooms her loving heart and caring soul shone for all who knew her.

She also did some very nice things for the staff by baking cookies, cakes, remembering birthdays and helping them with personal problems.

And Musket made dozens of new friends.

🐕 "I liked going to the Casa. Nanny had a room with a big bed. Sometimes I got on the bed with her. She liked that. The nurses were really nice to me and thought I was wonderful.

When we were leaving I tried to give Nanny kisses but the bed was too high for me to reach her face. If Daddy was there he lifted me and I gave Nanny kisses to make her happy."

Even Mom's memory or at least her good judgment was strained by her love of Musket.

Jane went over one day and gave Mom a snack bag of treats for Musket. "Make them last all day."

But when Jane looked a minute later, she saw her once strict and frugal mother feeding Musket one treat after another.

"Mom! Those are supposed to last all day!"

"But I love him," she said sincerely.

🐕 "Simmer down, Mommy. It makes her happy. We'll stop when she runs out."

Musket never protested the front-end treat loader.

🐕 "Daddy's gotta be kidding. What am I, insane?"

Mom was in the Casa during the October 2007 San Diego County wildfires. It was a scary time for all of us. Our home was between the paths of two major fires.

The air quality was pretty bad so I stayed home from work. We watched the news, wondering if our home was in danger. Houses only a mile away were being evacuated. I was no hero, but I pulled out all the garden hoses and filled the tub with water. Jane assembled a few important items and documents.

Dad was alone, so when Rancho Bernardo was threatened, we brought him over to stay with us. He didn't really understand what was happening but he had Musket all to himself.

🐈 "Mommy and Daddy were really worried. I could smell smoke. It was nasty and hurt my nostrils. Smoke always frightened me and made me think of burned fur.

But I had to keep Pop-pop calm so I played with him and let him give me treats. For the first time I ever remember, Daddy didn't try to keep Pop-pop from giving me too many."

The Casa was also threatened by the fires. When they lost power, Jane wanted to get Mom and bring her over, but that was impossible. The Casa evacuated all the residents to a place in La Jolla for the duration.

After a week it was over. Hundreds of homes had been lost; thousands of people were left without a place to live. The memory of that terrifying week will be with us forever. Musket was a wonder we could count on for comfort.

🐈 "I just did what had to be done. But for some reason I did gain some weight."

The Casa staff weren't happy to see Mom go home at the end of her therapy. Her sweet personality and Jane's sincere compassion made them popular. That and the joy Musket brought with him.

After Mom returned home, the strain on Jane became slow and relentless. As the sole caregiver for both of her parents Jane was over at their house every single morning from 7 to past noon, then again before dinner until they were ready for bed. I can't begin to relate all she went through but any reader who takes care of a parent with a serious disability will understand.

I'm proud of her for it, and even when she was sure she couldn't do it anymore, she pulled herself together and did it again.

🐈 "Mommy worked hard to take care of Nanny and Pop-pop. I went over and helped. Well, I tried to but then my 'beggar boy' evil twin made me do things Mommy didn't want me to do."

'Evil twin?' There's an original defense.

Jane joined some caregiver support groups. Being able to share her feelings and frustrations with others who were doing the same thing was a catharsis for her.

"Sometimes Mommy came home crying. But no matter how tired or upset she was, she always smiled when she saw me."

Jane had to remember a thousand things. It was easy to forget things like dates, names, what groceries were needed, or where she left the mortgage check.

She was the driver, shopper and primary cook. She did the laundry, paid the bills and organized.

For two houses.

I was the dishwasher, handyman, secondary cook, furniture mover, plumber, garbage man, housekeeper and gardener.

For one house.

And no, I didn't do any of them well. But I couldn't blame that all on my eyesight. I'm a guy.

"Daddy cleaned the house every two weeks. And even though I warned him again and again, he always managed to do the floors just before Mommy came home. So she had to come in on wet floors. When will he ever learn?"

Both Mom and Dad had frequent doctors' appointments and Jane took them to each, maintained their medications and treatments.

Sometimes she took them out shopping to give them a change. If I and Musket went along Dad followed Musket's wagging tail.

If someone commented on Musket Dad smiled, as proud as any grandfather.

One lady said Musket was adorable.

Dad, with his usual penchant for puns said, "No, he's not, he's Adoggable!"

Since then it was Dad's adjective for his favorite grandson.

"I know it was lame but Pop-pop laughed at it. So did everybody else."

Jane still had her sense of humor. She told me she was in a supermarket one day and noticed a woman her own age walking around with a glazed and confused look in her eyes.

"Are you taking care of your parents?" Jane asked.

The other woman nodded. "Yes. How'd you know?"

That must have been a moment of shared grim smiles.

Through it all there was one stable constant, one ray of light in the endless dark tunnel.

Musket's love.

Musket, like many dogs had a keen sense when someone was in pain or sick. He went right up to strangers in hospitals to see if they needed help. He was the perfect example of Unconditional Love.

Dad's dementia and Mom's health problems were probably obvious to him and he often lay down on the floor at their feet.

"Pop-pop was always happy to see me. If he was getting frustrated or angry at something I calmed him down.

'Where's my Musket?' he said. 'Musket a good boy? Yeah, Musket's a good boy.' He said it a lot and I loved hearing it. But I knew something was wrong with him.

The only good thing about Pop-pop's bad memory was that he forgot right away when he gave me a treat. So he gave me another one. And another."

As time went on, Dad repeated himself more frequently, even several times in an hour. We knew it was a common symptom of his illness but it made things hard for Jane and Mom. When he said 'Musket a good boy? Yeah Musket's a good boy' several dozen times in the course of a short drive to the store, it only reminded us of how much he'd lost.

"He was still my Pop-pop, and I loved him. I didn't know how to make him better and it made me sad."

Darcy's Gift

"Pop-pop took me on walks. Mommy said 'Dad, I think Musket wants to go for a walk.'

Then Pop-pop said 'Musket want to go for a walk?' Sometimes he forgot where he put the leash but Daddy had a spare. I always made sure we got back to the house safely."

Dad slowed down, got confused and frustrated easily, and began to have dizzy spells. He fell often enough for us to wonder what was wrong. The problem was he never remembered falling. Sometimes he just had a scrape or bump. But we lived in fear of when it would be serious.

"There was a time when Pop-pop fell and hurt himself. Mommy called Daddy on his cell phone and picked us up at the bus. Then we went to get Nanny. She was in a wheelchair.

When we reached the hospital, Daddy and I took Nanny into the Emergency area while Mommy parked the car. Then we found Pop-pop, complaining to the nurses, but when he saw me he smiled and said 'There's my Musket!'

He was in a bed and the doctors wanted to watch him for a while. Later he wanted to go home and got mad. Daddy lifted me on the bed with Pop-pop.

I sat down at his feet. Then Pop-pop calmed down and laughed. I was with him until they let him go home. Every time a lady nurse went by she said 'Awwww. Isn't that cute?'"

Musket brought out good and generosity in people. I didn't really understand what it was about him that set him apart from other dogs of his breed but I didn't question it either.

Jane often said Musket was a gift from Heaven, specifically her brother Darcy. He knew what she needed in her life. So he sent Musket to us.

Okay, I had to go blind first, but I think it was a bargain. Look what we got in return.

Given the choice between being blind and blessed with Musket at my side, or being sighted without him, I'd gladly choose the former.

Thank you, Darcy.

"Sometimes Mommy talks about her brother. Daddy said he was an amazing man. I don't know if Darcy was why I came to be with Mommy and Daddy but if so, I'm very happy he did."

Santa Musket

The holidays in Jane's family were a special time. The tradition was big, lavish meals and celebrations. Sometimes Kathy or Sue came to visit, but most of the time it was just the four . . . sorry Musket, five of us. Jane made fantastic Thanksgiving dinners. When Mom was in the Casa she cooked an entire 'meal on wheels' so to speak. All the entrees, sides, gravy, dessert and drinks were in Tupperware and Longaberger baskets. We brought the whole thing to the recreation room and Jane served one wonderful banquet.

It was a lot of work for her but the staff was very impressed, saying they'd never seen anyone do something so wonderful for their family. That was Jane.

She liked to get into the holidays especially Easter, Independence Day and National Scrapbooking Day.

Yep, there really is a National Scrapbooking Day.

The first Easter we had Musket we took him to have his picture taken with the Easter Bunny. But it turned out to be a real bunny! A cute little black bunny was placed on a pedestal . . ."

"Where I belong."

. . . and we put Musket close by. The girl who took the pictures was at first worried Musket might scare or eat the rabbit, but all he did was sniff it.

"Hmm, I think it needs salt."

The following year we found a 'real Easter Bunny,' a guy in a suit. But Musket liked the little one better.

"Thanksgiving was my favorite holiday. All that food! Mountains and mountains of wonderful, aromatic, delicious food. My mommy could cook better than anyone. When we had Nanny and Pop-pop or friends over, I scampered around the table from one person to another. Pop-pop was easiest to get food from. Nanny was a close second. Daddy was really mean. He almost never gave me anything but Mommy sneaked it to me."

Christmas in my own family was always in the Swedish tradition and for several years Jane and I kept the faith. But it became more our own way, starting our own traditions. We had a few obvious Musket-ish decorations, like Labrador ornaments and his own paw-shaped stocking on the mantel.

Every year I wrote one of those dreaded family newsletters. As you might imagine with my irrepressible sense of humor they were not typical holiday reading. In fact, since it was written from Musket's point of view, our friends really enjoyed reading them each year.

🐕 "Daddy's Christmas letters were funny but I don't think he really knew what I wanted to say, which was 'Send me food for Christmas.'"

I wrote a few Christmas song parodies. A couple of samples may be welcomed by those readers who haven't had anything to eat recently.

Irving Berlin I ain't.

🐕 "He's not kidding. It's pretty bad."

Sung to 'Rudolph the Red-Nosed Reindeer.'

You know Lassie, Benji, Checkers and Balto,
Rin-tin-tin, Snoopy, Old Yeller and Pluto;
But do you recall, the most wonderful dog of all?

Musket the bright-eyed Guide Dog,
Had a very wrinkly face,
And if you ever saw it,
You would swear he's part Shar Pei.

All of the other Guide Dogs,
Used to laugh and call him names,
They never let poor Musket,
Join in any Guide Dog games.

Then one sunny April day,
Daddy came to say,
"Musket with your eyes so bright,
Won't you guide me through my life?"
Then how the family loved him,
As they gave him hugs and treats,
Musket the bright-eyed Guide Dog,
You'll go down in history!

🐕 "I don't know this guy. He just grabbed my harness and made me go with him."

Or this one, to the tune of 'Grandma Got Run Over by a Reindeer.'

I got run over by my Guide Dog,
Walking home from work one winter's day,
He saw his Mommy wanting kisses,
I held on when he ran that way.

He'd been thinkin' about his mommy,
And I had to keep his mind on work,
But lo and behold he saw her,
With a bunch of treats and a smirk.

When they found me lyin' on the sidewalk,
Dizzy and bewildered from the pace,
There were paw prints on my stomach,
And wagging tail marks on my face.

Now we're all so proud of Musket,
He's the best Guide dog there is,
But it's just not safe to hold him,
When his mommy sez 'Mommy wants a kiss.'

I don't really mind when he does it,
He's so good at everything else,
He gives me plenty of love and kisses,
And a dislocated shoulder as well.

I tell all our friends and family
When they want to give Musket treats,
He's really very food driven,
So give me some warning first, please!

Note from the Editor: Please don't hold the publisher responsible for these pathetic attempts at songwriting. All complaints should be made to the author personally. Don't blame us.

Musket had a dog-sized Santa cap, reindeer antlers and a few Christmas scarves. Jane found them in those boutique 'shoppes.'

He was very cute in his holiday attire and I know he loved being the center of attention.

He wore them when we drove to Mom and Dad's, or the mall or wherever. Everybody who saw this serious, handsome working dog with a Santa cap on fell immediately in love. And he liked it.

Ho. Ho. Ho.

"Yeah. They thought it was cute to make me wear the Santa cap or antlers. Mommy was always buying 'the cutest thing she ever saw' for me to wear. I have a red and green plaid ruffled collar with bells on it. I hope to God none of my friends from Guide Dogs ever sees the pictures of me. I'll never be able to hold up my head again. Ho. Ho. Ho."

Jane's Singing Toys

Jane also had a habit of buying these weird singing plush toys. I cringed when she came home from shopping and said with a cheerful voice, "Look what I got, Honey."

From the bag she pulled a Santa which danced and sang 'Winter Wonderland,' or a Frog that warbled 'Jingle Bells, even a Turkey blaring, you guessed it, 'Turkey in the Straw.'

What did a frog have to do with Jingle Bells?

🐕 "I didn't get it. They wiggled and danced and sang but didn't give me belly rubs. What good were they?"

We really enjoyed Musket's birthdays. Every August 27 he received cards, small gifts, doggy food cakes and special attention. His friends at work came by my office to pet him and give him belly rubs and treats. And of course his Nanny and Pop-pop couldn't do enough for him.

Mom loved to buy gifts for her favorite grandson. One Christmas she told Jane to buy something for Musket from his Nanny. "The sky's the limit," the previously frugal mother said to her astonished daughter.

"So, $500 million, Mom?"

I'm sure Mom would have spent it if it would make her Musket happy.

I suggested a self-filling treat bin.

🐕 "Yeah! Wow that would be a great present!"

Mom bought him a very soft blanket with little paw prints and bones.

On cold nights he liked to be wrapped up snug.

Some winter nights were pretty chilly and we let Musket get on Jane's chaise lounge. He snuggled in and I put the blanket over him.

🐕 "How nice. It was like I had Nanny's love wrapped around me all night."

All night long he didn't move a muscle. When I got up to let him out he was still there, snug and happy.

He even came down the stairs with that blanket draped over his butt like a fluffy superhero cape.

🐕 "Just in case it was cold outside."

Farewell to Pop-pop

Jane finally decided to place Mom and Dad in a very nice retirement home in Vista. Mom was in the assisted living wing and given excellent care. Dad was in the Memory Unit.

It was very tough for Jane, but she knew it was the best thing for them. Musket was there to help keep him calm when we arrived. Dad only had eyes for him.

In April 2009, as I was writing this book, Dad died. He was 89 years of age. Musket and I were not able to be there while he was dying, but Mom, Jane, Sue and Kathy were by his side in his last hours.

He was lucid and talked to his family. Jane brought a small stuffed Labrador toy to give him. "Daddy here is Musket," she said, tears in her eyes.

What warms my heart is this man who had seen more than fourscore years of war and peace, raised four children, had three grandchildren and two great-grandchildren, held the stuffed dog in his hands and said over and over, 'This is my Musket. Musket gives me kisses."

A few days later the nursing home called and we rushed over, but he was already gone. Jane took Musket in to see him. In Dad's hand was that stuffed dog.

🐕 "Daddy, Mommy and I went to see Pop-pop. He didn't respond when I went into the room. But I licked his hand and said goodbye. I'll miss my Pop-pop."

We went to tell Mom, and Musket climbed onto her bed to comfort her.

On the table next to Mom's bed at the nursing home she kept that stuffed dog toy. In it she found comfort in the presence of both her husband and Musket.

She attended bible study, bingo, movies, exercise and sing-alongs. Musket went to visit her at least once a week. Needless to say, he quickly made a lot of friends among the staff and residents.

Some of the ladies didn't let him by without asking for a kiss from the most popular dog at the home.

🐕 "I liked going there. Daddy let them give me healthy treats which made them happy. Me too."

I'm glad Musket was able to give peace and happiness to so many people.

But that's just what he does.

He's adoggable.

Chapter Seven

NO DOGS ALLOWED WANNA BET?

"This chapter is really good. I'll let Daddy start if off. Wake me when he's finished."

'Where can Musket go with you?' The question was often asked, and it's time to answer it.

Let's get the legalese stuff out of the way first.

Service animal as defined by the Americans with Disabilities Act (ADA).

Any animal individually trained to do work or perform tasks for the benefit of an individual with a disability. Tasks typically performed by service animals include guiding people with impaired vision, alerting individuals with impaired hearing to the presence of intruders or sounds, providing minimal protection or rescue work, pulling a wheelchair, or retrieving dropped items.

Simply put, they help someone with a disability to be more independent, safe and healthy. Musket's job is easily defined. He's my eyes.

"Okay, come on. Let's get to the good stuff."

I generally use the term 'assistance' dog. A 'service' dog' is specific for physical tasks. Service, Guide, Psychiatric, Hearing Alert, or Signal Dogs are types of Assistance dogs.

A Service dog for someone with mobility or manipulative impairment may pull a wheelchair, pick up dropped objects, maintain their balance or do any of a hundred other physical tasks. An Alert dog has the ability to sense an oncoming seizure, diabetic shock or even bipolar episode.

There are animals trained to help children with Autism, hearing impaired persons and even to call 911 on a special phone.

Suffice to say Assistance dogs, and in some cases horses, cats, or monkeys are well-trained, well-behaved and intelligent animals.

One thing needs to be kept in mind. Assistance animals are NOT pets.

Guide dogs have been around for almost a century.

🐈 "Yada yada. I'm nodding off again."

Guide dogs are well-known to the general public. But many other trained Assistance animals are less familiar. In part this is due to what I call a 'hidden' disability. Being blind or using a wheelchair is pretty obvious. But a person who's hearing impaired or has Post-Traumatic Stress Disorder, diabetes or a traumatic brain injury might not be recognized as having a disability. Yet many of them have animals to help them.

Herein lays one of the more common conflicts.

The Americans with Disabilities Act states an animal trained specifically to assist a person with a disability has full access to all public areas, services and venues.

Any place a person can go, an Assistance dog may go. It's not my intention to detail the issue here but I'll mention a few examples.

Restaurants, stores, banks, offices, churches, libraries, theaters, parks, beaches, recreation areas, public transportation, airliners, trains and more. The only places they are not permitted are sterile areas like hospital ICUs, operating rooms, or food handling areas in restaurant kitchens, which was a relief to me and an annoyance to Musket.

🐈 "You can say that again. We need to change that law."

In my case and that of anyone with an obvious disability, the Assistance dog is not often challenged. Yet it does happen.

When someone with a 'hidden' disability the likelihood of a challenge or misunderstanding increases.

🐕 "Ah, now it's getting interesting."

The team in 2007

In my work at ISD I received dozens of calls a month from people who were refused access to a public place because of their animal, and business owners who asked if an animal must be allowed in their place of business.

The issue was usually resolved with a little judicious mediation.

I informed both parties of their rights and the rights of the other according to the law.

If a dog were doing its job to assist their handler in a manner directly involving their disability, then it was an Assistance animal. The business had to allow access, even if they didn't understand the disability or permit pets.

The business may ask if it s an Assistance dog, and if it helped with the disability, but no more. Anything beyond that is an invasion of privacy.

For instance I could be asked if Musket was a Guide dog and if he was working for me. If I said yes, that's as far as it needed to go. They couldn't ask my disability.

Besides, isn't it obvious? I'm a guy. They also can't demand proof of the disability.

The law does not require proof of disability, or of the dog's training.

Musket wears the California Assistance Dog ID tag, but again it's not required.

🐕 "But it does jingle really loud when I walk."

In some cases the dog may wear a harness or cape but some people don't want or need it. A hearing alert dog doesn't need a harness.

In the matter of the rights of the business, the dividing line was the behavior of the dog. If the dog was well-behaved, calm, non-aggressive and sanitary, there' was no reason it couldn't be with their handler in any public place.

If on the other hand it was barking, being aggressive, unsanitary, disruptive and not under control then the business had the right to ask the handler to either control the animal or leave. A handler must show respect for the rights of the business and other patrons.

Both parties should know the law.

It may be noticed I only covered issues which assumed the dog was a legitimate Assistance animal.

If it should be proven a person who stated they had an 'assistance dog' did not, or even had a disability and was faking it to bring their dog into a store, they were committing fraud. A felony.

🐕 "I'm still with Daddy. But let's get to the good part."

Such things did happen frequently and made it even harder for handlers with real Assistance animals.

Any business owner is in a quandary when faced with the decision of whether it is a real Assistance animal or not. They don't want to break the law nor do they want the dog handler to get away with fraud.

It's a tough call.

It's such a complicated subject I could write an entire book but far more capable people have done that.

This book is about Musket.

"Yawn. Huh? Oh, *now* he remembers me. Okay let's get on with it. You'll love this chapter, folks. Excuse me while I strrrrretch."

Want some Irony with those Fries?

Let's begin with an incident which happened to us in November 2007. I'd worked at ISD for nearly six years in the same location. The building was in Hillcrest in uptown San Diego. The neighborhood was mixed residential and retail, with some fast-food places.

Exactly opposite ISD, in full view of our office, was a McDonalds. They too had been there for many years. A lot of our staff and consumers went there, so people with disabilities going in weren't unusual.

"I like this story. I can't wait to get to the good part."

On that fine cool Thursday morning, Musket and I were on our way to work. Passing McDonalds, I suddenly had a craving for a McMuffin. Unusual for me, because I don't care much for fast food. I hadn't been in a McDonalds in about five years. But what the hell, I entered the door.

There was someone ahead of me, so Musket stopped.

Then it was my turn. Or so I thought. I asked for two McMuffins.

The girl behind the counter said something I didn't catch. I repeated my order and she repeated her statement. Then the customer waiting for her order informed me, "She says your pet can't be in here."

Okay, I knew how to handle this. I calmly explained to the girl Musket was not a pet, but a Guide dog.

She again said my dog couldn't be in the restaurant. Again I repeated it, stating I have the right under law, to be served.

Still no go. I was in the netherworld between wanting to get this misunderstanding sorted out and just saying to heck with it.

I don't like to quit. So I stayed.

She then said "You'll have to take your dog outside, I have customers waiting."

What was I, chopped liver?

🐕 "Ooh, I like this. Daddy really gets going."

After three more tries I did what I shouldn't ever have to do. I pulled out the laminated law card given to Guide Dog grads. I never had to use it, not in more than five years in cities all over the country.

I found out later that this was all on the surveillance tape. I could clearly be seen calmly removing the card from my wallet and showing it to her. She didn't even bother to look.

Wait, it gets better.

I said I wanted to speak to the manager. He'd get this straightened out, right?

🐕 "BZZT! Wrong answer, but thanks for playing."

He was just as obstinate. "Sir, we'll be happy to serve you if you go outside. Please take your dog out."

I wonder if the steam coming from my ears was visible on the tape.

I pointed out the window. "Do you see that building on the corner? That's Independence of San Diego. It's an agency which helps persons with disabilities fight for their rights. It's been there for nearly thirty years."

Then I dropped my bombshell. "I work there."

🐕 "Should have been a show-stopper, huh?"

Nope. He actually stepped from behind the counter and repeated I had to take Musket outside.

It was something from *Candid Camera*.

What was Musket, the source of all this angst doing? Was he being aggressive, barking and snatching food from tables?

Nope. Musket was being perfect. Quiet, calm. Just being a good Guide dog.

"Yeah, can you believe it? I was wearing my most cute look, too. I saw some people watching the drama. I could smell grilled meat and French fries. Even the vanilla shakes made my nose twitch. But I sat there, being a good dog."

Not a hint of backing down from the manager.

He even said "There's a sign on the door that says no pets."

I was finally fed up with these people. I told him I was going to call the police and fight for my rights. Not for a sumptuous five-course meal at the Four Seasons in New York, but a couple of McMuffins. The irony just bites.

"This was like mugging a cop in front of a police station."

After arriving at the office, I told my co-workers about the incident. Every single one was astonished.

"That's ridiculous!"

"Are you kidding? They wouldn't let Musket in? Are you going to sue them?"

All very good questions.

Was I going to sue? I was considering it.

"Want some fries with that irony? Listen to this."

One of my co-workers told me, "There is a sign on the door of that McDonalds. It says 'No Pets. We Welcome Assistance Dogs.'"

It was the very sign the manager told me to go and read. Funny, huh? Believe me I was splitting my sides laughing. For one thing, the man never made the connection that I had a Guide dog because I was blind.

"I told you it was a good story. And yes I'd like some fries."

I called that McDonalds and asked for the name and number of the franchise owner.

When I got the franchise operations supervisor on the phone he was stunned. He said he'd look into it. I think he might not really have believed me and thought I was just a hothead.

As the day wore on, I hadn't heard anything, so I decided to go back to McDonalds and get the names of the two persons from the morning shift.

🐕 "Are you ready for this?"

A new shift. New manager.

He refused to help me. Not only did he not give me the names he said I had to take my dog out. No dogs allowed.

I wonder if he could see my tonsils. That's how far my jaw had dropped. Then I heard him turn around and walk away.

Think of it. McDonalds, an American icon. A Guide dog. So well-recognized. And denial of access, the denial of a basic civil right.

You bet I fought it.

I stepped aside and pulled out my cell phone telling him I was calling the police.

He said "Go ahead. I'll sue you."

Dig that grave a little deeper. I called and was told a patrol car would be by shortly. Then I called my office and spoke to our executive director. He and three managers showed up. That's what I call supportive.

Then the cops showed. The manager wilted. I'm sure he thought I was bluffing. He gave me the names. First names only.

I thanked him and the officers and returned to work.

No I still hadn't eaten.

🐕 "Neither had I."

I called the operations supervisor again and told him what had happened. This time he seemed to take my story much more seriously.

I contacted the newspaper and asked a contact there who I might tell about this. Before the day was out, my phone was ringing off the hook.

I had already written a detailed account of the incident, with times and names.

The next morning I found a message from a *Union Tribune* reporter. I invited him to come by. We discussed the details. Then the phone rang. The McDonalds operations supervisor was across the street and wanted to meet with me.

The reporter suggested he go first and get some coffee and see how they reacted as I came over. He'd be incognito. I liked the idea.

I was still determined but not angry, and was willing to hear these people out.

After ten minutes Musket and I went to McDonalds. Musket was as sweet as always.

🐈 "Well duh."

Three men opened the front doors and welcomed me in as if I were the Governor. They introduced themselves. Both the operations director and the owner of the franchise of 15 restaurants had come to meet me.

They were very nice and offered me breakfast. I declined.

🐈 "That's the part of the story I don't like."

Then I told them in detail what had happened the previous day. All were stunned and very apologetic. It was then I learned about the surveillance cameras. They clearly showed the rude behavior of the staff.

They asked me what I wanted. Then I introduced the reporter from *Union-Tribune*. That felt really good.

They took it well and openly admitted their culpability. Then I dropped my bombshell.

"I don't want to sue. I only want to make sure this never happens to anyone again."

I could hear relief in their voices. The owner told us he'd only bought this particular restaurant a few months before and the re-training of the staff was way behind schedule. No kidding.

It was one of the worst-run and operated McDonalds in the city, and the incident was the perfect opportunity to do something about it.

I again reiterated I had no wish to sue them. That would take a long time and benefit no one. My co-workers thought I was nuts. But I also knew I had been given a 'Golden Arches' opportunity. Sorry for the pun but I couldn't resist.

Considering what I did for a living, and how I felt about frivolous lawsuits, I told the McDonalds officials I would like to be involved in the re-training of the staff and managers for the whole franchise in disability awareness and access.

One of the men was very interested in Musket and asked a lot of questions. Musket was perfect, presenting himself in the manner a well-trained Guide dog should.

"I wanted to be nice. This guy had access to *tons* of food."

The story came out in the newspaper on Sunday. By Tuesday a local news station wanted to interview me. Of course I said yes. Good publicity for ISD, and to set an example of self-advocacy. It was also a great chance to show the general public that not all disabled people sue.

Of course Musket was given a lot of attention.

"They shot lots of footage of me but the only close-up was of me yawning. It was a little embarrassing. I looked like Old Yeller."

My phone rang like crazy for days. Our center received a lot of good exposure.

After a few months McDonalds and I had worked out the details. I knew an excellent diversity trainer named Diana Carson, who said she'd be glad to help.

We set up a presentation, of which I would do the Assistance animal and access section. In front of managers and shift leaders of the whole franchise, we did a 4-hour talk about disability awareness and universal access.

It went very well. For what it resulted in, I was a lot more satisfied than if I'd taken them to court.

The incident was one of those once-in-a-lifetime opportunities which if handled right, can make a difference to a lot of people. The moral high ground is a nice place to be. The original issue, being denied access because of my Guide dog was something I was willing to fight.

And I'm glad to say the management of McDonalds took the issue very seriously and were sincere in their willingness to address it. I was grateful for their cooperation. Some of my co-workers have been to that restaurant several times and told me the service and access has greatly improved.

It worked out well. I still get calls resulting from the original coverage. I guess Musket was pretty photogenic.

To read the actual story just Google 'Disabled man not lovin' it after snubbed at McDonald's.'

🐈 "That was fun. Daddy tells it really good."

Cluelessville

San Diego unfortunately had a reputation for having a lot of uninformed, inconsiderate and even hostile people thinking they had a god-given right to challenge a person with an Assistance animal. Oh, the stories I could tell.

Here are a few things people have asked me. Remember, these things really happened.

In a line at Costco a man turned to me and said, "So, what's this? You're supposed to be blind or something?" His tone was as if I were wearing a Halloween costume he didn't quite understand, I shrugged. "No, I'm not supposed to be but it seemed like a good idea. I really enjoy taking advantage of all the wonderful opportunities and chances for advancement I can get from being disabled."

I don't think he got it. A woman behind us was laughing. She got it just fine.

We were passing a supermarket driveway one night when a car blocked us.

Driver: "Are you really blind?"

"Yes I am," I said.

Driver: "How do I know that?"

Sigh. "Let me drive your car. I hope you have good insurance."

For some reason he didn't take me up on the offer.

At a bus stop, a man was standing near me and said, "Is that one of those blind dogs?"

Oh, what I could have said. 'I sure hope not. I'll have to get my money back!'

I answered him honestly.

My favorite. A man was ahead of me waiting for a bus. When the bus pulled up, he stood by the door and actually bowed slightly. "After you, Mr. Blind Person, sir."

No, I didn't tip him, but I was tempted.

Believe me I couldn't make this stuff up. Life was far more interesting.

🐕 "I remember these guys. The one in Costco was a jerk. I don't know why people had to act so self-important all the time. Didn't they know it was all about me?"

There were some very nice and helpful people out there and I was grateful for their kindness. I believed most people were basically nice and meant well.

I was able to get around by myself. Blind people don't want someone to grab their arm at a street crossing and say 'Here, I'll help you.'

Somewhere in their kindness was a misplaced belief the blind persons are helpless. We're not.

We'll ask for help if we need it.

🐕 "But Daddy almost never does. He has me."

I sometimes used GPS to navigate in unfamiliar areas. It doesn't replace the cane or a Guide dog or good Orientation & Mobility skills. It was just a tool to increase mobility.

🐕 "I didn't trust it. It talked to Daddy and he did what it said. Actually he told me to do what it said. If I can ever find it I'm going to bury it in the yard."

As the only Guide dog handler at ISD I had become the default 'expert' in the matter of Assistance animals. They had access to all public transportation like buses, trains, planes and taxis. It was rarely a problem but once in a while it did happen.

Sometimes it was an improperly trained driver or even caused by another Assistance dog handler.

A few years ago I was stepping onto a bus heading downtown. I didn't often take that route so the driver didn't know me.

"Have you got identification for the dog?" the driver asked.

I must have looked confused. "He's a Guide dog," I said.

"I need I.D."

"His name is Musket." That didn't satisfy him.

"No you need a Transit System I.D. card with his picture to prove he's a working dog.

Here we go again. "No, you don't. There is no such thing."

"Yes there is, sir and I can't let you on the bus until I know he's a working dog."

We were holding up the bus, so I said firmly, "I have the State I.D. tag. And that's all he needs. Now let's get going."

Finally he relented and we took a seat right behind him. While we rode, I asked the driver what he was talking about. "A transit system I.D. card?"

"Yeah," he said sullenly, sure I was breaking some sort of law. "The dog's owner has to have one."

After a few more questions, I learned what was going on.

Apparently some dog handlers had gone to the transit office and had cards made with the dog's name and picture. Maybe they thought it was cute but I believe it was because they might have had a hidden disability. Drivers had challenged their dogs' legitimacy.

So the cards issued by the transit company were their statement of authenticity, so to speak.

Because the driver was just doing his job, I wanted to clear it up. "Okay, there is no such thing. The cards are not transit system policy. I've worked with the director of training and he never mentioned it. It's not required by law either. When you get back to the office, please ask the training director to tell you."

The driver clearly didn't believe me but I had tried. What worried me were the hundreds of other Assistance dog handlers who might be forced to get one of these 'I.D.' cards just to ride the bus.

When I returned to my office I called the director of training for the transit system and he assured me there were no such things as the cards and weren't transit company policy.

I asked him if he would make sure the drivers were informed of this.

Just doing my part for the cause.

"Daddy was really good at that, especially when he knew something was wrong."

When we were in Atlanta for a conference in 2006 a shuttle van picked us up at the hotel to bring us back to the airport.

As I attempted to climb into the van's open side door, the driver stopped me.

"I can't have your dog on the van, sir."

I gave him my usual reply. He continued to refuse, even to the point of being rude.

Finally one of the hotel's clerks came out and tried to help. No go.

He gave me the number of the shuttle service and I got a supervisor on my cell phone. After explaining the situation I handed it to the driver.

After a few minutes he gave in and warmly welcomed me into the van.

During the ride I asked him why he had been so dead set against Musket being on the van.

"I might have a passenger who is allergic to dogs," he explained. His voice was thick with worry. I think his supervisor must have reamed him out.

"Okay," I said, "I understand, but that can't be a reason. If you have an allergic rider, tell the dog handler and have another van dispatched. Easy." Then I told him I wasn't mad and it would be okay. While we were at another hotel making a pickup, I called the supervisor again and made sure the driver wasn't in trouble. The supervisor was nice and we agreed some extra training was the best course.

Upon reaching the airport the driver, who felt better, unloaded my bags. I shook his hand and thanked him.

In my hand was a nice tip. Some things just worked out better with a little communication.

🐕 "I think Daddy did the right thing but it could have been a lot worse. That driver just didn't know any better."

Airports and commercial airlines are a big enough subject for a whole chapter, so we'll leave it for now. But it's amazing. Musket and I have been all over the country and that dog has more flight attendant girlfriends than Dean Martin could ever dream.

🐕 "I loved it. They always asked Daddy if he wanted something to drink. But they offered me belly rubs."

The Doggy Under the Table

Some businesses got it right. They considered an Assistance dog a sort of canine celebrity. I wonder where I heard that before? They welcomed us in with sincere smiles.

To be fair most people we encountered fit this category. And I appreciated every one of them.

As unofficial representatives of Assistance dogs and persons with disabilities, Musket and I tried to set the best example for the general public. I wanted the next Assistance dog handler to be welcomed in because the business owner had seen how well-behaved these dogs are.

🐕 "Well behaved, but none are as cute as me."

Only a few times over the years we were challenged. They were resolved by a short conversation with the owner or manager. Chinese restaurants seemed to have the most problems understanding. But in every single case it was cleared up and we were welcomed. It was a good thing since Jane and I loved Chinese food.

🐕 "I liked the Won Tons and fortune cookies."

When Jane took care of her parents, we often ate out to give her a break. We had a few regular haunts and they knew the three of us pretty well.

When we went to a place we've never tried before, I was just a bit more alert.

Sometimes it happened, most of the time not.

Generalizations are hard to avoid, but it seemed when a lady was at the front counter, we were welcomed with no questions. If it was an older man, then I was often asked if Musket was a service dog.

"He sure is," I usually replied.

"Come on, Daddy let's get to the food part. I loved restaurants. They were magic. We went in and people just gave us food. It was so fantastic."

When we went into a dark restaurant Jane followed the waitress and I hung on to Musket who became increasingly eager to get to the food part.

"You betcha!"

Waitresses were the first to fall under Musket's spell. "Oh, she's so beautiful. I love dogs."

"Again with the 'she.'"

Musket went right under the table and got into position.

"I had to be able to take French fries from both Mommy and Daddy. I got a sore neck from twisting my head around."

When the food arrived Musket became more alert. The waitress usually asked if he might want any water. Most of the time we said yes.

"Okay, since Daddy brought this up, I have a question. Why did everybody assume because I was a large breed I drank a lot of water? My bladder is only the size of a kiwi fruit. They never brought a small bowl. It was always a vat, a pool, a tub of water, sloshing all over the place. When I saw that I was puzzled. Was I supposed to drink it or take a swim?"

Musket's sense of smell was very acute. He knew there was food on the table, and his nose was buzzing.

Through the meal Jane and I surreptitiously slipped Musket a few fries, his favorite. But he stayed under the table.

It worked on the same principle as mob protection money. If I gave him fries, he didn't make no trouble.

If I forgot to pay attention to him he put his head on my knee.

Impossible to ignore.

🐕 "Resistance is futile. You will feed me."

As related previously the issue was Musket's behavior. He was quiet, not being a disturbance to other patrons, and not unsanitary. When we paid the check and stood to leave, the best indication was when other diners exclaimed "I didn't even know there was a dog in here."

🐕 "The swimming pool under the table hid me from view."

Musket should be seen and not heard. Sometimes irony fits perfectly. But he was like that and never been a disruption.

We were always welcomed back. Okay, Musket was welcomed back. I doubt the staff even noticed Jane or me. It must be the big soulful brown eyes.

🐕 "What was your first clue, Sherlock?"

On a day trip to Temecula, a wine and cheese community north of San Diego, we went to a western-style place called the Texas Grille. That was one time I really regretted being blind. The waitresses were all babes with short skirts and full bosoms. Like Hooters but with more class.

Jane only told me this *afterwards*. I'll get her for that.

Anyway, when we entered the girl at the front said we'd have to eat outside.

This was prior to the McDonalds incident. I actually didn't hear her because the Country Western music was loud. But Jane heard and told the girl Musket was a Guide dog. The girl again said we'd have to eat outside on the patio.

"We would rather eat inside, not with the smokers," Jane said. She put her foot down and got our table.

Then Jane, of whom I'm always proud, asked our waitress if we could see the manager.

A moment later the manager, a nice woman, came to the table. "Is there something I can help you with?"

Jane and I told her what the other girl had said, that Musket would have to be outside.

"I don't believe it," she exclaimed. "I've trained the staff about this. I raise Assistance dog puppies. That should never have happened. I'm very sorry."

All was well and after she'd gotten a kiss from Musket, we had our dinner. Great food. I really recommend the chicken fried steak and potatoes.

And a bright light so you can see the girls.

"I have a question and I'd like it answered by anyone who can do so. If it's called a 'Doggy Bag' why don't the dogs ever see it? Hmmm?"

One day at work I called a local Italian place and ordered a meatball sandwich. Then Musket and I walked the two blocks to the restaurant.

And guess what we walked into?

A television restaurant review. I told you, some things just happen around Musket.

The reporter from a local station recognized me from years before when as a re-enactor I had escorted him around one of the military history encampments in San Diego.

He asked if we'd like to be on TV and of course I agreed.

"He had to ask? Daddy was a bigger ham than me."

He did a quick interview, asking how I liked the food there, but Musket was in the shot most of the time. The guy even teased him with a pizza. He doesn't know how lucky he was I had a firm grip on the leash.

The reporter commented he remembered when I had a different musket.

🐕 "And just who was that, Daddy?"

In the end, I was given the meal free, probably because I said on TV the food was the best in town.

After I returned to the office I called Jane to tell her about her budding television star dog.

🐕 "Daddy didn't' give me any of the sandwich, though."

We took Musket when shopping in grocery or department stores, malls or those cute little 'shoppes' women liked so much.

In most stores it was easy for him to guide me. The aisles were wide and unobstructed with plenty of room to maneuver.

I noticed in some stores his keen sense of smell was fooled. Walking down an aisle with bleach, soap and cleanser, that crazy dog was sniffing it as if he expected it to be edible.

🐕 "So what do I know? I couldn't read the labels. Tide looked delicious."

In some large department stores, it was easy for me to lose Jane.

(Insert a Jane 'sigh' here).

I said to Musket, "Where's your Mommy? Let's go find Mommy!"

It worked every time. I don't know if he remembered which way she went, or if he could follow her trail by scent or what. But he always found her.

It was easy to tell when Musket found her because his tail started to wag furiously and I could feel it in the harness handle.

"There's my Musket!" she said happily.

🐕 "Okay, I'll tell the secret. Mommy gave out warm love rays I could follow."

In the 'shoppes' it was a different matter. Jane said, "Maybe you should stay out here, Honey. It's kind of tight in there."

"Okay, no problem." I found a bench to sit on and waited.

Without fail she called me. "Honey I just found something really cute I want to show you."

So in we went, doomed. But Musket was perfect as he neatly threaded me through a tight maze of tables, displays and highly breakable merchandise. He never steered me wrong or knocked anything down. I was careful of his wrecking ball tail, though.

The proprietor often commented on Musket. Then Jane, wanting to spread his joy said, "Would you like to meet him?"

"Oh, can I?"

After making sure there was nothing valuable on the counter, I patted it and said "Paws up."

He stood and put his paws on the counter to get a pat from his new friend. Worked every time.

🐕 "I made more new friends that way."

The face that launched a thousand friendships

He wasn't fond of shopping, especially when we went to several stores. The first clothing store, he was fine. Alert, tail wagging.

Then we entered a card shop. Still going but just a bit slower.

A bath and linen store. Tail was drooping slightly, enthusiasm waning.

By the fourth or fifth store, his head was low and he was dragging his tail.

🐕 "Can I help it if I don't have any shopping stamina? I'm sure if I were a girl dog it would be different."

Hmm. I never knew Musket was a chauvinist. Confessions indeed.

🐕 "I'm not a chauvinist. What's a chauvinist?"

I kept a few treats in my pocket to keep him going.

To be honest I did like to shop with Jane but at times I could get bored.

That was when my penchant for irreverent humor and social or political commentary came out. Jane never paid attention to me, but merely said 'Yes dear' every few minutes.

I got some great story ideas in stores.

I understand Albert Einstein had the original idea for the Theory of Relativity while shopping with his wife in Wal-Mart.

Well it could have happened.

I just heard a sigh again.

The only store Musket liked was Costco. And I'll give you the reason in two words.

Free samples.

It didn't take long for a smart dog like Musket to realize every time we reached the end of an aisle at Costco, someone was handing out food. And he wasn't shy about asking for samples.

Hot links, pizza, tofu, yogurt, cheesecake, teriyaki chicken, Vienna franks, tapioca pudding, scrambled eggs; the list went on and on.

No, I didn't let him have any of those things.

I ate them.

🐕 "Well, you just try and walk around Costco next time without me, pal."

As a blind guy, once in a while I accidentally walked into a Womens' restroom. Really, by accident.

🐕 "Anybody believe that?"

In most cases a strange (and they don't come any stranger than me) man were to suddenly appear in a womens' restroom it would be cause for alarm and calling security.

But when I was with Musket, all that happened was I heard a kind female voice saying "I think you're in the wrong place. Oh, what a beautiful dog. What is his name?"

Need I say more?

"It wasn't my fault. I couldn't read the signs."

Kids with Dirty Faces

In stores we met a lot of kids with their parents. The first indication was when we heard 'Doggy!' or 'Mom, there's a dog in here!"

"They didn't say it quietly either."

If Jane was with us she often turned and said "His name's Musket. Wanna say hi?"

It was pretty much 100% yes. The kids came over and I dropped the harness handle, the signal that he was off duty and could be a dog.

His tail was wagging as he met his new admirers. Little kids were a favorite for several reasons.

"First of all, they were just my height. I didn't have to reach to kiss them. Second, most kids were messy eaters, especially babies. They always had food on their faces. I performed a public health service by washing them."

It's probably good to mention Musket's mouth. I brushed his teeth for him, although it wasn't high on his list of fun things to do, and chewing on his bone kept his teeth clean. He had very nice breath for a dog.

"Better than Daddy in the morning from what Mommy said."

Ahem. Anyway as I was saying before I was rudely interrupted, Musket had nice breath. I know how dogs wash themselves, but he was a very clean dog. In all the years we've had him he never had fleas. And he drank a lot of water, even away from restaurants. So getting a kiss from Musket wasn't a health hazard. Dog saliva was supposed to have some medicinal properties too. I think. Or was that Mothers' spit?

So Moms didn't have to freak out when he gave their babies a face wash. The kids loved it. A giggling child with Musket snuffling and licking them was a definite Kodak moment.

🐕 "Oops, I missed a spot. Hold still."

Some children were afraid of Musket, and didn't want to get near him. I really didn't blame the little tykes. Musket was a big dog and when he was excited his mouth was open, baring his lower teeth. And that could be a bit scary. I never encouraged kids to approach a strange dog without a parent's permission.

Some dogs aren't as friendly as Musket. I didn't want any child to assume since Musket was so sweet, all others were the same.

I often cautioned children and their parents to be careful.

🐕 "No kid should be afraid of me. But I know better than anybody there are some mean dogs out there. Daddy will tell that story in the next chapter. Back to the kids."

Coming home on the bus one evening, I was sitting several rows back when the driver, cut off by another car, had to stop short. The momentum of the bus caused every rider to surge forward and a little girl of about seven fell off her seat and was hurt. Not badly but she was crying and very miserable. The driver attended to her and after a few minutes we moved on. At the next stop I brought Musket forward and we sat across from the wailing tyke. Musket went over to her.

"Do you want to say hi?" I asked.

Her mother said, "He's a nice dog. You can pet him."

In a moment the little girl was stroking Musket's head and we all realized she was no longer crying.

🐕 "Poor little thing was just unhappy. I made her smile. But she didn't have any food on her face so only one of us was happy."

In our daily work, we've encountered parents who don't want their kids near me. I've heard them saying either out loud or in hushed whispers, 'Stay away from him! He's blind.'

Once, outside a supermarket a little girl asked me "Mister are you blind?"

It was a perfectly honest and frank question. She was curious and had a right to know.

I never got to answer her.

The girl's mother grabbed her and snarled "Don't ask such stupid questions!"

I felt bad for the kid and resented her mother's inability to accept reality. Some parents think they're being respectful by not asking a person with a disability about themselves.

Some are afraid of something they can't cope with or don't understand.

Sure they want to protect their children but making them look away, or worse, run away from someone with a disability is insulting and gives the child the wrong impression.

With Musket nothing bad ever happened. Most of the kids he met liked him and wanted to pet him until his fur was flying off. Parents were often impressed by his being a Guide dog and how well-behaved and quiet he was.

Oftentimes someone told us they had a friend or family member who raised an Assistance dog. I always said 'Please thank them for their good work.' I meant it. Puppy raisers are wonderful people in my book.

When I was graduating from Guide Dogs, I met several puppy raisers who'd trained over a dozen dogs. The highest number for one couple was 21. It had to be a true labor of love, raising, training, loving a growing puppy, only to give it up after a few months. I could only guess it would be like sending a nearly-grown child off to college.

"I have a PhDog Degree in Begging."

Children asked about Musket's harness and how it worked, which I explained to them. Jane was pretty good at it too. But always their parents wanted to know about the little blue nylon pack attached to the harness. It was about the size of an éclair.

"That's where he carries his poop bags," I told them.

The usual reaction was surprise, as if they'd never heard of picking up dog poop. And judging by the piles Musket frequently steered me around, many people never have.

"If I have to pick it up, he should at least carry the bags," I said with a smile.

🐕 "Daddy picked it up. That was his job."

Inside the pack he also had his business cards. Yes, business cards. I designed them myself. They listed Musket's name, 'Musket Carlson, PhDog' and his title 'Blind/Low Vision Mobility Specialist and Stress Relief Counselor.'

The tag line was 'Squishy-face kisses a specialty.' And so on. It even listed his pee-mail address.

I gave them out to his fans, which always earned a laugh.

🐕 "Working dog with a business card. It's a no-brainer."

When someone asked about how to get an Assistance dog for themselves or someone they knew, I gave them my own card. It wasn't only my job, but my pleasure to help others with the independence an Assistance dog brings.

Given that Musket and lots of other Assistance dogs attract people, I noticed a few things over the years.

Most people respected the dog/handler relationship and asked me if they could pet him.

That was always the best way. If it was a safe situation like not in the middle of the street, I almost always dropped the harness handle and said "Sure you can. Thank you for asking."

After they said hello to him, they moved off, satisfied.

I was pretty easygoing about letting people pet Musket.

🐕 "I know by scent if they're dog lovers. My schnozz is never wrong."

But some Assistance dog handlers aren't. It's their right to refuse. The person asking shouldn't take it personally. In some cases the dog might be too easily distracted, or the handler doesn't want the dog to have contact with another person.

An Assistance dog is as important to a person with a disability as their wheelchair or cane. It provided them with mobility, safety and independence. Think of it the same way as asking a total stranger if you could drive their car. Or not asking and driving it anyway.

All Assistance dog handlers are proud of their dogs and think of them not as pets but their eyes or ears or hands.

🐕 "What was I to you, Daddy?

Musket is of course my eyes, my guide and my protector. He kept me safe. But he is also my little buddy. I love him very much.

🐕 "Whew. He had me worried for a moment there."

I realized the difference between Musket and other dogs a few years ago when walking with my brother David in Solvang, a Danish-themed tourist town in central California. David had Beamer, a Golden Retriever. There were plenty of people around and we of course attracted attention.

David made a comment I still remember clearly. "I can't get over how many people want to meet Musket, but don't even notice Beamer."

🐕 "Ah, well some dogs got it, and some dogs don't got it."

And Musket sure was full of it.

🐕 "Hey, did Daddy just dis me?"

Sneakers and Honkers

It was truly wonderful how Musket attracted people. We made new friends and even been given better service. All because of him.

🐕 "Well, it wasn't hard to imagine why."

A man once asked me, "What um, make of dog is he?"

I knew he meant breed, but you know how sometimes you just can't get at the right word? He laughed at himself and continued. 'What make and model?"

I grinned. "His make is Retriever, the Labrador Model. A 2000 Labrador from Guide Dog Motors of San Rafael."

We both shared a laugh at that. But it wasn't enough for me. "We ordered the vanilla color, with caramel trim."

"Oh, well. Daddy has to get his entertainment somewhere, I suppose."

We've encountered some pretty interesting types of people. I'll try and list them by name, habitat and gender. First, the difficult types. Then I'll list the wonderful ones.

Genus: The Overeager Dog Lover
Canus Amorus Enthusiasticus

Species: The Sneaker
Habitat: Bus stops
Gender: Male

This type knew I couldn't see him, and had no respect for me, so he snuck up slowly and reached out to start petting. I could usually tell because Musket quivered a bit. I reached out and felt the hand on his head. "Please don't touch my dog. He's working." That usually did it and he went off, miffed at at being caught and not apologizing.

Species: The Step Right Up
Habitat: Bus stops, in line at stores
Gender: Male

These just walked right up and said nothing as if I wasn't there or worth talking to. They thought someone with a disability was a 'non-entity.' My reaction wasn't hard to guess.

I often responded with "Don't touch my dog. He's working. Touch my eyes, they don't work."

That usually drove them off. I didn't mind because respect for another human being wasn't in their nature.

Species: The Attaboy or Hi, Doggy

Habitat: Guy places (bars, pool halls, sporting events)

Gender: What else? Male

Not hard to guess what this type did. They were usually harmless, sometimes drunk and just wanted to meet Musket. They thought he was like any other dog. They just bent over and ruffled his fur. "Hey, puppy! How are you?"

My response was as in the Sneaker. Not angry, but firm.

Often the Attaboy apologized, accompanied by burps and hiccups, and I let them meet him properly.

A subspecies was the Attitude Attaboy. They resented me telling them not to touch him. "Why not? What's it to you if I do?"

If they got belligerent, that was it. All bets were off.

Species: The Charmer

Habitat: Everywhere

Gender: Both

These individuals used compliments to get at Musket. "You have a beautiful dog."

"Thank you," I replied.

Then, feeling they've paid the toll, they moved in and started petting.

Again not bad people, just uninformed.

Species: The Does He Bite?

Habitat: Bus Stops

Gender: Often female

Very much like the Charmer in one respect, they asked if Musket would bite, then began petting. They apparently felt that was all which was required to pet him. When this happened I replied, "He only bites people who pet him without asking."

Believe it or not some of them didn't see the irony.

Another version of The Does He Bite? are people who were afraid of dogs. I respected their fear and told them he never bites and was very friendly.

Once on a sidewalk by the bus stop I heard a woman say "Don't let it bite me! Keep it away from me!"

"Miss," I said calmly, "he won't bite at all. He's very friendly. Please don't be afraid."

She continued to act as if Musket were foaming at the mouth. "You keep that dog away from me!"

I finally made him lie down and she passed, while I tried to explain he was a Guide dog not an attack dog. It made no difference. I could only assume she'd always been afraid of dogs or had been attacked, or was just paranoid. In any case I respected her feelings.

🐕 "I wanted to say hello and show her I was a nice dog but she wouldn't believe us."

The characters mentioned above were real and I'm sure several of my fellow Assistance dog handlers have encountered them. I said they may be uninformed or even indifferent.

Species: The Jump in Front

Habitat: Outside bars, sidewalk cafes

Gender: Definitely a guy

This only happened once. But once was enough. We were walking in downtown San Diego, passing several sidewalk cafes. I was moving at a pretty fast pace to catch a bus.

Then the Jump in Front struck. I can't even describe it. One minute moving along, the next instant BAM! He was right in between me and Musket, petting him. I pretty much fell over the guy. Musket had no warning.

The man never even acknowledged me.

"What the hell are you doing?" I said, not bothering to keep the anger out of my voice.

"I wanted to meet him. What's wrong with that?

"He's working! He's a Guide dog."

"Well I don't have a dog. My condo doesn't allow it." That was lame and didn't help matters.

"Smart move on their part, not letting you have one."

Still he didn't seem to get it.

"Leave him alone," I said. "Didn't you see me? I almost fell over you."

I loved his next line. "It's okay. I'm a lawyer."

Well what was I thinking? That made it all better, didn't it?

Just to set the record straight I did NOT retain him for any future legal needs.

🐕 "Daddy is telling the truth. We met some real bozos. He treated everybody the same if they respected us. We've met some really nice people too."

The idea that because someone had an Assistance dog in a public place it was open season on the dog, ticked me off. When the Step Right Up or the Sneaker attacked, I felt like saying 'Hey, would you want a total stranger hugging your kid?" That's the way it was for us.

🐕 "I know Daddy wanted to protect me. We didn't know those people; we just wanted them to respect our rights."

A related genre to those mentioned above could be found anywhere. And frequently were.

Genus: The Attitude
Oblivio Socialius

Species: Hey I'm Walkin' Here
Habitat: All across America
Gender: Both

Well there have to be a few nuts in the great trail mix of life. Musket and I have met our share of them. The kind of people who just walked right in front of us, not even noticing Musket and then having the gall to make me think I was the rude one really took the cake.

Life would be a lot better for everybody if those people would slow down, shut their cell phones, put away the Starbucks triple latte, turn off the boom box and pay attention to the world the rest of us inhabit with them.

Lecture's over. Thank you.

🐕 "Whew. You got off lightly. He usually goes on forever."

A species which doesn't fit exactly into the category is still worth mentioning. Even though they don't interact directly with dogs they do have serious effects on them.

Species: The Thoughtless Smoker

Habitat: Everywhere

Species: Usually male

I'm not a smoker but I have no problem with those who are. To each his own.

One day Musket and I were waiting for a bus. A smoker was nearby, puffing away as I kept upwind from him.

Then the bus pulled up. The smoker took one long last drag and stepped on board in front of me.

Then Musket stepped on the glowing butt. He shrieked in pain, twisting around and hobbling.

I didn't know what had happened. A woman behind me said "He stepped on that cigarette. Poor puppy!"

I helped Musket onto the bus. He sat and held his left front paw off the floor. I found some napkins in my backpack, which I soaked with water to wash and soothe his burned paw. I didn't think it was serious but it had to be painful.

Several other riders were asking if he was okay, if I needed their cell phone to call a vet.

Then the same woman, who was sitting next to me, said, "He was the one who dropped the cigarette without grinding it out." The smoker was sitting directly across from me.

I didn't say anything. But neither did he. No apology, nothing. Either he didn't accept responsibility or didn't care he'd caused injury and pain to a dog. I'm sure he could feel the other riders glaring at him.

I kept the wet napkin on Musket's paw for several minutes until he licked my hand, which told me he appreciated my attention.

"I did. My paw hurt a lot. I don't know what I stepped on but I could hardly walk on it. Daddy took good care of me."

A few stops later the smoker got off. Then the woman next to me said, "He lit up the second he hit the sidewalk."

I actually felt pity for the smoker who was so hooked he had lost any compassion for others.

I called Jane and asked her to pick us up. I didn't want Musket to walk home that night. I also didn't tell Jane what had happened. She'd have freaked out. Musket was walking fine the next day but since then I've been wary of smokers at bus stops.

There is yet another genus.

And they could be aggressively malicious. They were the misguided animal rights activists.

Nothing funny about them. I'd been working with Musket almost two years when I first began to hear about incidents of Assistance dogs being targeted by individuals wanting either to free or steal them.

Deliberate interference with a working Assistance animal was a felony. And the theft of one was a serious felony, not to mention the obvious catastrophe to the handler.

Apparently people actually went to a harnessed guide or service dog to release it. Setting it free of its servitude and bondage if you can believe it.

The incidents had apparently occurred in various parts of California, where animal rights are taken seriously.

And to top it off, the people doing this were supposedly from a well-regarded animal rights organization. I'm stating here and now, I do not believe that organization nor any of its members were involved, but that was the rumor.

When I heard about this I called the local office of the group. The woman I spoke to had not heard of this matter but would look into it.

🐕 "I don't want to be taken away from my mommy and daddy."

It remained in the back of my mind. What if someone did try to take Musket away from me? First of all I'd fight like a tiger and scream bloody murder. That person would be committing both a serious crime and a moral outrage. If they want to 'free' a working dog and allow it to roam feral in the idyllic woods like Puck from 'A Midsummer Night's Dream,' they're forgetting they are not wild dogs able to survive on their own.

Musket would die without care.

🐕 "I sure would. I don't know how to get food by myself. And who would snuggle with me?"

The organization I mentioned and will not name out of respect is an excellent group dedicated to assuring animals are treated humanely. I loved all animals and felt real pain when I heard of people inflicting abuse on innocent creatures.

The idea of a dog being 'forced' to work was ludicrous. Assistance animals are loved, cared for and part of a team. They like what they do.

When I held the harness out for Musket he actually looked around to make sure there was an audience. He liked to show off.

🐕 "Mommy, do you see how good I am?"

As it turned out the rumors were probably exaggerated, but to this day Jane still gives Musket his morning spiel with the line 'If anyone touches your harness you bite their butt!'

🐕 "You can bet on that Mommy!"

So far in this chapter I've related meetings with people. But there are a lot of cars in our daily life too.

Americans without disabilities who drive everywhere often don't realize some people are full-time pedestrians.

This was often an issue when I called for directions to some location I had to go for an outreach or meeting.

Remember, I was a blind guy going to do a talk about Assistive Technology and Guide dogs.

"Can you give me directions?"

The person on the phone said, "Sure, take Highway 8 east to College Avenue and drive up the hill to the second light, right for 5 blocks and . . ." Not a clue.

I often had to ask for bus routes and more useful information. But most of the people I talked to had no idea what bus route served their location.

Anyway, on our daily route to and from work we had to cross a few intersections. The problem wasn't Musket, who was very good at that.

The problem was the Genus distantly related to the Jump In Front type mentioned earlier.

Genus: The Clueless Driver
Automobilius Imbecilius

Species: The I Can Stop Where I Want
Habitat: Crosswalks, intersections, driveways
Gender: Nearly always male

These people also had a disability. Their legs were too short to reach the brake pedal.

They found it impossible to stop their vehicle before the first crosswalk line. Or even the second. Their bumper protruded into the intersection.

This posed a real dilemma for us and for anyone using a wheelchair or walker or even pushing a baby stroller.

Try crossing the street with your eyes closed sometime.

🐈 "I had a job to do getting us across the street safely with some bozo blocking the crosswalk. I had to stop while Daddy figured out what was in the way."

Then the driver opened his window and said one of four things.

"Hey, can't you see me?"

"Don't touch my car."

"Hey, there's a car here."

"Can't you just go around?"

🐈 "They even honked. I knew Daddy didn't speak Honk.

It was very dangerous because we were still in the intersection and the light was going to change. The only way was to walk around the car into the cross traffic and get back between the lines.

Daddy never yelled at those people. He had a far more subtle way of making his point. He said "Let's go around, Musket."

Then we went as conspicuously as possible so all the other drivers would look at this twit and think 'What a jerk that driver is.' I think Daddy's way was best, if we moved fast."

Species: The Whistler

Habitat: Crosswalks, intersections

Gender: Male

One other denizen of the crosswalk was the Whistler. They didn't block the crosswalk but they did call out to Musket. Some intersections are on wide, busy roads. And suddenly I heard 'Thweeet! Hey puppy! C'mere, boy!"

Musket couldn't help looking around for the source of the noise. That kind of behavior was just plain idiotic. Couldn't the driver see what was happening? I'm not saying they were bad people, just clueless.

"I didn't like it when someone whistled at me while I was working. I got confused and had to know if Daddy wanted me to go over there."

Now that I've listed the bad and ugly, I'm going to turn around and express some praise and gratitude.

Genus: The Social Conscience

Sensibilus Americanus

One other occasional encounter was more amusing than anything although it did illustrate the image the general public had about blind folks.

Species: The Shy and Curious

Habitat: All across America

Gender: Both

I'm not totally blind, and pretty mobile. This often led to a familiar question. "Are you training him?"

Inwardly I chuckled. They were asking a legitimate question and deserved an honest answer.

"Nope, he's working for me."

Then I heard a slightly awkward pause while they tried to work this out.

"Oh, well you don't look blind."

It's true and they weren't the first nor I hope the last to think so.

"Thank you, but I'm legally blind. I really need him."

This relaxed the questioner who was apparently relieved they didn't have to conduct a citizens' arrest.

"How much can you see?"

"Not a lot, believe me. If you could see what I do, you'd freak out."

Species: The Respectful Person

Habitat: Not nearly enough places

Gender: Both

This species is wonderful. They asked about Musket, kept their distance and waited until I invited them to pet him. Some said "I know I'm not supposed to pet him when he's working."

I really appreciated their sincerity and always dropped the harness handle. "Please come and say hi. He's not working right now."

It felt good to meet these people. No pity, no fear, no attitude. Just nice folks who wanted to meet a working dog.

🐕 "I liked them the best. We made some great friends that way."

Meanwhile, back on the road.

Species: The Considerate Driver

Habitat: Crosswalks, intersections, parking lots

Gender: Both

There have been times when a crosswalk was blocked by a car. And as Musket and I approached, instead of the wisecracks, the driver backed up, clearing the crosswalk.

Even a huge 18-wheeler driver once did it.

I know it was difficult and even dangerous. But I very much appreciated it, for myself and any disabled or senior who depended on a clear route across the street.

To all who took the time to back out, thank you from all of us.

🐕 "When a driver moved back or stopped to make sure we were clear it meant they cared about other people. And dogs."

But no matter how careful we were, sometimes fate just put us in the wrong place at the wrong time. And it happened very fast.

We have been run over. Twice. But neither incident was serious. Walking home from work one day we were on a residential street. As we passed one driveway a car backed out on my right. Musket and I were just coming behind it. He tried to push me back but at first I didn't realize what was happening.

Then the car's bumper shoved against me and I was knocked over. I remember letting go of Musket so he wouldn't be hurt as I pounded on the moving car's trunk lid. Then it stopped.

The driver came out and saw what she'd done. I was on the street holding my right arm. It was hurting from the impact and fall. Musket was okay, and came over to me. The woman was horrified, and began to cry.

I sat down on the curb, checking my arm. No injuries.

She was kneeling beside me, crying and very upset at nearly running me down.

I wasn't mad and told her I was okay. Soon she calmed down and I introduced her to Musket.

It was an accident and could have happened to anybody. I'll never forget the feeling of that heavy car backing up and I couldn't get out of the way.

I didn't press charges because I knew she would never again back up without looking.

"Daddy tried to keep me from being hurt. He took good care of me. I remembered that place every time we passed it and slowed down just in case."

The second time happened in downtown San Diego where we'd just gotten off the bus and were preparing to cross a busy intersection. The two right-turn lanes in front of us were both blind turns and in order for us to be seen by oncoming cars we had to practically be in the middle of the road. At rush hour a lot of cars didn't pay as mush attention as they should have.

"Daddy waited until he heard the traffic stop and said 'Forward.' I moved out and we passed a stopped car in the right turn lane and into the second lane which was empty. Then I saw a car coming at us. I stopped, and Daddy did too. Then the car was almost on us. I saw the driver was looking to her left and not ahead. Daddy tried to step back but the car bumped into him. Then someone honked their horn and the driver stopped. Daddy got us back on the sidewalk and the woman came over to see if we were okay."

Fortunately she wasn't going fast. I had time to move back, thanks to Musket.

She worked for the city government, which might have earned her some scathing remarks, but I again didn't press charges. Maybe I was too soft sometimes. But she was really nice and offered us a ride to work. But I declined. I got her card and after getting to work I called her. Some things just had a way of working out. She became my contact in the city government and a great help in reaching other officials for local legislative issues. Sure it was probably from guilt but I didn't mind.

"We were okay. I even gave her a kiss. I remembered when Peter O'Reilly tried to run us over during training. I guess I learned. And that's what a well-trained Guide dog does.

Just remember we're out there, stores, restaurants and everywhere else. If you want to meet us, feel free to ask. And don't forget the treats. 'Just look for the Guide dog label . . .'"

Chapter Eight

A Dog's Life

"I look like a dog, smell like a dog, act like a dog, and sound like a dog. So what am I? I'm Musket the Guide dog. But I'm a dog first. I'm proud of being a working dog.

Daddy has done a lot of the writing, and I know I'm in every chapter, but this one is All About Me. Go for it, Daddy."

This chapter is about Musket the duckbilled platypus.

No, just kidding.

This is by his own request, so don't blame me.

It's about his life 'off-duty.'

When I or Jane took Musket for a walk, I used my cane, so he could just be a dog.

On those walks his inner personality changed. He became self-indulgent, even a bit disobedient.

"I don't believe it. We're only on the first page and already he's dissin' me!"

If he just wanted to go out, I opened the door for him. There was a small plot of common ground by the front walk, which never did well with any plants. I wasn't sure if the acidity of the soil was off or what. Ivy, ice plants, bushes, boxwood, nothing grew there. Not even weeds.

The Homeowners' Association did the gardening in the common areas.

Since 1995 I took it upon myself to fertilize, plant various hardy shrubs, turn over the soil, you name it. Nada. Zilch.

In 2009 we received a letter stating we would have to take 'our dog somewhere else to relieve him,' because he was killing the plants.

I didn't blame them for thinking so but I knew better. We'd had him for just over seven years. For eight years prior to that nothing grew there.

He wasn't the problem, and I wrote back stating this. But I will admit he did tend to target the new plants.

"Well someone planted them in MY spot!"

When I put his leash on, Musket knew he was going for a walk. Out the driveway he started pulling, looking for the holy grail of grass.

The sidewalks in our housing development are lined with slopes of ivy groundcover and oleanders running for about a quarter of a mile.

But before we went five inches he began power sniffing. His nose twitched so much it buzzed like a rattlesnake's tail.

When he buried it into the ivy it looked like he was trying to vacuum the greenery.

Once he apparently inhaled something irritating, and spent the next ten minutes sneezing. A dog's sneeze is funny but I finally got a paper towel and gave his nose a firm wiping. That seemed to clear it up. The reason it took ten minutes is because that's how long it took me to stop laughing.

"Firm, he called it. It felt like he was trying to pull my nose off."

We tried to be patient. After all it was his walk. But progress was s-l-o-w. Roughly a foot a minute.

With the wind at our back. Downhill.

Musket was in no hurry. And he had lots of pee saved up. I hope this won't gross anybody out, but I presume most of the readers are dog lovers.

Musket, as mentioned peed like a girl. He didn't lift his leg, but sort of squatted. His vet told me it was because he'd been neutered as a puppy.

🐕 "You can say that again. I never learned how to pee like a boy. So give me a break."

He plodded on, still sucking the plants into his nose. Sometimes I was in a hurry and needed him to go, but he wouldn't move.

A dog who didn't want to move could dig its claws into solid concrete. It was like dragging a 100 lb. bag of gravel with a rope.

Like a lot of dog owners I was leery of having Musket's collar too tight, not wanting him to be uncomfortable. But it backfired when he dug in his heels. One pull and off it came over his head.

🐕 "You go on ahead, I'll catch up with you."

To add to this he often reversed course and walked back several yards. His nose caught another scent.

🐕 "My nose was very sharp. I mean I had a sharp sense of smell, not like it was pointed. And I could follow a scent from across the street. Daddy was amazed when I did that, even after it rained."

A walk took us past dozens of condos. A few had barking dogs in yards or on balconies. I don't know about most people but I find dogs who bark incessantly very irritating. It was as if they thought it mattered. Musket was totally unimpressed and kept right on sniffing. Sometimes he stopped and looked at the barking dog.

🐕 "Give the vocal cords a rest, killer. If you look really close you'll see I'm not quivering with fear."

His actions as he was getting ready to 'do his business' were pretty consistent. A lot of turning, twisting, stopping and moving on. I could almost read his mind.

'Okay this looks good, no, here is better . . . ah, no let's try over here. I like this. Wait, I'm thinking. Okay this is it. Really. Ahhhhh.'

I felt his back and tail when he was going. During a pee his tail had a hook in it you could hang a hat on. For a poop, it was straight as an arrow.

🐕 "Ah, Daddy this is kind of private. Do you have to tell the whole world?"

Well, you asked me to write a chapter about you as a dog. Live with it, Musket.

For such a smart and well-trained dog he reverted to his base instincts when he was on the leash. When we were in a strange city or region of town, he sniffed like crazy. "Musket I can pretty much guarantee you'll never meet that dog."

🐕 "So what? A dog's gotta do what a dog's gotta do. And yes I take my time selecting the perfect spot. I'm not like humans. Humans use the same place again and again. Boring. How do you mark your territory? With a magazine?"

It annoyed me when I had to skip around some other dog's poop because their sighted owners were too lazy or inconsiderate to bother. I felt like saying "Hey I'm blind and I pick it up!"

At Guide Dogs we were advised to set the right example. So I pick it up.

His routine in the grass where he usually goes followed a pattern. He went to the same places in sequence every time, sniffed, peed, and moved on to the next spot.

Most of the dogs in the area used the same lawn, and Musket was seeing who had been there, how long ago and if they had anything new to say. Sound familiar?

Musket was checking his 'pee-mail.'

🐕 "Cute. I'm a dog, not Bill Gates."

Sidewalk Smorgasbord

The one thing I had to look out for besides some other dogs' poop was food on the ground. Musket would be strolling along and in an instant his head ducked like he stepped on his tongue.

He reached the Sidewalk Smorgasbord.

I know just what happened. He found a French fry or potato chip or something. And that dog had Zero Willpower. He scooped it up without even thinking. Usually it was too late for me to stop him. I used to stick my fingers into his mouth and tried to get it but most of the time it was too late.

🐕 "That got old real fast. After a few of those episodes I learned to swallow fast. I suppose I might not have picked up the food but some other dog would get it. I couldn't allow that."

I was anxious to stop his 'grazing' because he had a sensitive stomach and got sick from some foods. And God only knew what was on the sidewalk. He wasn't exactly a discerning gourmet.

🐕 "You want a gourmet? I wouldn't turn down Beluga Caviar."

Spoiled Rotten Dog

Kahoots, a pet supply store, had really nice employees. The only problem was their policy of giving treats to dogs.

Musket learned that REAL quick. When Jane and I went to Kahoots I used my cane and had Musket on the leash. He sure wasn't going to be any use as a Guide dog, except to lead me to the counter. Besides I had to carry the 40lb. bag of kibble.

And he knew just where the dog food aisle was.

🐕 "Follow me, Daddy. We turn right here; go to Aisle 4, then twenty feet on the left to the bottom shelf. That's where they keep the treats."

Another problem with pet stores was Jane. She was so in love with Musket she couldn't walk past the toys without saying "Oh, look at this. Musket, do you want this toy?"

🐕 "Sure! I don't have enough toys at home."

The other thing she couldn't resist was doggy beds. Musket didn't need a comfy poofy bed. He could fall asleep on a pile of broken brick.

But Jane insisted on wanting to buy these fluffy, overstuffed poofy things with lace and tassels.

No dog of mine was going to sleep on a bed Louis XVI would consider effeminate.

She got a lot of catalogs in the mail. They saw her coming a long way off. Over dinner one night I heard the dreaded words "Oh, Honey we have to get this for Musket!"

I listened but my feet were tensed for immediate flight while I made sure my credit cards were safe in my wallet.

What she found was a doggy pool in the shape of a bone.

Wait, it gets better.

With an awning.

And a treat tray.

Only $175 bucks.

She wasn't kidding.

How could I resist?

"Yeah how could you?"

I managed to prevail upon her common sense.

The Sound of Sizzling

San Diego is known for its warm sunny weather. I liked walking barefoot at home. But outside on the blacktop pavement, it wasn't a smart thing to do.

But being a guy, my third disability, when I needed to get the mail sometimes I didn't feel like putting on my shoes. So I did the quickstep to the mailbox and back. Jane just shook her head and said, "He's all mine, girls."

Hot as the parking area got in the summer sun, it never fazed that dog.

Musket was a true southern California sun worshipper.

Remember Garfield in the comics could never walk past a sunbeam without falling asleep?

That's Musket. If I had the garage door open he saw that blazing, melting, searing smoking, frying pan of a driveway and . . .

Flop. A dropped egg would fry in two minutes.

I know all dogs love the sun, and they have a normal body temperature of about 105 degrees but . . . wow. He fell asleep on his side, contented and comfortable.

I swear if I listened hard I would hear sizzling and smell the odor of burning fur.

"Turn over pal, that side's done. What am I going to do with you? Crazy dog."

"Huh? Oh, thanks Daddy. Yawn."

Remember the 1960s phrase 'Happiness is a warm puppy?' He was happy.

"Daddy thought it was hot out there. But it was just right. I felt the sun warming my body like the sun was giving me a belly rub."

What's in a Name?

I still thought he was a crazy dog.

This brings me to names. Musket is his true name.

"Uh, Daddy? I think there's more."

Oh for crying out loud. Okay. Lord Musket Carlson, PhDog. But past that, he had dozens of nicknames we've given him over the years. Some were descriptive, but all have been appropriate. At Guide Dogs I was calling him 'Little Buddy,' a clear term of endearment.

But after he came home he earned some new ones.

Fuzzy butt, Buzzy futt, Mopey-pants, Einstein, Lightning, Zippy, Sleepyhead, Beggar Boy, Beg-O-Matic, Begomeister, Spud Muffin, Musk, Little butt, Musket-tusket, Musketeer.

Pretty self-explanatory. Zippy and Lightning came up when he was less than quick in moving. He was also a crazy dog, screwy pooch and a nutty mutt. As in 'You're a crazy dog.'

Jane liked cute names like Bubbalicious, Bubba, Bubbabutt, Bugaboo, Bugglyboo, or something like that.

Since his name was part of a command, sometimes I often used an abbreviated 'Bug,' or 'Butt.' "C'mon bug, up."

And he responded just fine. It was the tone that did the trick. The word was not as important as the tone and action.

If I said 'Carwash' to Musket with the hand signal for 'sit' in a firm tone, he did it. I'm sure he'd give me a puzzled look.

Some commands have been shortened, partly out of laziness partly because it's cute. 'Up you go' became 'upago.' 'Go to Mommy,' was 'GoMommy.' He knew 'paws up' means to jump on the bed or stand on his hind feet.

There were times when I needed to give him a command without words, in church or during someone's speech. I've taught him to associate snapping my fingers and raising my right forefinger to mean 'sit.' A flat hand meant 'stay.' A thumb jerked up meant 'up.'

He learned just fine and it impressed people.

🐕 "Okay can I talk now? Thank you. This is my chapter, remember?

I didn't mind the weird names. I was still Musket. 'Butt?' Sheesh. I could live with it. 'Bugaboo?' Okay, Mommy loved me. But calling me a nutty mutt was going a bit too far. For one thing I don't have any nuts.

Daddy taught me the hand signals a long time ago. I learned fast and all he had to do was snap his fingers to get my attention. I knew he wanted me to do something and I did it. Because if I was a good boy he rewarded me with a treat."

Soggy Doggy

I've been an avid swimmer since I was about three, and always loved the water. In high school I made the Varsity swim team specializing in the 100-yard Freestyle.

Up the road from our house was a fenced-in pool and patio for the residents.

Hot summer days were great for a swim and I brought Musket with me one Saturday afternoon.

He caused a stir among the other residents when we entered the pool area. I planned to put him on leash tie-down but the other people, some of whom knew Musket urged me to let him run free. There was a fence, so I did. The towel was right by the pool's edge. I put my hearing aids in a shoe.

As soon as I dove into the pool Musket went nuts. He ran back and forth while I did my laps, and every time I reached the end of the lane there he was, licking my face. I'm not sure what he thought was going on.

"It was just a lot of fun and Daddy was easy to reach."

I had to keep him from trying to drink the water. But the real fun was when one of the other residents suggested Musket might like to jump in.

"I don't know if that's' a good idea," I said.

"Come on, he'll love it."

I called Musket and he lay down with his front paws in the water but no further.

Then he slid in. What a splashing episode that was. He could swim just fine, but he acted as if he was about to go down for the last time.

It wasn't safe to get near him because his front claws were going like Freddie Kreuger after ten cups of coffee.

"Swimming with Daddy was fun, but he wouldn't get near me. Finally I climbed up the steps and shook off."

He soaked up the water like a furry sponge. I swear the water level dropped three inches when he climbed out.

Shaking *it off he w*atered lawns on the other side of the road.

"He's exaggerating. But some people had to wring out their towels."

We took him to a friend's home and put him on their pool chaise lounge. He loved it! Jane said he looked like a movie star.

"I wonder what the working dogs are doing today?"

Lots of other dogs of all breeds lived in our neighborhood. It was all condos, so there wasn't much yard space. They were mostly small dogs, in the 20-40lb. range. Beagles, Welsh Corgies, Dachshunds, Scottish Terriers, Pugs and other breeds.

It was an eclectic bunch and in a short time Musket was one of the gang. He wasn't the only retriever, or even the only yellow Lab, but he was the sole Guide dog.

As you might have guessed, Musket was pretty mellow. 'Mellow Yellow,' like the 1960s song by Donovan. Yes I just aged myself.

He was never aggressive or hostile to other dogs, no matter their size. That being said, when he met other dogs, Musket assumed they were as friendly as he.

Dogs of course had a way of meeting and sizing each other up. They sniffed. I'm rather glad people didn't do that. A handshake worked fine for me.

Musket, if he was off harness, went to a strange dog and they sniffed each other's noses, which was a little pointless, if you stop to think about it. I wondered how they kept from getting stuck together like two suction cups.

"Hmm, yeah I think Daddy is right. It was pointless. I for one never smelled anything from another dog's nose. But we couldn't overcome a few million years of evolution and instinct. So we did it."

Then they worked backwards to the business end until they looked like the number 69.

"We were interfacing, if you want to use Daddy's computer lingo."

In any case he got along with most dogs. He was more than mellow to some, even submissive. Dogs instinctively protect their soft and vulnerable belly from other dogs. They must trust the other dog or be submissive to allow it.

If Musket felt safe he just lay on his back and said "Do me!"

"I'd like to make a point here. Daddy's right. I have to trust another dog to do that. We played and had fun. Sniffing was the best way to tell another dog's mood and intentions. I could tell when another dog was feeling aggressive or playful, just by scent.

But sometimes I never had the chance."

The Attack

Most of the dogs in our area were friendly, with responsible pet owners. They ranged from hyperactive yappers to jumping playful mid-sized, and big easygoing plodders.

But a few were not so friendly.

I suppose I might as well get this story out of the way. It's not easy to write about, but here goes.

"It's okay, Daddy. I'm right here. You tell it."

It was in late 2002, and we were going home after work. Being mid-winter it was long dark as we walked up Ted Williams Parkway. The sidewalks were not illuminated on the stretch which bordered a shallow gully of scrub brush.

I sensed a change in Musket's pace. I could tell he'd spotted another dog ahead. I tightened my grip on the harness handle.

Then it happened. Musket reared back. I heard a loud snarl and Musket's shriek of pain and terror. I couldn't see what was happening. I yelled, "Musket, oh my god, Musket!" I grabbed at the other dog that had Musket by the throat. Musket was desperately trying to get away. The other dog's owners, who sounded like a man and woman, were saying "Stop that! Come on!"

I yelled at them to get their dog off Musket.

"I was really scared. The other dog was mean and trying to hurt me. I didn't know why. I never wanted to hurt him. Daddy was yelling and even hitting the other dog on the head."

Then after a lot of growling and pulling it was over, and I put myself in between them. I was shaking as I got down on my knees to find out if he was hurt. His throat was wet and sticky. "He's bleeding," I said to the other people. "I have to get him to the vet!"

I asked them to help me find out where the blood was coming from.

But other than Musket's panting and the passing of cars, I heard nothing. "Help me, I think he's hurt. Where are you?"

Gone. They had run off.

"When it was over the bad people with their bad dog ran away."

Deep inside me two emotions fought for supremacy. Dreaded fear of Musket being badly hurt, and a searing rage at the craven cowardice of two irresponsible dog owners.

Angry, I screamed into the night. "Come back you bastards! Your vicious monster attacked and hurt my Guide dog! You rotten sons of bitches!"

But Musket came first. I comforted him, trying to decide what to do. Feeling around his neck I began to realize it might not be blood but saliva from the attacker. He seemed to be okay, but shaking like an aspen leaf in a high wind. I was too, and since at that time I didn't have a cell phone, knew I'd have to get him home by myself.

After about ten minutes he had calmed down under my caressing, and even gave me a kiss. "Wanna go home to Mommy?" Another kiss.

"Okay little buddy. Let's take it slow."

We got home and I called for Jane. She could tell right away something was wrong, since my face had to be as white as a sheet.

Musket of course was happy to see her. While he gave her kisses I told her about the attack.

She was cooing softly to him as she examined his neck. "I think he's okay. There's blood but it's not too bad."

She went to get a towel, and I examined his harness. There were deep teeth marks and scratches on the chest strap. I realized it had kept that monster's teeth from getting into Musket's flesh.

"Daddy took care of me. I think that was when I really bonded with him. I knew he was my good and loving Daddy and I trusted him.

Mommy checked to make sure I was okay. My throat hurt for days. Why do people want to have mean dogs? The world would be a better place if all dogs were nice."

We gave him a lot of love and attention that night. I remembered during the attack trying to pull the dog off Musket with my bare hands. He felt like some short-haired mastiff, maybe a Pit Bull Terrier or Rottweiler. I'm not making generalizations, but in my opinion people who owned Rottweilers or Pit bulls, knowing of the reputation they had, were more likely to condone that sort of vicious behavior. It's as if they were proud of having a dog breed known for being mean.

For any readers who have calm, gentle and loving examples of those breed, please don't be offended. Just keep up the good work.

To let an aggressive dog attack a friendly dog is reprehensible. But to run away like sniveling cowards is unforgivable. To run away from a blind man and his Guide dog who might be critically hurt? The newspapers would have a field day with such a story.

An attack by one dog on another is bad enough. Musket being a Guide dog made it even worse. But there are legal issues. Allowing an attack by a dog on an Assistance dog during the performance of its duty is a felony and carries a very stiff fine.

I would have voted for the guillotine.

🐕 "Too soft as far as I was concerned."

If the people who ran off ever read this, I have this to say. You are cruel, stupid and beneath contempt.

🐕 "For months afterward I was nervous on that stretch of road."

The Dog Pack

I'm glad we got that out of the way but it needed to be told. Musket was a sweet dog by any standards and like any good daddy I had nightmares of him being hurt or frightened.

The bond really started then. I think he felt it and our teamwork improved.

I was always cautious when Musket encountered another dog, but most people, with those two already noted exceptions were responsible dog handlers with friendly dogs.

Note I didn't say well-trained, but you can't have everything. As long as they weren't dangerous. Musket had a lot of canine friends.

His best buddy ever was my cousin Chick's Doberman, Cassius, a big, strong and seriously motivated dog. Chick owned a three-story condo overlooking San Pedro harbor.

The first time we brought Musket to meet Chick, who as I said, had a lot to do with my decision to get a Guide dog, she fell in love with him. But he and Cassius were instant friends. The entire time we were there the sound of two big dogs charging back and forth, up and down, and around the furniture made the building shake. They romped, cavorted and even frolicked.

Cassius liked to take Musket's whole head in his mouth. That scared us at first but Musket enjoyed it. I said he's submissive, and it's not possible to be the dominant one over Cassius in his own home. Musket never yelped or whimpered. All he had was a lot of dog spit on his head.

🐕 "That's okay. I wiped it off on Daddy's black velour jacket."

It was fun to watch but conversation was impossible.

When we left, Musket rested his head on the back of the seat, looking forlornly out the rear window.

"Aw, he misses Cassius," Jane told me.

🐕 "Cousin Cassius was cool. Like a big brother. A really big one. He outweighed me by about 25 pounds, but he never hurt me. However, I don't think I should ever eat out of his dish."

On the other side of the weight scale, no pun intended were Pippin and Katy, two more members of the Dog Pack.

Pippin was also a Dobie. Sort of. He was a Miniature Pinscher, or Min Pin. His mommy and daddy were Crystal and Jameson Reinek, both teachers who lived a few doors away. They were young, active and wonderful people. Crystal had a horse in Poway, a nearby semi-rural community. Pippin was a tiny snapshot of a Dobie. He weighed about 10 pounds. Musket was his big buddy. At least we thought so. I'm not sure what Musket thought. Let's ask him.

🐕 "I'll tell you in a minute. Finish your story."

Okay. Pippin barked when Musket and I knocked on their door. Before we went in I asked to make sure Pippin's food was off the floor.

🐕 "So that's why I never found it. I thought he was small because he didn't eat."

Pippin was thrilled to have his big buddy over and he jumped like a dropped superball. Musket didn't mind, and soon lay down to paw and play with Pippin.

Pippin was also a favorite of Jane's. "He gives me Nanas," which is what Crystal called Pippin's kisses. His tongue was about the size of a Q-Tip and could hardly be felt but his fervor never faltered.

🐕 "I liked Pippin, even if he was a bit jumpy. But he never bit or nipped me like some other dogs I could name.

When we saw Pippin's mommy or daddy I always got excited. Jameson was lots of fun to play with."

Another friend was Katy, a West Highland Terrier owned by Pat, one of Jane's crafting friends. Katy was typical for her breed. In short, she was jumpy, yappy, happy and impossible to slow down. Musket quickly learned to dread going over to Katy's house in Rancho Bernardo. When he went in the door it was open season on Musket.

🐕 "Katy was in love with me. She told me so between yaps. I liked her but not in *that* way. She was about 1/50th my size. And she bit me! I mean really. I had these big dewlaps and soft ears which she thought are perfect to nip on. I was just a big chew toy to her. I usually gave her about ten minutes then that was it. I walked away. I didn't growl, bite or scare her. But I had my limits."

Musket was patient with Katy. He never bit or even snarled at another dog, except for a coyote Jane saw when going to the mailbox one day.

Musket stood in front of his mommy and let out a huge bark. Two things happened. Jane jumped and the coyote found a quieter place to go.

Jane said Musket brought that bark up from the bottom of his feet.

That's when we learned how protective he is of his mommy.

Back to Katy. We loved buying toys for Musket. And one of them was a sheepskin gingerbread man with a squeaky thing in it. Sorry, I don't know the technical term. Musket loved squeaky toys and chewed it to shreds. Guess what we named it?

Yep, Katy.

I think it was a sort of therapy for him even though he'd never hurt another dog.

🐕 "Never. But boy, I've been tempted."

Since we're on the subject, I have a rhetorical question, which means you don't have to write in and tell me the answer. But if you want to, go to www.musketmania.com.

What is it with tiny dogs yapping and growling at big dogs? Does that make any sense at all? Never mind what the owner is doing. This is between canines.

🐕 "I agree with Daddy here. I'll continue with his question. If a dog the size of a Kaiser roll tries to antagonize something as big as a mid-sized auto but with more teeth, that would seem evolutionarily counterproductive, wouldn't it?

Would any sane human poke a full-grown Tyrannosaur with a short stick?

That little dog's owner shouldn't be surprised to find themselves holding a leash with the other end in Cujo's mouth.

I guess those small dogs must procreate very fast. Like a fifteen minutes gestation period. Even if I'm gentle that doesn't mean Cujo or Fang or Satan the Bloodfiend down the street are. But the psychotic little terrors go right on yapping away. "Let me at him! I'll nip his toes off! Let me go!"

It's a mystery isn't it? I just had to ask.

🐕 "And the other question is, why were all the TV Lassies supposed to be boys but were played by girls?"

Cisco belonged to a man who lived up the street from us. Bob was a former USAF B-52 pilot who'd served in Vietnam. He was a large guy, easygoing and liked western six-gun shootouts as a hobby. Cisco was a Vizsla, a lovely breed from eastern Europe. They're like large greyhounds but have a beautiful brownish-purple coat. Cisco was one of the most hyperactive big dogs I've ever met. He was like a runaway tornado, only louder. Remember the cartoon Tasmanian Devil? That was Cisco. He barked and jumped and went nuts when he saw Musket. They played like two ping-pong balls in a paint mixer.

Musket was a playful dog but not for long. He had short bursts of energy and then slowed down. Cisco was way too active for him. I think Bob put Jolt cola in his bowl.

Just kidding Bob. Don't shoot me.

🐕 "Oh, Cisco. Whoo, that was one fun dog, but I couldn't keep up with him. I tried to show him the tricks of sniffing and begging but he never slowed down. He sometimes went right for my daddy. He almost tore a hole in Daddy's pocket trying to get at the treats he smelled there. At least I waited."

We took Musket to the local dog park. A bunch of regulars met there on Saturday mornings. At first it was fun and Musket ran around, chasing the toys, romping with the other dogs and making new friends. The other handlers thought it was cool to have a real live Guide dog around and asked me a lot of questions. Jane and I stood there with our Starbuck's mugs and enjoyed the dog talk.

But I learned a few things. Musket does have some male dog urges. He once fell for a gorgeous white Great Pyrenees. She was definitely not interested in him.

The woman who'd brought her said to me. "Is that your Guide dog humping my dog?"

"If it's a Guide dog, it's mine," I said, embarrassed.

🐕 "Well, I admit I got carried away with that white dog. But she wasn't interested even after I told her I was safe."

Musket was neutered as a puppy. When one woman asked me if she could have a puppy if he ever sired any, I told her, "Sorry, he's got the hardware but the software was downloaded years ago."

For some reason Musket didn't seem to find this as funny as everybody else.

🐕 "Duh. I wonder why? I still jump when I hear someone using a pair of scissors."

The Toy Obstacle Course

He loves toys. In the living room we had a large wicker basket under a table. In it were dozens of doggy toys. Rubber balls, Kongs, Nyla Bones, real bones, Katy, rubber bones, cloth Frisbees, sticks, rope toys, you name it.

When the doorbell rang, he charged down the stairs and waited by the door, tail wagging furiously.

Unless I knew the visitor I held Musket back. "It's okay he's very friendly. Are you afraid of dogs?"

We haven't had a single visitor uncomfortable with Musket's attention.

As soon as they came in Musket ran to the basket to grab a toy at random. Then he brought it to them.

"Oh, you brought a toy!"

It didn't matter if it was a friend, an Avon Lady, a window washer or a plumber. Musket wanted someone new to play with him.

"When we had visitors I was really excited. I liked meeting new people. I grabbed a toy to give to them. Sometimes I forgot I had it in my mouth."

He often left his bone on the floor near the kitchen. And when I or Jane came down the stairs I heard him pick it up. But I really don't think he remembered it was in his mouth. Jane laughed. "Would you like me to light that for you, sir?"

He did have one other trait associated with his toys. He pulled one out and played with it. Later he got another one and chewed it. Soon there were several of them scattered through the house. I've even found them out on the ground where he pees at night. He picked one up and totally forgot it was in his mouth.

He Never Put Them Away!

"I'm a DOG, Daddy. I wasn't trained to put my toys away. That's your job."

Life as a guy with legal blindness was tricky, but Musket set up an obstacle course of dozens of toys all over the house. A minefield had to be safer.

I played with him every weekend. I'll say this right now. He's not a retriever no matter what his breed.

If I had to survive by hunting ducks I'd spend an awful lot of time in the water feeling around for my ducks. That would be a funny sight, come to think of it.

"The only way Daddy could hit a duck with a shotgun is if the duck sat on the muzzle."

It was a hypothetical situation. Frisbees and the Kong were the best, because I could get some real distance with them. Musket watched it in my hand and I let fly. He ran off and I could hear him skidding on the pavement as he snatched it up.

He brought it to me, where I grabbed at it and we started pulling.

The reader may recall our first day at Guide Dogs when he pulled me over the bed. He is one strong puppy. What I got playing with him was a serious upper-body workout.

Then I threw it again and he retrieved it. But that was about it. He got bored quickly. And if I was stupid enough to throw it again, I had to go and find it myself, which was always lots of fun.

"Fool me once shame on you fool me twice shame on me. That's why I didn't run after it any more than that. It dawned on me I was doing all the work. Daddy just stood there."

I spent a lot of time muttering 'crazy dog' to myself until I found a neighbor to help me.

Nancy Martin, a wonderful lady helped me get the Frisbee out of a tree. She became one of Musket's sweethearts. She barbecued meat on her balcony overlooking the parking lot and tossed bits to him. Ever since then he associated Nancy with food from heaven.

He loved Tug-of-War. And I think I know why. Jane was reading to me from a book about Labrador retrievers. Apparently they weren't really hunting dogs but worked with fishermen on the island of Labrador.

The dogs were bred and trained to help pull in the nets. They developed the strong neck muscles and jaws. In a way it explained a lot about Musket's behavior and strength.

In any case it wasn't a game for wimps.

"You got that right. I could drag an RV if a rope toy was tied to the bumper. But when I played with small kids I didn't use all my strength. I didn't want to hurt them."

He played with a little neighbor girl once and he was gentle, as if he could tell what her limits were.

I often wondered if he might have a couple of other breeds in him. Of course I knew he was purebred. That's what the school told me. Purebred Labrador retriever. He had the thick dewlaps of a real Lab, and the heavy otter tail of a real Lab.

But his face had so much extra flesh I wondered if one of his antecedents slept with a Shar Pei. I'm not kidding. One of Jane's favorite things with Musket is to show someone 'Squishy-face.'

This is for real dog lovers.

"Okay let's get it over with. Sigh."

She gently put her hands on either side of his head, and then slid them forward towards his muzzle.

"Squishy-face!" she said.

Musket's face was buried in furry folds. It was really cute.

"Mommy made me do Squishy-face for people. When a child was crying she did it. Got them laughing every time. Okay I admit it, I liked the attention. But it was a little embarrassing."

When Musket was sleeping flat, his forehead drooped, making him look as if he was frowning.

"He doesn't look happy," people told me.

I already knew why. Sometimes I slid his flesh back and showed how he really looked.

"See what I have to put up with?

The extra flesh made some people think he was overweight. Musket was about 70 pounds when we brought him home. At that time he was 20 months old. Over the years and the changes in his diet he hovered between 75 and 80 pounds. I've met Labs in the 100-pound range. But he looked fat.

🐕 "I wasn't fat. Daddy didn't feed me enough to make me fat. I'm big-boned."

Dinosaurs are big-boned. What is you, Musketsaurus Rex?

The Sound of Musket

The other challenge to his purebred status was his bark. Want to know what was interesting about it?

He doesn't have one. He almost never barked. Since 2002, he's barked half a dozen times, as when he saw the coyote or when was startled by someone knocking at the door. Then he let out a loud 'WURF!'

That's it, that's the whole show, thank you for coming. I wonder if the Shar Pei had a Basenji girlfriend.

🐕 "Daddy is casting aspersions on my parentage now. I have plenty to say and that's why we wrote this book."

He did make sounds. When he was over at Mom and Dad's and wanted to go for a walk he let Dad know. He had a deep strident moaning whine. It was pretty startling to hear.

The other sound he made was 'The Sigh.' Musket was the master of sighs. I really think he picked it up from Jane.

Being my wife, she had a lot of reasons to sigh. If I left a task I promised to do undone, I heard . . . The Sigh.

If I bumped into a wall, she sighed.

Musket knew how to use it. If he was sleeping and I wanted to play with him or pet him he let his feelings show.

He was out and didn't wish to be disturbed. He took a long deep breath. And let it go in a manner calculated to convey deep resignation. It didn't take a rocket scientist to figure out he wanted to be left alone.

🐕 "So, while we're on the subject, why didn't he ever leave me alone? He knew my bedtime was 8:00. After that I was no good to anyone. I needed my beauty sleep and he was being playful?"

He snored, too. I took my hearing aids out at night. No good. I still heard him. His snore was deep and resonant.

I'm not making this up.

The windows vibrated. We could be watching a war movie or Jane's favorite, *Independence Day* and we had to turn it up.

Because we couldn't hear it!

🐕 "Sheesh, Daddy snored louder than I did and I didn't have hearing aids to take out."

A couple of years ago Musket began to . . . oh let's say 'let one rip.'

He never farted when he was young. Jane told me of one early occasion when he was sitting by her and she heard a tiny 'pup.' Musket spun his head back at his rear end as if to say 'Did that come out of me?'

And the smell? Whoof. He could clear out a stadium during a monster truck rally on Beer and Chili night if he wanted to. A bomb scare would take more time.

🐕 "Har-dee-har har. Pull my paw, Daddy."

Putting Words in His Mouth

The other sounds were probably unique to him. The first was The Snort. This was like 'aloha' or 'dude,' and had several applications, such as irritation, resignation or impatience.

If he was in the way on the floor I told him to move. He did, accompanied by The Snort.

If he was begging at the table I told him to lie down and again came The Snort.

When he was at my heels, urging me to make his food. I heard several snorts.

Lately, he started waking us by putting his cold wet nose in our face and snorting. Sound icky? Go with that. And totally impossible to ignore.

"I only have one thing to say to that, Daddy. Snort."

If he was really excited he panted rapidly. He panted like a steam locomotive. I swear if you didn't see him doing it, you'd be looking for the 20th Century Limited pulling into Grand Central.

"I'm not sure if I should feel complimented or insulted."

The last sound was The Grumble. This sometimes accompanied The Snort. The Grumble was also an indication of displeasure at something I wanted him to do.

The Grumble was not quite a growl, but close. It was more like he was clearing his throat in an insolent manner. The Grumble and The Sigh were almost interchangeable.

"I knew exactly when to use each of them. Daddy gave me lots of reasons."

Despite not being able to talk Musket did have a voice.

Jane and I were his interpreters. Or should I say ventriloquists?

Our friends and family got used to this strange idiosyncrasy of ours. In any given situation where a comment or question from Musket was appropriate, we supplied it. In the Ed Norton voice. And we did it pretty much everywhere. Jane did the voice pretty well.

"I just wish they'd stop putting words in my mouth and put food in there instead."

Bathing Beauty

When still at Guide Dogs we were told a dog only needed a bath about once a year.

Sure. What planet are you from and is there oxygen there? They base that on one thing.

Grooming. Every single day.

Right.

Let's move on to a place where reality has more effect. Anybody who groomed a Lab or a Golden knew it was time-consuming. Throw a full-time job and commuting on the bus into the equation and priorities change a lot. We were out twelve hours a day. But I took good care of my fuzzy butt.

He shed a lot in the late summer and late winter. But no matter how often or how diligently I groomed him, he shed like an explosion in a wool mill. Friends told me they could tell where Musket had been by the trail of fur.

"Well excuse me! I couldn't help it. I suggested Daddy use hair spray but he didn't go for that."

When I could feel big tufts of fur on the floor and carpet, it was time to clean house.

And we knew whose fur it was.

"Oh sure, blame it on the dog. But before you jump to conclusions, remember this. Daddy was losing his hair too."

My hair wasn't blond. If any readers are considering getting a Lab or a Golden, or any long-haired breed I have two suggestions: The Furminator and a really good vacuum cleaner.

Jane bought the Furminator. I'm plugging it free of charge. It worked GREAT. The teeth were very short and fine and got in deep. A good grooming and that dog didn't shed for weeks.

I got so much fur I'm saving it to make another Musket.

"Uh, what was that? Another Musket?"

Labs, because of their drooping ears were susceptible to ear infections and needed frequent cleaning.

"I hated having my ears cleaned. Daddy did it because he wanted to keep me from having infections. He squirted this cold stuff into my ear. I couldn't stand the feeling and I tried to shake it out but he held me so I couldn't. Then he used a baby wipe. Talk about degrading. They're for cleaning a baby's butt."

Does anybody know a dog who likes getting baths? Please e-mail me so I can have them talk to Musket.

He got a bath about once a month. We first tried it in a large tub outside with cold water from the hose.

Bad idea. It was like trying to hold a bucking bronco. With teeth.

When Carrie was raising him she took him into the shower with her. That seemed like a good idea so I did the same thing.

No I don't mean I put him in the shower with her. I mean with me.

The trick was to keep the flying water in the shower stall, not on the bathroom walls and ceiling.

I had to do some brisk drying before I let him out to the balcony where he could lie in the sun. But doggone it, no matter how I held him he always got in a good shake right by the mirrors.

Then he did it again passing the bed and TV on the way out.

But did he do it when he was outside and it was the perfect place?

Give me a break. Not my dog.

🐕 "Payback time! Baths. I was the most miserable pooch you ever saw standing there in the shower with Daddy. And if you took four hours to dry off you'd hate it too.

Mommy and Daddy took me to the beach a few times. I loved that. I ran and played and romped and jumped in the water. It was great.

But Daddy made me stand under a shower. I guess I might have been a little sandy. And smelly. And dirty.

I had to stay in the back seat wrapped in a towel until we got home. Then I got another shower. I don't think the fun was worth it."

We found a place in the city which provided the bath, grooming materials, shampoo, conditioner and dryers at a good price. For an Assistance dog was half price. When Jane's Dad was in the early stages of Alzheimer's we took him along, knowing he'd enjoy it. Jane and I had a ball giving Musket a bath and taking pictures. Dad laughed the whole time.

🐕 "Well at least somebody enjoyed it."

Their signature was, and again I'm not making this up, Blueberry Facials.

Read it as many times as you want, it's still the same.

Blueberry Facial.

After the bath and rinse I rubbed the stuff into his facial fur. I don't have to read Musket's comments to know what he thought of that.

"You can bet your last buck on that bud."

Jane, however, loved it. She thought he smelled nice. I thought he smelled like a wet hairy blueberry muffin. It could have been worse I guess. It could have been raspberry. I hate raspberry.

"Well eating them has to be better than having them rubbed into your hair."

They had huge blow dryers, and Musket stood there while I dried him off. He didn't seem to mind, but I wondered what he was thinking.

"Down in the valley, valley so low

You missed a spot Dad-dy, hear the wind blow.

Hear the wind blow, sigh, hear the wind blow, my butt is still sog-gy, hear the wind blow.

Hear the wind blow whoo, hear the wind blow, my ears are flap-ping, hear the wind blow."

When Musket has been bathed and groomed his fur was soft and poofy. I mean like bunny-soft. I had to be careful he didn't sit in something sticky or dirty. Again the problem was he didn't know what his butt was doing.

"At least I had a butt. Daddy doesn't. I don't know how he kept his pants up."

Food Driven

We found a lot of things to laugh about with Musket. Not all of them were recurring. Sometimes it was just once. His love of food sometimes got him into a tight spot. Literally.

I once dropped a treat on the floor and it went under the bed. Didn't stop that dog. He crawled on his belly like a soldier going under the barbed wire. Then he could go no farther and he stretched. And strained.

And got stuck.

We could tell he was jammed in there. Most dogs and most people would have given up the attempt.

"Well as long as I was under there I might as well get the treat."

I lifted the bed while he snatched it up and slid out. That was one determined dog.

He might have a great memory and learned things but as far as food was concerned there was no future, only 'now.'

It was now or never.

While writing this chapter he again gave me another good example.

"Just doing my part for the cause."

Next to my computer desk was my oak TV cabinet. The bottom edge was about half an inch from the carpet. In front of it was my barbell with (weight number edited since no one would believe it anyway) pounds on it.

Yes, I sometimes actually used it. Don't let the cobwebs fool you.

I gave Musket a few kibble and dropped some. Then I resumed writing.

A few minutes later I noticed he was still right next to me, lying on the floor. I knew he was focused on the dropped kibble.

Not until I heard snuffling and bumping did I reach down to see what he was doing.

One, just one kibble the size of a Skittle had rolled under the cabinet. And that dog was lying on his side, muzzle shoved under the barbell bar, trying to get his tongue into the narrow space.

Even though it was at least two inches back, he was determined to get it.

"It might have been ages until he picked up that barbell. So I went for it. It's my instinct for survival."

He once fell asleep on the floor behind me, and I heard a weird bubbling noise. When I turned around, I found he'd fallen asleep with his head in the water bowl. I guess a formal education didn't automatically confer brains and common sense. For a smart dog he's—

"You can stop right there, pal. You don't want to dis me."

Sing-along with Musket

I've always wondered how dogs drink water. The mechanics of it baffled me.

Musket was no different from any other dog, but he could drink from a bottle. When we were out on hot days we took bottles of cold water with us. Musket could slurp under the flow while we poured it. Jane was better at this than I. Musket always gagged when I did it.

Just the other day Musket was drinking from his Longaberger bowl. He made a lot of noise and left a big puddle around him. Nothing dainty about his drinking.

But the rhythm of the drinking reminded me of a song.

Yes, again. But this is a good one. Honest. Come on, at least try it.

The tempo was exactly the same as The Tokens' 'The Lion Sleeps Tonight.'

The slurping goes like slop-a-dop, slop-a-dop . . .

'Aweemoweh, Aweemoweh, Aweemoweh, Aweemoweh, Aweemoweh, Aweemoweh . . .

Got that? Now the verse.

In the kitchen, in Mommy's kitchen

The Guide dog begs tonight
In the kitchen, his Mommy's kitchen
The Guide dog begs tonight!

Aweemoweh, Aweemoweh, Aweemoweh, Aweemoweh, Aweemoweh, Aweemoweh . . .

Near the table, the kitchen table
The Guide dog begs tonight
At the table, the kitchen table
The Guide dog begs tonight!

Aweemoweh, Aweemoweh, Aweemoweh, Aweemoweh, Aweemoweh, Aweemoweh . . .

Sit my doggy, don't beg my doggy
You have eaten once today
Down my doggy, my hungry doggy
I'll give you some any-way!

🐕 "Oh god, someone please shoot me!"

Okay, that's it. See what that crazy dog brings out in me?

🐕 "He's calling *me* crazy?"

During the writing of this book I asked friends to relate any stories they had about Musket, any anecdotes which defined his character.

And guess what I learned? Guess what a certain dog, I won't name any names, but his rhymes with 'Tusket,' has been doing for nine years?

🐕 "Oh-oh. This doesn't sound good."

I found out through a good friend, Linda Stull, what my loyal, devoted and well-trained Guide dog has been doing, literally behind my back.

"Daddy, can I have a drink of water? I'm really thirsty. You can even sing that great song while I drink."

It often happened at night when my sight was at its worst. I opened the door of Linda's car and let him out. Then I retrieved my backpack. Meanwhile, he was sniffing the grass. Then I called him to me.

"Erp. I think the jig is up."

I was bending over, reaching out and calling him, even snapping my fingers. And guess what my sweet little loving pooch was doing?

Staying behind me. Linda said that as I turned around reaching to find him, he was watching and staying in my blind spot.

"Busted! Well, Daddy did have a big blind spot. That was funny, wasn't it?"

I had to use my sharp tone of voice and say "Musket! Come!"

And he sauntered up to me as if he'd been right there all along.

This had been going on all these years and I never knew it.

"I'm shocked. How could he think such a thing?"

There'll be a few changes. I can guarantee that.

At the end of the day he was done in and asleep by 8:00. That's not to say it was the last we saw of him. As mentioned before he found some pretty inconvenient places to lie down. One of them was my side of the bed.

We had a queen-sized bed but it might as well be a baby crib for all the space it had when he was sleeping on it. He stretched out all four paws, covering as much area as possible. If I tried to lie down on an unoccupied space, he expelled The Sigh and The Grumble, then shifted to block me.

I'm not kidding. He was still sound asleep.

After I settled in, his feet were on my back.

Pushing.

"Well, ex-cuuuse me! I was asleep and not responsible for my actions. Besides I was there first. And I liked to snuggle with Mommy."

Sometimes it was the opposite. I was lying on the bed listening to a book when Musket jumped up and came over. Picture this big panting Labrador hovering there, demanding attention.

"What?" I asked.

He answered by planting his big paws on my chest, slobbering me with kisses. It was impossible to ignore.

🐕 "Hello? Anybody home? Why is it that all Lassie had to do was bark and Timmy's family instantly knew the kid had fallen down a well or was abducted by aliens, but my daddy couldn't figure out what I wanted?"

Oh, I knew what he wanted. To go out and to get a treat. But I usually played dumb because it drove him nuts. "What? What do you want?"

🐕 "You mean you did that on purpose?"

It wasn't easy to breathe with a 75-pound dog standing on me but I liked it. The only drawback was when he was climbing down and accidentally stepped on various delicate parts of my body. Oof.

🐕 "What makes you think it was accidental, Daddy?"

So far in this chapter I related nearly all of his quirks. But there was one I held off on because I can't do it justice. I've been trying to figure out how to describe it.

Here goes.

🐕 "Hmm, what is Daddy up to now?"

Imagine you're driving down a narrow alley. There is just enough room for two cars to pass one another if they each hold to their side of the alley.

With me so far? Okay, you think you're the only car in the alley and are not quite in the middle but off to one side. And suddenly another car, a sports car appeared ahead, and wanted to pass.

Did it choose the wider space?

No. It aimed for the narrowest slot and squeezed through, scraping the wall and the paint off your car.

That's what Musket does. When I walked down the hall to the TV room, I tended to hug the right wall, trailing my hand along it for a guide. He got up from the floor of the TV room and came towards me. And even if there were three wide unobstructed feet of clearance on my left, he always aimed for the six narrow inches on my right.

Only I didn't know it until I felt his furry butt jamming himself past me.

Does that make any sense at all?

🐕 "Well, you have to understand. There is a reason but it's hard to explain. Really, you're better off not knowing."

Sure. I'm convinced. Thanks for clearing it up.

Another example of his apparent feeling of entitlement happens in the car. Sometimes Jane had books or magazines, boxes or bags on her side of the back seat.

Musket didn't like anything to be on that seat and made a deliberate show of lying on top of whatever was there, no matter how uncomfortable it was. The entire rest of the seat was empty.

🐕 "I was making my point. I was going to lie there and be miserable and it was your fault."

Musket's fixation on self-gratification extended to belly rubs. He could be very persistent, rolling over and inserting himself into the personal space of others. We found out no one had any personal space around Musket. Zilch. Recall what I said about his butt? He sat on my feet.

🐕 "What's yours is mine and what's mine is mine. That goes for feet, too."

When all was quiet and we were asleep he moved from his bed to the floor next to Jane's side of the bed. I really believe he loved her more than anything in the world.

🐕 "Yep. That's my definition of Heaven. Being with my mommy."

CHAPTER NINE

FLYING THE FURRY SKIES

What do Gettysburg, Philadelphia, Washington DC, New York City, the Grand Canyon, Catalina Island, Denver, Albuquerque, Louisville, Atlanta, Chicago, San Francisco, Sacramento and Los Angeles all have in common?

"I've peed in every one of them."

That dog has gotten around.

We've traveled for work and pleasure all over the country. With Jane we've flown back east, what Californians call the far side of the world, and visited friends and famous places with Musket at our side.

On airliners Musket did not ride with the baggage. We never considered making him do that. Since Musket was a Guide dog he rode with me.

Airline travel with a Guide dog added a few new wrinkles to the equation of 'getting there is half the fun.'

In the summer of 2003, we flew to Pennsylvania to visit Jane's friends Lisa and Peter Herman, who lived with their three kids near Harrisburg.

It was our first long-distance trip with Musket, so it was also a learning experience.

Several of our friends, including Sharon from work offered to take Musket for the time we'd be gone. That was sweet of her. And come to think of it, just a bit greedy. But the whole point of having a Guide dog was to be more independent.

🐕 "Dang. It would have been a whole week of being fed and pampered."

Guide Dogs' advice was to limit Musket's food and water intake the day before and the day of the flight.

🐕 "Grumble. Snort. Sigh."

The reason was so he wouldn't have to be relieved at an inconvenient moment, like 30,000 feet over Des Moines.

🐕 "I knew something was up when Daddy stiffed me on breakfast."

I packed a few toys, treats and several days' food for him.

Arriving at the airport, I took Musket to a small grassy area to give him one last chance to go. Next stop, Chicago. I had to literally make him go.

🐕 "I didn't have to go but Daddy was so insistent, I faked it."

After checking in the luggage, the agent asked if I needed any assistance. Like a complete nincompoop I said, "No, thank you."

Then the fun began. Seasoned travelers know what I mean.

Yes, the bane of all air travel.

"I thought you had the tickets."

No, just kidding.

SECURITY.

Long lines crept through the barriers like the doomed cattle in *Hud*.

But the memory of 9/11 was still pretty fresh, so no one complained.

When we reached the front of the line we were told to remove all metal objects. Musket posed some new challenges.

The first guard began running his hands over Musket, feeling for anything odd. I wasn't sure what, but they had a job to do. He felt the small pouch on his harness. "What's in here?" He asked.

"His poop bags," Jane said.

The man's hands jerked back as if shocked with 2,000 volts.

"Don't worry, they're empty."
That was the funny part.

🐕 "I thought he wanted to pet me."

Guide Dogs told me what to do. I removed his harness and collar which had metal in them.

A man on the other side of the metal detector waited. I said, "Call him. His name's Musket."

🐕 "That was really smart of Daddy, huh?"

Yes. A Musket on an airliner. They didn't say anything but I'm sure the security people watched us carefully.

Ever since then I've said his name was Fred. It worked just as well.

The guard called and Musket, followed by his wagging tail went through. Then it was my turn. And of course I bumped the side.

(Insert a Jane sigh soundbite here). I had to do it again. Even so, they went over me with the Dustbuster.

🐕 "They made Daddy hold out his arms while they searched him. I wanted the guard to see if they could find any treats in Daddy's pockets."

Musket was waiting for me when I was guided by another guard to the bins where my things were waiting.

I harnessed Musket and after we picked up our carry-on we walked to the gate.

Jane and I didn't agree on everything but on one thing we were in perfect harmony. We were always early for a flight. We never waited until the last minute.

The gate agent checked us in and asked if I needed pre-boarding.

I really didn't need it but in the years since, I used it not only for my own convenience, but that of other passengers. With pre-boarding I was seated and Musket at my feet out of the way.

But on that first flight, Jane was smarter than me. She cut me off and said yes before I could open my big mouth.

When the flight was called we got in line and went down the jetway. Musket was very curious and excited, and when we reached the door of the plane he flight attendants saw his wagging tail. "Oh, what a lovely dog. Welcome aboard."

And it began. 3,000 miles of Musket adoration.

🐕 "The flight attendants were very good at making me comfortable."

We were in bulkhead seats in coach, where there was more floor space for Musket to lie down. He was a good traveler and went right to sleep. The flight attendants were very considerate and often asked if he or we needed anything. But Musket snored right through the takeoff. Never even flinched.

🐕 "A lot quieter than that brat 8-year old behind us."

Jane read and slept, and I had a book on tape. *The Great Bridge*, by David McCullough. The history of the Brooklyn Bridge. Terrific book.

The 5-hour flight was uneventful, with the usual salty peanuts and soft drinks. They offered Musket water, which he eagerly drank. He was thirsty from the dry cabin air.

🐕 "I was getting bored and stiff, and one of the attendants asked if I might to stretch my legs. Daddy said that would be great and the attendant let me walk down the long aisle. I made lots of new friends.

A 'Blind' Pilot?

When the attendant took Musket for a walk at 30,000 feet I heard the other passengers exclaiming about how beautiful and well-behaved he was. We just smiled.

Finally we descended into the approach for Chicago's Midway Airport.

We'd asked that someone be at the gate to escort Musket and me through security and outside so he could relieve himself. He'd been holding it for at least six hours, reduced food or not.

The flight attendants complimented us on our wonderful dog.

Then we hit the first snag.

The girl waiting for us at the gate had a wheelchair. "Mr. Carlson?"

Jane and I both sighed. "Yes," I said. "I need someone to escort me past security."

She didn't get it. "Why?"

I indicated Musket, who was crossing his legs and clenching his teeth. "Because he has to go and it will take too long for me to find the way outside. We have to catch another flight in 45 minutes."

The girl didn't know what to do.

Then a wonderful thing happened.

A United Airlines Captain came over. "Hello, I overheard what you were saying. Can I help? What's his name?"

"His name is Musket."

He was very nice. Jane explained the situation. He smiled and said he had an idea. "Do you think he'd go with me? I can take him down to the tarmac. Will he go there?"

What did we have to lose? I told the pilot Musket would follow him.

"Hey Musket," he said, a definite dog lover.

🐕 "He was really nice and said he liked Labradors. I took to him right away. His uniform was dark and clean and I was aching to shed on it.

Daddy told him what to say to me and we went off. He took me through the terminal, past crowds of people. I don't know why they were all staring at us."

Musket with his new friend in Chicago

Imagine it. An airline pilot in uniform wearing sunglasses, walking through an airport terminal with a Guide dog.

Ah, I wish I could have seen it.

And some people probably wish they hadn't.

"We went through a door and down some stairs and outside.

The concrete was hot, dry and very big. "Do your business, Musket," he told me. And boy did I! Peed so much it looked like a lake. But it felt soooooo good. I'm glad I made a new friend."

That story is one of those amazing things Musket just made happen. You can't plan or arrange them. And I sure couldn't make them up.

🐈 "I bet the number of people at the flight insurance machines tripled."

We arrived in the City of Brotherly Love on time.

Lisa and her kids were waiting for us when we came out and the usual hugs and greetings were exchanged.

Jane said, "And this is my baby, Musket."

The girls, Sonia and Madeline, took to him as expected. Brian, the only boy thought Musket was really cool.

The town the Hermans called home was semi-rural with rolling green hills and huge yards surrounding colonial-style homes.

Peter, Lisa's husband introduced himself when we exited the minivan. "Hi, I'm Peter. Want a beer?"

I liked him immediately.

🐈 "I really enjoyed their house. Lots and lots of room to run around, with big lawns and new scents. Peter even grilled some venison for Daddy who'd never had any before. I got a few bits and loved it."

Over the next week we visited, with Peter behind the wheel, Gettysburg, New York, and Philadelphia.

Jane was having a good time with Lisa, catching up on their friendship, hitting craft and quilt shops, but Gettysburg, as you might guess, was a place of pilgrimage.

Arriving at the historic town I was pretty much in awe.

Lisa, who knew I was a serious Civil War buff asked me to be the narrator and I was only too happy to oblige.

Well duh.

Jane? She slept in the van. Just another field. It was almost sacrilegious, but she never slept well on strange beds.

To Musket Gettysburg, the iconographic battlefield of the bloodiest war ever fought on American soil, was a great big sniff-fest. He smelled the grass where Pickett's men charged on July 3 1863, he sniffed the brush on Little Round Top where Joshua Chamberlain's 20th Maine fought off several determined Confederate attacks, and he tried to pee at the base of the Virginia Memorial on Seminary Ridge where Robert E. Lee made the fateful decision which doomed the south.

Sigh. Some Musket I brought to Gettysburg.

“Simmer down, Daddy. I drank a lot of water that morning.”

The Great (I think) Bridge

New York City was another odyssey for this history buff. 9/11 was almost two years in the past, but not in the memory of New Yorkers. Arriving in the city via a tunnel under the Hudson River, I recognized the tall shapes of skyscrapers reaching heights which San Diego could never dream.

We toured the huge somber pit of Ground Zero, and I tried to imagine the immense buildings which had once stood there. Even when I had good sight I’d never seen a skyscraper taller than 40 floors, mere toadstools in NYC. I craned my neck but couldn’t visualize the lost glory of the Twin Towers.

Musket seemed to understand the solemnity of the moment and was very quiet and respectful.

“Everybody was very quiet and seemed sad.”

We went to the Battery and let him play in the fountain. New York City in the summer was everything I’d heard it was. Hot and muggy and crowded and loud.

And really exciting.

Then we went to the Empire State Building. Okay, maybe it wasn’t a very imaginative destination but I was a tourist on my first visit to the Big Apple. Sue me.

And there another small Musket miracle happened.

The lines to the 86th Floor elevators were long. Jane was astonished by the $11.00 price. Not like when she was a little girl and her grandfather took her there for 90 cents. I won’t say the year but it was during the Kennedy Administration.

“I don’t think Mommy liked that.”

We stepped into line and just then an attendant came over to me. “You don’t have to wait. Please follow me.”

I didn't get it at first, and when I did, wasn't sure it was fair. Jane thought so.

She took me by the hand. "Come on, Honey."

🐕 "I followed Mommy because Daddy was in one of his 'Duh' moments."

We were taken to the head of the line and went up to the Observation Deck. And there before us was all of New York City.

Wow. That's all I can say. Wow. Sorry, I'm not Hemingway. But I was stunned. Now I'm sure the reader is asking, 'What can a blind man see from the top of the Empire State Building?'

Good question.

Answer? Not a lot. But the biggest, most enormous, vast incredible, immense and awe-inspiring not a lot I've ever not seen.

🐕 "I think Daddy was trying to be funny there."

Seriously, I could manage with Jane's help, to make out the shapes of the Chrysler Building and other landmarks. But it was just being there that mattered.

A Guide dog on the Observation Deck wasn't something people saw every day and Musket attracted a lot of attention. People wanted their pictures taken with him.

Jane took a picture of Musket on his hind legs, looking over the railing. I don't think he liked it.

🐕 "Waaaaay too high for me. And to make matters worse, I saw a hot dog cart on the sidewalk below. Whine."

Jane showed me Rockefeller Center, where her grandfather had taken her to see the Christmas tree, and she told me stories of her childhood visits to New York. I loved those stories.

We had lunch at Lombardi's in Little Italy, the oldest pizzeria in the U.S. I'd heard about it on the History Channel. They have a huge brick coal-fired oven and I could hear it blazing in the rear. We had the Lombardi's Classic. Thick slabs of hot fresh melted mozzarella and steaming tomato and meat sauce on fresh crust. Jane was always stating I'd never had a 'real New York Pizza.' Okay, now I have. Wow again.

🐕 "I like pizza crusts. I've never had the other part because Daddy wouldn't give it to me. But he didn't know a waitress gave me a big piece of mozzarella cheese. Abon-dog-za!"

After lunch we drove to . . . Brooklyn.

Yeah, Brooklyn. Yougodda problem wid dat?

I wanted to walk over the bridge.

Jane and Peter drove back to Manhattan and waited in City Hall Park for Lisa, the kids, Musket and I to walk over the East River.

That was a dream come true for me. I was having a ball on the trip but the walk over Washington Roebling's bridge was unforgettable.

Lisa asked me to tell her about the bridge. What did I do? Talked her ears off.

They're still ringing. To Musket it was just a long, long concrete sidewalk over a lot of water. He was looking forward to the grass of the park.

🐕 "All that water made me want to pee."

There is an irony in most things and my walk over the bridge had a great one. Finally I was there, actually able to touch the steel cables and granite towers. But because I was telling Lisa about it, I was over the river and in Manhattan before I realized I'd never even looked at the bridge under me.

I guess I have to go back.

🐕 "I kept trying to tell Daddy. But he was blabbing away, oblivious."

Patriotic Pup

Philly was a place both Jane and I wanted to visit. The brand-new National Constitution Center had just opened, and we enjoyed the theater-in-the-round presentation. Very much worth it and very accessible to people with disabilities.

Musket slept through the show. Patriotism isn't really high on his priorities.

In one large hall there were life-sized figures of Adams, Jefferson, Washington, and Franklin, who was holding his hand out as if making a speech. But Musket must have thought he was offering a treat. So he begged from one of our nation's founders. That's my boy.

🐕 "That's a politician for you. They hold out their hand and give you nothing."

Musket has a better grasp of politics than I thought. Across the street the Liberty Bell awaited a long line of tourists. A row of metal detectors made everybody aware of the new world we lived in.

Once again Musket was a star and we were moved up in line. All of us.

When a group of about 30 people was brought into the hall to view the famous old bell, the ranger giving the presentation took me by the arm. "You can come through the barrier," he said kindly.

And I, a blind guy from San Diego California and Musket's Daddy, got to touch the Liberty Bell.

Ain't being disabled great?

🐕 "I didn't know what all the fuss was about, but everywhere we went, someone brought Daddy and me up front. They must have thought he was a celebrity or something."

Independence Hall, the birthplace of the Declaration of Independence was a fascinating place. But as much as I enjoyed the history and the very ambience of the old building, one thing really impressed me

A wheelchair ramp outside the door. Independence indeed. God Bless America.

Lisa drove us to Washington DC with Sonia, her oldest daughter. Musket slept in the back all the way through Baltimore and into the capital.

The first stop was at the National Academies, where a colleague I'd been corresponding with was as a researcher. Joan Esnayra PhD also had an Assistance dog, a lovely Rhodesian Ridgeback named Wasabe, like the Japanese spice.

In addition to her research work she started the Psychiatric Service Dog Society (PSDS) an organization which advocates and informs people of the advantages of Assistance dogs for persons with mental illnesses.

Sonia was a future Senate intern, eager to make contacts in the capital. So I introduced her to Joan.

Musket and Wasabe met, and as well-trained Assistance dogs, behaved themselves, while the humans talked.

"Well, I could tell it was Wasabe's territory. I respected that."

Wasabe's job for Joan was to be her alert dog for her Bipolar Disorder. In order to alert her to hypo-manic episodes he would tap his nose repeatedly on Joan's elbow until she acknowledged the alert. Road rage was a periodic feature of her episodes. Wasabe gave her an alert for aggressive driving by a particular look that she learned to interpret. That look told her it was time to get off the road, NOW.

Joan Esnayra and Wasabe
Photo courtesy Dr. Joan Esnayra

🐕 "Doesn't it seem like an awful lot of people could use one of those dogs?"

Joan and I stay in touch and discuss her encounters with people who didn't understand why she, an obviously sighted person needed a dog.

She related a story too good to keep to myself.

While walking through an airport with her dog one day, a man saw her and asked "Is that one of those hearing dogs?"

But Joan was in a hurry and couldn't take the time to respond.

Then the man, assuming she hadn't heard him, cupped his hands around his mouth and yelled, "IS THAT ONE OF THOSE HEARING DOGS?"

Joan's newest and most promising project began when the PSDS received a grant from the U.S. Army to work with returning Iraq and Afghanistan veterans with Post-traumatic Stress Disorder (PTSD), or what in a more innocent age used to be called 'battle fatigue.' The veterans would train their own psychiatric Assistance dogs.

Walter Reed Army Medical Hospital was to be the host of the project and it could be a great benefit to many wounded and mentally disabled veterans.

Joan and I have managed to get together since then and I met her two new dogs, both Ridgebacks, named Kenji and Rainbow. Her work has a real chance of making a great positive difference in the lives of a lot of mentally ill people.

But to date, Joan and her organization are still struggling against bureaucratic red tape and downright hostile interference by other so-called Assistance dog groups. For more information about her wonderful work, go to: www.psychdog.org

Or the reader may wish to read an article I wrote about Joan, 'Guide Dogs for the Mind, which may be found at www.barkmagazine.com

🐕 "We've seen dogs do amazing things for veterans. Daddy and I went to the San Diego Naval Medical Center to meet some soldiers who'd been hurt fighting far away from home. They were just kids. A few other Guide dogs and I were allowed to play with them, because they sometimes respond better to animals than people.

That made sense to me. I liked making them laugh."

Back to our vacation.

Jane and I toured some of the Smithsonian while Lisa and Sonia toured the Capitol Building.

Jane wanted to see Julia Child's kitchen and I was eager to find out if I could see the Star-Spangled Banner under restoration. No, sorry to say. It was just too dark for me. But that's life.

Flying home tired and content after a wonderful trip, we were given another treat.

"Did he say treat?"

There were a few empty seats in First Class, and the flight attendant offered to bring us up so Musket would have more room. Jane didn't mind at all. And to add some frosting on the cake—

"Now he said cake. Where?"

Sheesh. The attendant said Musket could lay on one of the seats. Talk about luxury. The only thing they didn't offer him was champagne.

"Champagne tickles my nose. That was wonderful. About time someone knew how to treat a celebrity dog."

But with all windfalls there had to be one small glitch. Another attendant named Andrew was very rude and made no secret of the fact that he didn't want Musket on the seat, nor should he even be allowed in the cabin.

Not a dog lover, but even more, a serious jerk.

"I wanted to piddle on his foot."

We ignored him because the senior attendant was the one who brought us up to First Class. But its guys like that who make life harder for people.

Chicago to San Diego was much better. No First Class but we met a truly wonderful lady named Maureen who was a Senior Flight Attendant for the airline. Jane lost no time in telling her about Andrew.

As Maureen listened, she asked a lot of questions about Musket and fell in love with him. Musket has always seemed to attract blondes.

🐕 "She was so beautiful and rubbed my belly from Chicago to Denver. Ahhhhhh."

The Reality Check came when we arrived in San Diego. Recall previously I described San Diego as being a non-friendly city to Assistance dogs?

Yep. After all the wonderful and special treatment Musket had been given back east, the driver of the shuttle from the airport to home said "The dog will have to ride in the back with the baggage."

Welcome home, little buddy.

🐕 "Mommy and Daddy didn't let it happen. They and even the other riders made him back off and I rode with them."

Musket and I traveled on business trips to Atlanta, Washington DC, Louisville, Sacramento and Los Angeles. Since I was on my own it required a little more forethought, arranging transportation and knowing the itinerary. Somehow everything seemed to work out in the end.

🐕 "I really missed Mommy when I went somewhere without her. But Daddy did take good care of me."

We flew to Atlanta for a week-long conference in 2006. I always wanted to visit where Scarlett O'Hara lived. Remember I read *Gone with the Wind* when I was ten?

It was a hot sweltering week in the Georgia summer sun. We stayed at the Hyatt Regency courtesy of the agency's travel budget, and were treated royally. But first I wanted to locate a nice grassy spot outside to relieve Musket.

🐕 "Peeing was number one in my book. No pun intended."

How I found it was rather funny in retrospect. After we'd checked in I went to the concierge and said, "Hey, can you tell me where I can find some grass?"

The man behind the desk asked me if I could repeat myself, which I did. Word for word.

"Ah, um, I'm not sure I can help you, sir," he said.

"Are you sure?" I asked. "Just a small bit of grass is all I need."

"I heard every word of that and I tried to get Daddy's attention. Then he caught on."

It finally dawned on me what I had been asking. And after I stopped laughing I explained what I meant. The concierge seemed very relieved and told me about a small plot of grass near the entrance.

"Daddy never made that mistake again. I wish Mommy could have been there to see it."

Perish the thought. She'd have sighed for a week.

The room was on the 18th floor overlooking a courtyard, but I couldn't quite make out where Rhett and Scarlett rode out of the city when it was burned by Sherman in 1864. Dang.

One thing about hotels with room service, the guests left the trays on the floor outside their door.

And guess who didn't know about this?

Me.

Guess who found out before I did?

"Me! That was great. How nice of the other guests to leave their food scraps outside for me. Daddy kept pulling me away. And for some reason he kept muttering, 'Crazy dog, it's not a smorgasbord.'"

Musket handled the heat better than I did, but on our last day there I believed he was getting overheated on our walk. Passing an outdoor fountain on Peachtree Street I took him to the water's edge. He sniffed and looked at me with puzzled eyes.

"You want me to go in there?"

I used the leash to make him walk into the six inches of cool water. He resisted at first but then he didn't want to get out. He liked it.

🐈 "Can you blame me? The pavement was 160 degrees!"

Louisville was very much like Atlanta, a southern city with old-fashioned manners and gentility.

Guide dogs are very welcome in Louisville, because the town had a long association with blind persons. The Kentucky School for the Blind and the American Printing House for the Blind were in Louisville. APH was a major institution which designed assistive technology for blind and low vision users, and was also one of the studios for talking books of the National Library Service.

Musket and I visited APH and met many of the people I'd only known from phone calls and e-mails.

A man from the product design division showed us around. He even let me examine a few of the new devices APH were putting on the market in the next year.

I was fascinated by the Bill and Color Reader. The gadget was about the size of a pack of cigarettes and could read any American currency, identifying it with an electronic voice. It was a real nice thing for a blind shopper to have.

But it also read colors with amazing accuracy. I held it to my sky blue shirt and it stated 'Light Blue.'

I told the designer it should have one other teensy feature. Since it would be used to identify the color of clothes, it should also have a 'Wife Opinion' setting. If I put on a green shirt and blue trousers and then checked the colors, a voice should say 'You're not leaving the house dressed like that!' And then it should suggest a pair of Khaki slacks.

Just a suggestion. Even if I could see, I would still dress like a dork. After all, I'm still a guy.

🐈 "Mommy sighed every time Daddy picked out his own clothes. They were nice in Louisville."

We traveled to Yale University a few years ago with a friend, professor in Public Health named Emily Moore. We were there to speak at an international conference of health professionals concerned with blindness in developing countries.

Yale was an amazing place and Emily, who had done some post-graduate work there showed me around campus. I'm glad we went. Musket met dozens of students and doctors from all over the world. I think he had a thing for a very sweet girl from Bombay.

"Now that you mention it, I did. She said I had the most beautiful eyes. She revered me but I don't think it had anything to do with her religion."

We took several photos of Musket and I on the campus, which Jane used in a scrapbook entitled Yale-Oh Lab. It's one of her best creative efforts and I think it's great.

"Mommy has me in every one of her scrapbooks. Daddy might be in there too. I think."

The Scent of Strange Dogs

Jane and I have traveled by car as well, but the freedom of our own timetable and ability to go where we please had its own drawbacks when one of the persons in the car was blind.

I don't mean I drove.

I mean I don't drive.

Jane did it all. The trips related here were with her behind the wheel the entire time.

If I had to guess what would be the hardest thing about being married to a blind guy, it would be that I couldn't share the driving.

"Daddy's forgetting his bad jokes. That was the second hardest thing."

But it's not like I haven't offered to drive.

"Oh, sure. I can't wait to try that sometime. I'll run alongside the car, and tell Daddy where to go."

No. Musket would not be trotting alongside the car, guiding me.

I'd drive using the Braille method, using the row of bumps on the lane and keeping the left wheels on them.

Bubabubabubabubabubabub . . .

🐕 "I'm sure they got it Daddy. Snort."

Actually I did drive once, sort of. Roberto Frias and I did an outreach together. Roberto, a wheelchair user was really amazing. He rolled up to the van, opened the sliding door and his driver's door, then hoisted himself up to the seat and reached back to put the chair in behind him. He didn't really need a Disabled parking space.

But he did need to be able to open the friggin' van door.

When we were leaving he discovered his van door was blocked by some bozo's car. I mean really close.

He couldn't get in. So I suggested I drive the van out for him.

Bless his heart, which must have skipped a beat or two he agreed. I climbed in and ever so carefully drove out far enough for Roberto to get at the door.

🐕 "That scared me. Roberto, who was really nice, held my leash while Daddy drove. And he never flinched. I nearly fainted."

When Jane and I took a trip of several hundred miles, it wore on her. I sat next to her, making sure she had what she needed, like water, cough drops, or the MapQuest directions.

We both listen to books on CD, and they helped a lot. But all I could really do was keep her company.

Musket needed to stretch every couple of hours and sometimes Jane wanted to take a nap so I took him out at rest areas for a little while.

Then he was off, sniffing and surveying the recent users of the grass.

🐕 "I wanted to meet some of those other dogs. One smelled very interesting. I think it was a Border Collie from Arizona. And over there . . ."

By the time we were home Jane might have driven a thousand miles. That was a lot and she was worn out. I usually told her to take a shower and go to bed.

What drove her nuts, no pun intended, was that I was tired too. It wasn't easy sitting there and doing nothing. I wish I could help but it was my job to unload, pump the gas and change the CDs or whatever. If we had a flat or some problem, I was Mr. Fix-it. And in emergencies I was usually the one who kept his head.

Musket was supposed to give her kisses every fifty miles or so.

"Just doing my bit for the cause."

Cambria is a small seaside town in central California near Hearst Castle.

We loved it there. The shops, excellent restaurants, quiet streets and friendly people have managed to avoid being taken over by chain stores and fast-food joints.

There's not even a Starbucks.

Last time we stayed a the Cambria Shores Inn, a beachfront motel with tasteful, comfortable rooms. They were also pet-friendly. A statue of St. Francis of Assisi stood outside the registration office, holding a tray with doggy treats.

Fortunately it was out of Musket's reach.

That would be a fallen saint indeed.

"I would have been careful, but Daddy never let me near him."

They couldn't have been more friendly, and welcomed a real Guide dog. All the restaurants and shops were equally accommodating.

Everywhere we went we found smiles and open arms.

We took a walk along the beach. It was the time of year when the Elephant Seals were giving birth and the beach was covered with the immense brown beasts, some weighing as much as 3 tons.

Musket wasn't sure what to make of them.

"Yeah. I heard barking and thought there were dogs nearby. But all I saw were these huge monsters that looked like potatoes."

We found one large male by himself and Jane took some pictures of him. We named him Edgar.

🐕 "I didn't want to get too close to him. He was as big as our car. He might have been trying to find a quiet place away from all the barking."

Jane and I drove to Sacramento to see Carrie, his puppy raiser. She was a licensed vet, and showed us around her clinic.

There was a tiny cat that had been hit by car crushing its hind legs. The cat, named 'Squishy,' had been adopted by the clinic staff and moved around on its front legs. Her back end was supported by a small wheeled frame.

Musket went right up to the little kitty and gave her a kiss. Only the most hard-hearted person wouldn't cry at the sight.

🐕 "I felt so sorry for her, even if she was a cat."

Carrie took us and her dog Shana to Lake Folsom. Shana was Musket's older 'sister' while he was with Carrie.

Carrie picked up a long stick and threw it into the water. Shana went right in after it.

Musket did too, but not *quite* as far. He waited in the surf until Shana had brought the stick almost all the way.

Then he took it from her.

🐕 "Look what I did, Mommy!"

A few times he 'helped' her bring it to shore, with the stick in both of their mouths. Finally Shana caught on to his tricks.

🐕 "I thought she was tired and I only wanted to help."

I held on to Shana and told Musket to get the stick himself. The look he gave me had to be one of incredulity.

🐕 "You're kidding, right Daddy? She likes to get the stick. Why should I take that joy away from her?"

Sleeping Through a Robbery

Musket has been to Disneyland, courtesy of our friend, Linda. She was retiring from AT&T after thirty years. The company had a deal with Disneyland. She could have guests and lunch at Club 33, an exclusive, and I do mean exclusive restaurant in New Orleans Square. Since Linda is crazy about Musket she asked if we'd like to go. Of course, being a Disneyphile, I said yes.

🐕 "He had to struggle almost three seconds with that one."

It was just before Halloween and about ten of Linda's friends arrived in the park for a day of fun and food. I had known about Club 33 for years but never knew anyone who'd been there. The membership is way up there with Fortune 500 types. But in we went, to a lovely *fin de siècle* New Orleans restaurant. Linda described it as all dark carved wood, real crystal chandeliers and elegant furnishings. It was so quiet you'd never know that just outside the windows was Disneyland full of guests. It was like being in another world.

Musket was welcome and given a crystal bowl of chilled water.

🐕 "Ah, this is the way it should be."

As far as I was able to determine, he was the first Guide dog to enter the club's hallowed halls.

🐕 "It's about time, don't you think? I could only add some class to the joint."

After a fantastic lunch we toured the park. The first thing I did was to buy Musket a set of Mickey Mouse ears. Well, I had to.

🐕 "No, he didn't have to. But he did. In case you didn't guess, Daddy's like a big kid."

You'd have thought Mickey, Goofy, Chip 'n' Dale and the other characters weren't even there. Musket stole the hearts of every person we passed. Progress was slow because they all wanted to take his picture!

🐕 "All I heard all day long was 'Oh, look at the dog, he's so cute!' and 'Can I get a picture of him?' You'd think no one ever put ears on a dog before. Donald Duck had his picture taken with me, which had so many people snapping away it sounded like a swarm of crickets. I never met Pluto. I wanted his autograph. Goofy said hi, though. I was puzzled. He sure didn't smell like a dog. What's up with that?"

When the cameras really started clicking
Photo courtesy Linda Stull

We went on several rides. One of our party stayed with Musket since he wouldn't have liked the Haunted Mansion or Big Thunder Mountain Railroad. But I did take him on the Pirates of the Caribbean, my all-time favorite. I could remember it pretty well, even though it was all dark to me. The only glitch was I'd forgotten about the splash after the drop into the caverns. Musket was at my feet and was drenched. Oops.

"Oops, he says. That water was cold! All around us were these deranged people singing and dancing while I was shivering. The nice attendants got some towels for me and Daddy dried me off in the sun. It took me a long time to forgive him."

After a long day at the Happiest Place on Earth
Photo courtesy Linda Stull

In April 2011 Jane and I went to the Grand Canyon for our anniversary, which was on our Bucket List.

We drove to Williams, Arizona where the Grand Canyon Railway began. A hotel stay and breakfast had us at the depot where a 1950s-era passenger train awaited us. The attendant for our car was a lovely lady named Sherry, who, of course fawned over Musket.

"Here we go again. Adoration. It's such a burden to bear. I don't know how Leonardo DiCaprio endures it."

The train ride was fun and Sherry was a great tour guide, describing all the local scenery and attractions as we neared the canyon.

When we stepped off the train we took a tour bus for a drive along the canyon's rim. The driver, a fun and ebullient lady, helped me down and made sure Musket was okay each time we stopped.

🐈 "Daddy and I posed for Mommy next to this great big ditch. It was huge, I mean really big. I could smell a lot of strange scents, but the people we met were even stranger. I met folks from France and Italy and even farther off places. Like California. One little French boy learned my name and said it every time he saw me. 'Mus-kat! Mus-kat!' He almost got it right."

We enjoyed our stay at the canyon. I had a minor 'guy' moment when we were in the Hopi House, a shop with Hopi Indian crafts. Jane was shopping, and my mind began working on an idea.

🐈 "Oh, no. Here we go again. Hang on, it's pretty bad."

Jane came back and I said, "Honey, you know what they should do here?"

Jane said, "What?"

"They should open an International House of Pancakes next door."

"Why?" she said, not seeing the trap.

I hit her with the zinger. "They can call it the HOPI IHOP!"

🐈 "I warned you, didn't I?"

Spectacular scenery, wonderful people, great restaurants and great service were hallmarks of our trip, but what I remember most was the train ride back.

We were boarded by train robbers.

Jane told me "Honey, there are some masked men on horseback out there."

"Great," I said as the train came to a stop. "Maybe they'll rob us."

They came on board and started 'taking' valuables from the excited and laughing passengers. Only in America will people pay good money to be robbed.

Then the desperado who asked me for my money saw Musket. My dog was growling, snarling and lunging at the man who threatened his mommy and daddy.

Just kidding. You readers should know him by now.

🐕 "What robbery? I slept through it."

Musket sleeping on a glass bottom boat at Catalina Island, 2011

Cannon, Porpoises, Warbirds and Bonnie Hunt

Planes are one thing, and Musket did fine on trains too. But boats? Well that was another matter and one I'm not too proud of.

I'm only going to relate it because I promised I'd be honest in this book. I could be guilty of errors in judgment, even where Musket was concerned.

"Oh, yeah I'll go along with that."

Jane learned there would be a pair of 19th-century revenue cutters sailing on San Diego Bay, having a naval gun battle.

"Do you want to go?"

Duh. Of course I wanted to go.

"What about Musket?" She asked.

I thought about it. I had to bring him along. Not that I HAD to, but I just HAD to. Get it?

A couple of years before we had gone to the Holiday Bowl in Qualcomm Stadium. I don't recall the teams, but we'd gotten the tickets free. Musket slept through the game. Then the fireworks began. We were right under them.

I'm not making this up. He slept through the fireworks booming right over our heads. Even I was stunned by them.

That was on my mind when Jane asked me about bringing Musket along on the bay cruise.

"I think he'll be okay," I said. "He never minded loud booms before."

"Well I'll have to admit up to that point I never minded them."

On a perfect sunny Saturday morning on the San Diego waterfront, the *Californian*, a topsail schooner awaited us. 145 feet long, she and her sister the *Lynx* were sleek and beautiful. When we brought Musket on board, the mate at the gangplank cautioned us about the cannon fire. I told them Musket doesn't mind loud noises and as a former re-enactor I knew how loud cannon could be.

The sail out to the center of the bay was glorious. I even helped to haul lines to raise the main boom.

Then the *Lynx* came into view. The cannon, small 2-pounder bronze smoothbores were run out. Then they opened fire.

Musket took it well at first. I'd even gotten some earplugs for him but as the firing went on and the two ships circled each other like boxers in the ring, he began to get uneasy. I took him belowdecks and gave him treats. He remained calm enough but I knew bringing him was a mistake. I regret it to this day.

"Shiver me timbers! That was a loud day for me. I didn't like the booms. Daddy took care of me and covered my ears so it wasn't too bad. But I was glad to get my paws back on solid ground. The first place he took me was a big lawn. Oooohhhh, it felt good to drain my bilges."

He's been on other boats since, but as long as there were no cannon he didn't mind it at all.

Another 'boat' we visited was the *RMS Titanic*.

There was an exhibit in Los Angeles of *Titanic* artifacts and displays of the ship's interior.

I'm also a major *Titanic* buff. Jane led, explaining the artifacts and displays to me. I have to say Jane indulges my sometimes childish whims and love of history. And I really appreciated her for it.

"But to be fair, Daddy indulged her hobbies. Mommy couldn't visit any town without going to the local craft stores. And next to her was Daddy, me at his side."

Even though she wasn't as deranged as me about such things she was fascinated by some of the objects recovered from the bottom of the Atlantic.

The centerpiece of the exhibit were full-sized re-creations of the ship's famous rooms. First Class staterooms, Steerage berths, the Café Parisien, and even the Grand Staircase were indistinguishable from the real thing. When we walked out of a First Class corridor and entered the A Deck Grand Staircase Landing, I stopped in total awe.

It was beautiful. The sweeping wrought-iron and bronze balustrades, the elegant clock of Honor and Glory crowning Time, and even the floor tile were perfect to the last detail.

Then Captain Edward J. Smith came over and held out his hand. "Hello," he said in an elegant accent. "Welcome aboard."

I almost felt as if I was on board the real *Titanic*. All that was missing was the vibration of the engines under my feet.

'Captain Smith' asked about Musket. Probably the first Guide dog ever to set foot on the great liner.

Okay I'm acting weird but that's what it felt like.

"That Captain man was very kind to me. Daddy gave him a treat to give to me. I'm really sorry he drowned."

King Tut also came to Los Angeles and made Musket's acquaintance. Sharon McCabe from work went with Jane and me. But the only subject Tut and Musket could discuss was their Mummys.

"Groan. I heard that coming but I couldn't stop him. Sorry.

By the way I just thought of something. This book is titled 'Confessions of a Guide Dog' but Daddy's done most of the talking. I have an idea for a book and this is the place to mention it. It will be entitled 'Pee-Mail: A Dog's Travel Guide to Great Places to Pee from San Francisco to Washington DC.' Look for it in your local bookstore or order it online. Thank you. Back to you, Daddy."

Oh, God. What next? Where was I? For my birthday two years ago Jane bought me a very unusual present.

She kept it a secret from me and even on the morning of, all she told me was to bring a swimsuit.

We drove down to Mission Bay and pulled into the Sea World parking lot.

I hadn't figured it out yet, but I was getting ideas. It might have been to swim in the shark tank. I don't know if my life insurance would have considered that accidental death or suicide.

"I'd go with sudden insanity."

Jane led me to the DIP tank. "DIP?" I asked, not sure who it meant.

"If it had said 'DRIP' then Daddy would be sure."

The Dolphin Interactive Program was a great opportunity for ordinary folks to swim with dolphins. To say I was pleased is an understatement.

I was thrilled and excited beyond measure.

The trainers, wearing tight wetsuits, gave the 11 people with me that morning instructions on what we were going to do. They were very helpful and I never felt uncomfortable or concerned about my vision.

My hearing was another matter.

I was shown the mens' locker room where I stuffed my butt into a wetsuit. I think that was the day I decided to start a diet and weightlifting program.

Believe me, it wasn't pretty. I'm lucky no one tried to harpoon me.

"Daddy wouldn't let Mommy take any pictures of him out of the water. He looked like a black and red sausage."

Musket of course could not go in with me. I don't think they had doggy wetsuits.

"I saw these really big fish all swimming in a huge pool."

My trainer, who didn't look like a sausage was a cute redhead named Lindsey. I left one of my hearing aids on but quickly realized I wouldn't need it. Lindsey spoke directly into my ear.

"Mark, take my arm and we'll step onto the pool ledge."

The ledge was in about a foot of water at the edge of the pool. Lindsey told me what to do. And with her first signal to a large female in front of me, I knew wearing a hearing aid was a mistake.

I was suddenly under a wave of green water, kicked up by the huge mammal.

You know what seawater tastes like?

Yuck. And it was cold!

"How cold was it, Daddy?"

I'm not Johnny Carson. The wetsuit protected me from the worst of it. But I took the now-sodden hearing aid out and placed it on a shelf.

Lindsey showed me how to signal the big female, who was named Toby, how to jump, turn over, stand on her tail and spin, slap the water with her flukes and other behaviors. They're not called 'tricks.'

The best part was being able to hug her and rub her belly.

🐈 "I saw that! Daddy was rubbing that big fish's belly instead of mine!"

They took pictures of Toby and me. I carried one in my wallet for nonbelievers.

The entire experience was one I'll never forget. Jane really outdid herself for a birthday present.

I was just expecting some DVDs.

🐈 "Daddy was smiling when he came back to us. But he also smelled like seaweed."

The rest of the day we toured Sea World. I worked there in 1985 and was amazed at how much had changed. The Shamu Stadium I remembered was long gone, a mere puddle compared to the immense lake they have now.

We took our seats within 10 rows of the clear Plexiglas tank wall. I was having a pretty good eye day and was able to see some of the show.

I wasn't having a good ear day, though. My left hearing aid needed some serious blow-drying.

Musket was under our seat, probably dreaming of tuna fish sandwiches.

We knew we might get splashed. What the hell, I was still wet anyway.

🐈 "But I WASN'T!"

And then it happened. Shamu leapt from the water right in front of us and came down like a black and white mountain falling over. Green seawater rushed over us like a tidal wave. And poor Musket never saw it coming.

🐈 "Yeah, you could say that. I was sound asleep when that oversized sardine tried to drown me. I came up from under the bench, shaking and completely soaked. Happy birthday Daddy."

For Jane's birthday, I got tickets to the Bonnie Hunt Show.

She didn't know what I had planned, but since she was driving she might have guessed when I told her to drive to Culver City. Next time I'm getting a limo. Live and learn.

The show's Public Relations people had called me the night before the taping to tell me we couldn't be at the 2:00 show because Bonnie, ever the dog lover, would be doing a dog adoption segment. They offered to have us at the 6:00 taping instead. I wasn't happy because it would be we'd be getting home pretty late, but since Kyra Sedgewick, one of Jane's favorite actresses would be on that show, I knew it was worth it.

When we arrived at the studio, a nice lady came to us and said, "You must be Mark, Jane and Musket."

🐕 "I guess she knew how to treat celebrities."

We were given great seats in the third row of the Dean Martin Theatre and Jane was getting very excited. Then Bonnie came out.

🐕 "I, on the other hand was on the floor by Daddy's feet. Couldn't see a thing."

It was a surprise when Bonnie herself came into the audience and was standing only a few feet from us. I got Musket to put his paws on my lap and Bonnie saw him. She came close and petted him, asking his name. I explained we were there for Jane's birthday. Jane got a handshake from Bonnie Hunt and Musket made a new friend.

🐕 "Yeah, she was really pretty and I could tell Mommy was excited."

Bonnie came back at the end of the show and again saw Musket. She even had the cameras zoom in on his sleepy face. And the audience, seeing my now-groggy doggy on the overhead screens, all said 'Awwww.'

🐕 "Okay I was half asleep. It was way past my bedtime."

We were sure it would get on the show but it only made the previews. Yet it was fun and Jane got to meet her favorite TV star.

"Any idea what you're going to do next year, Daddy?"

I'm working on it.

Jane managed to top herself when for Christmas she bought me a ride in a World War Two trainer plane.

And on a wonderful Saturday, we drove out to Gillespie Field in El Cajon.

I was wearing my A-2 leather bomber jacket. Had to look the part.

When it was my turn, I was led out to the plane, whose engine was running in idle.

A North American AT-6 Texan, it was a twin-seat trainer was built in 1943 as a primary flight trainer for the Air Corps. It was powered by a Pratt & Whitney 1,300 hp Wasp radial engine. The plane was in natural aluminum finish with Air Corps insignia. She was beautiful.

Yes, I'm a warbird buff too. I hope you're keeping track of my hobbies. There will be a test at the end of the book.

A ground crewman led me up the port wing into the front cockpit where I was strapped in. The instructions they gave me were detailed but due to my sight some things weren't going to be possible.

"Daddy went out to the airplane without me. I always went on a plane with him but Mommy said I had to stay with her. I looked at Mommy and wanted to know if Daddy didn't need me anymore."

I wore a headset so I could hear the pilot, whose name was Kevin.

My hearing aid had dried off by then.

Then we taxied onto the runway, my heart beating like a machine gun.

By the way, I did have a parachute. These were the instructions I received on the use of a parachute: "In case of an emergency you will slide the canopy all the way back. Then you will use your left hand to remove the headset. Release your safety belt and stand up in the seat, facing the starboard wing. Grab the 'D' ring of the chute, step out onto the wing, and let yourself fall off the back edge, while pulling the 'D' ring. Got it?"

Yeah, I had it but there was one tiny question.

"Um, what happens to me after I leave the plane? Don't I get any instructions on how not to fall into Lakeside Reservoir? Or how not to break the same neck I was silly enough to place in your care?"

Don't you just love it when someone laughs at an important question but never really answers it?

The flight was only 15 minutes but I loved every single second of it, from the roaring takeoff to climbing high over Lakeside Reservoir, and soaring in the iridescent blue sky.

What could I see? About the same as I saw from the Empire State Building but it was the thrill of being in a real WWII aircraft, the power of that mighty Wasp engine thrumming into my bones.

The pilot and I talked about the plane, flying and history. Jane hadn't paid for the extended aerobatic flight but Kevin seemed to like me.

"Are you an adventurous kind of guy?" I heard in my headset.

"I'm not sure I should answer that," I replied. Still grinning like an idiot.

He told me to close the canopy and hang on. "I'll throw in a roll."

On most occasions that phrase means getting bread with your meal.

What an incredible feeling, the entire world spun around my head. The flight is on video, from outside and in the front cockpit.

The microphone even caught my scream.

I'm rather glad it wouldn't show me puking.

"Daddy came back okay. I wished I could have gone with him, because he was smiling and must have had a good time."

Chapter Ten

MY FURRY CO-PILOT

While I was in the air with Kevin I told him about my weekend pastime.

In the winter of 2006 Jane suggested I consider volunteering as a docent at a museum.

That sounded like a good idea, but I suspected it might have been motivate by her need for a day alone once in a while.

🐈 "I wonder why she'd want that?"

I first took a tour of the *USS Midway* a late-WWII aircraft carrier, which had been turned into a San Diego museum. But it didn't take long to realize the steep ladders, low headroom and high door sills would lead to a painful experience for this blind guy. And Musket could never have negotiated some of the tight spaces.

I guess WWII carriers weren't meant to be ADA-compliant. How in the world did the pilots in wheelchairs ever get into the planes?

Then I thought of the San Diego Air and Space Museum in Balboa Park.

After calling and arranging to meet the volunteer coordinators, I took Musket to the museum.

The new SDASM Docent and Dogcent

SDASM was a 275-foot round Art-deco structure built as the Ford exhibit for the 1935 Pan Pacific Exposition.

Ross Davis and Tom Cooke showed us into the docent lounge. I was a bit nervous.

🐕 "Daddy seemed excited when we entered the museum. I had no idea how much time we'd eventually be spending there."

Tom and Ross, really nice guys, asked me a lot of questions about my interest in aviation and if I could handle the volunteer work. It went well but Musket had a little accident.

🐈 "No, not that kind of 'accident.' I was bored with all the airplane talk and moved to find a place to sleep. My harness handle caught on the spigot of the water cooler and I couldn't move. I got scared and tried to get away. Then the whole thing came crashing down. It was a mess."

I was sure the water cooler crash would put a quick end to my hopes of becoming a docent. The idea of a blind docent tour guide in a museum filled with irreplaceable airplanes and valuable aviation memorabilia was just a little farfetched. But Ross and Tom were great and said it was okay.

They must have terrific insurance.

🐈 "I was glad they weren't mad at Daddy for what I did. Ross was really nice and rubbed my belly."

The training required book study, 100 hours of time at the museum and taking 20 tours with different docents.

I explained I would have to study on the computer or on tape. As for the hours and tours, I could be there every Sunday.

It usually took a new trainee about a year or so to complete the training. But like my days at the Davidson Program in 2001 I was in a hurry.

I ordered every single audio book I could find on aircraft, aviation technology, the space program, early flight, and military aviation from the Braille Library.

I generally read about 100+ books a year. Since I could read on the bus, in bed, around the house or wherever, I could do a lot of reading.

🐈 "I almost never saw Daddy without his headset."

I dove into the project, taking tours and meeting lots of nice people with an interest in aviation.

Musket was a novelty but quickly became well-known. Total strangers started coming up to us. "You must be Musket."

"Yes, he is," I replied.

"And you are . . . ?"

Sigh. Well, that's the way it goes.

🐕 "Beauty before brains, Daddy."

Are you sure that's what you meant, Musket?

David Hardy, despite his having been in the U.S. for more than thirty years, is my perfect image of an educated, mannerly and cultured Englishman.

He even taught me how Cricket was played.

Yes it actually has rules and does make sense.

David took care of the Supermarine Mk XVI Spitfire, a sleek shark of a fighter, the terror of the Luftwaffe during the Battle of Britain.

David was a good friend, even if he liked his beer warm.

🐕 "Daddy had fun at the museum and we made a lot of friends. Grace was my sweetheart, a really nice little old lady. She told Daddy she was afraid of dogs but I got her over that really quick.

David soon became a good friend of Daddy's. Bob, Don and Jerry also took us on tours, teaching Daddy about the planes and things."

Since the museum was very dark, I couldn't see anything. I may not have been able to see the aircraft but I could feel them. As a seasoned aviation buff I could tell the difference between the smooth aerodynamic nose of a P-51 Mustang and the blunt air-cooled cowling of the Gee Bee racer.

"Gee they're just my size!"
Photo courtesy Linda Stull

"We got to know our way around the museum. I learned when and where to stop for each airplane. Daddy felt around until he recognized what plane it was and told me, "Here, Musket. Stay." Then he patted my head so I'd associate that plane with praise. I got to like going there, even if the only scents were metal, fabric, dust and oil."

Most of the volunteers were over 70 years old. Several were World War II Navy and Air Force veterans. A 'target-rich environment' for a military history buff like me.

Don was a pilot for United Airlines far back enough to have piloted propeller-driven DC-3s.

Ross flew helicopters for the Navy in Vietnam. Jerry worked on the original Pan American Boeing 314 Clippers in the 1930s.

Bob Klees was another longtime docent and a great guy. He took me on several tours and was good at assisting me in learning my way around the museum.

Bob let me sit in the *Spirit of St. Louis*.

The plane we had in the Rotunda is not the original, which is at the Smithsonian, but it was built by Ryan Aeronautical in San Diego where the real plane was constructed in 1927.

While talking about Lindbergh and the New York to Paris flight, Bob asked me if I'd like to sit in the pilot's seat.

'No, thanks' was NOT my reply. He got a ladder and assisted me into the cabin. It was one mighty tight fit, the seat so low my knees were almost up to my shoulders, the instrument panel only a foot from my face. Yet tight as it was, I knew Charles Lindbergh was four inches taller than I, and sat in that cabin for 33 hours.

"I watched Daddy get into that silver plane while Bob held my leash. And I wondered again why Daddy didn't take me along. Was it my breath?"

The final exam consisted of conducting a tour with Ross and Tom, and a few warm bodies pulled at random.

"It was our first tour with me guiding the guide, who was guiding the other head guides. It was like being a locomotive at the head of a train."

So Musket and I did our first tour, starting outside at the Convair Sea Dart jet seaplane and the sleek Lockheed A-12 Blackbird, precursor to the famed SR-71.

We proceeded through the exhibits as I, with Musket's uncanny skill of stopping in the right places, related the history of aviation.

The only glitch was I hadn't heard when Tom told me I would only have an hour.

A good tour lasts about an hour and a half, covering the 70-odd planes in the collection. And by the 45-minute mark we were only up to the mid-1930s. I began to speed up, shortening my talks and eliminating some of the planes whose history I'd labored so hard to memorize.

But we finally emerged from the Space Gallery into the main Rotunda at a few minutes past the hour mark.

🐕 "Daddy kept making me move faster and I got confused."

"Whew," I said, not exaggerating. "That was a whirlwind."

Ross and Tom felt I had what it took to be a full-fledged docent and welcomed both Musket and I to the Museum's staff.

I was given a badge with my picture. Even Musket got one.

🐕 "Daddy put my badge around my neck when we went to the museum. Everybody thought it was cute. I don't. I'm proud of being the only Guide dog docent in San Diego."

Guided by Delight

We enjoyed giving tours to the public.

When I showed up with Musket I could feel the raised eyebrows. "Is that blind man and his dog going to give us the tour?" I heard one man ask Tom at the front desk, "Is this a joke?"

Tom, laughing, said "No, he's one of our best tour guides. Have fun."

My humor helped a lot. I introduced myself. "Hi, my name is Mark. Welcome to the museum. And this is Musket. He'll do the walking and I'll do the talking."

That broke the ice every time.

🐕 "Daddy liked to use me in the tour. I guided him in the dark museum and stopped at the right places, but we also did something cool.

When we reached this one big plane, (they're all big to me) he talked about its history. Then after a moment he leaned down to me like I got his attention. "What is it, Musket?" A second later he stood up. 'Oh, that's right. Musket reminded me the pilot of this aircraft's call sign was 'Jig Dog.'"

It always got a laugh and I got a treat."

I was often called in when a group of blind students was coming.

We provided them with white gloves so they, unlike other patrons could touch the aircraft and exhibits.

Many of the docents were 'Plane Captains' and given the privilege of caring for one of the aircraft. My plane was a 1911 Deperdussin (Deh-paw-du-*sahn*) Militaire. She was my sweetheart. I like little old ladies, and 100 years just fit the bill.

A French monocoque monoplane from the pre-World War One era she had fabric wings, an open cockpit and 60-hp Gnome rotary engine.

I dusted her once a month, which led to some humorous incidents.

Musket slept under the wing while I dusted. One day I heard a woman patron asking "Why would they have a seeing-eye dog as part of the display? Was the pilot blind?"

Musket was sleeping so soundly they thought he was a stuffed dog.

"I woke up when Daddy called me and the woman let out a little yelp. Served her right. Stuffed dog!"

Having Musket along during museum tours was always memorable. He calmed fidgety children and amused adults. It's not too farfetched to say his presence made a visit to the San Diego Air and Space Museum a truly exceptional experience.

From The Moon to Musket

Wally Schirra, one of the original seven Mercury astronauts, had been a member of the museum's board for many years. When he died in May of 2007, his memorial service was held in the museum's central Pavilion of Flight.

It was attended by hundreds of friends, aviation legends, astronauts, celebrities and veterans.

Musket and I helped in whatever way we could. The line of guests streamed in and mingled, with wine and hors d'oeuvres, talking about Wally and sharing stories.

We heard speeches and tributes by some of Wally's friends and fellow astronauts. Even Bill Dana, the man who had made famous the now politically incorrect Jose Jimenez, the cowardly Latino astronaut was there for Wally. For the first time in nearly 30 years an audience heard the reedy, scared voice saying "My name, Jose Jimenez."

It was an emotional event.

"Daddy was really excited that night. I met nice astronauts and more little old ladies."

Barbara Woodbury, the President of the Navy and Marine Corps Association knew pretty much everybody in naval aviation and NASA.

Well, since Musket played a strong role, I'll let him talk for a bit.

"Oh, okay. A lot of people were interested in me. Then Barbara came over. "Oh, he's so cute. Can I meet him? What's his name?"

Daddy let go of my harness and told her my name. I thought she was sweet, very beautiful and elegant.

Barbara took several pictures of me. And Daddy too, I think. Barbara explained, while petting me, she'd known Wally and all the other astronauts for years.

Daddy asked if she would introduce him to any of them.

And that's how we were introduced Gene Cernan, Tom Stafford and Jig Dog Ramage."

Gene Cernan was the last man to walk on the Moon on Apollo 17 in 1972. Rail-thin, white-haired and dignified, he flew with Tom Stafford, John Young and Jack Schmitt.

And he instantly liked Musket. Barbara took pictures of us together and Gene later autographed one

'To Mark and Musket from the Moon, Gene Cernan.'

Is that cool or what?

With Apollo 17 astronaut Gene Cernan
Photo courtesy Barbara Woodbury

"Daddy said Gene walked on the Moon. Okay that's fine, but he gave me a piece of his sandwich. That's why I liked him."

Tom Stafford flew with Wally on Gemini 6, and commanded Gemini 9 and Apollo 10 with Cernan. He was also the commander of the American crew on the 1975 Apollo-Soyuz mission.

I was in awe of the men who'd made important strides in the journey to, and in Cernan's case on, the Moon.

Where no Guide Dog has Gone Before

The museum hosted the 40th Anniversary Gala of the December 1968 flight of Apollo 8. Over a dozen of NASA's most famous personages attended, including Neil Armstrong and the crew of Apollo 8.

Musket and I were invited to be VIP Docents, a true honor. Along with David Hardy, we escorted the gray-haired dignitaries through the collection.

A short man with a Texas accent came up to me and asked to meet Musket.

I happily said yes and the older gentleman, whom I didn't know, knelt down to say hello. Musket recognized a dog lover right away. His tail beat against my legs.

"He's very mellow and nice,' the man said, stroking Musket's fur. "Very friendly dog." He said it as 'dawg.'

"Yes, he is."

Finally I asked him his name.

"Alan Bean," he said, shaking my hand. "Glad to meet you, Mark."

I gasped. "It's really nice to meet you too, Captain. Welcome to the museum."

Al Bean was the fourth man to walk on the Moon with Pete Conrad on Apollo 12, and the commander of the Skylab 3 crew, which stayed in space for 59 days in 1973. Today he's a respected artist of moonscapes and Apollo history.

But at that moment Al Bean, astronaut and artist was a new friend of Musket.

"He said, 'I'm sorry Musket I don't have any treats for you,' but Daddy took care of that. Daddy seemed real excited about meeting him, but Al was just a nice older man who gave me a treat."

The press was there, and of course Musket made the news again. He was recovering from some surgery and didn't have his harness on, instead wearing a red shirt which said 'Who's Your Santa?' If you want to see it go to Youtube and type:'Apollo 8 40th Anniversary.' You'll hit the video shot by the museum and there is my crazy Guide dog in his Christmas shirt.

🐕 "Daddy was using his cane that day and I was on leash. It felt strange but all my friends from the museum were glad to see I was doing well. There were a lot of cameras and people moving around. I thought they were there to see me."

The crew of Apollo 8, Frank Borman, Jim Lovell and Bill Anders did a re-creation of their famous reading from Genesis on Christmas Day 1968 while in orbit around the Moon.

Musket and I were witness to this historic moment and it sent chills up my spine.

The Star Trek Exhibition was at the museum then, with props and artifacts from all the series and movies. The centerpiece was a full-scale set of the starship *USS Enterprise* bridge. The Apollo astronauts were like kids, sitting in Captain Kirk's chair and having their pictures taken.

Gene Cernan came over and said hello to me and Musket, and while talking to him I bumped into another man. "Sorry," I said, moving aside. I asked, "Who is this?"

Cernan smiled. "Neil Armstrong."

Armstrong held out his hand and I shook it.

Musket and I, on the bridge of the Starship *Enterprise*, met the first man to walk on the Moon, standing next to the last man to walk on the Moon.

Ain't life grand?

🐕 "Mr. Armstrong was polite but my friend Gene was happy to see me. Daddy for some reason was very quiet."

Old Sailors

Barbara had also introduced us to Ginger Ramage, a sweet, warm-hearted older woman who wanted to meet Musket. I brought him over. Then she turned to her husband. "Jig, do you want to meet Musket and Mark?

A large older man turned towards us and gave Musket a pat on the head and shook my hand.

Barbara told me who I was chatting with. Rear Admiral James D. 'Jig Dog' Ramage, USN. He was a retired veteran of World War Two, Korea and Vietnam, and holder of the Navy Cross.

Jig, as he prefers to be called, had been a dive bomber pilot aboard the *USS Enterprise* and dropped bombs on the Japanese shipping at Truk Lagoon in February of 1944.

He was Air Group Commander on *USS Oriskany* during the filming of *The Bridges at Toko-Ri* with Fredric March, William Holden, Grace Kelly and Mickey Rooney.

Jig told me about meeting Holden was amazed at the complex and dangerous work the Navy did in Korea.

Mickey Rooney, ever the ebullient Irishman generously entertained the crew with nightly shows of music and comedy.

Now that's what I called a war story.

Since then Jig has been a good friend.

My friend Linda, who is as plane and veteran crazy as me, took Musket and I to meet Jig and Ginger at the Coronado Ferry Landing for coffee.

"Jig and Ginger went there every day with friends. Ginger thought I was the most wonderful dog in the world. Who was I to argue? She bought some healthy dog treats for me and I was in doggy heaven. Warm sun, treats, belly rubs and treats."

On one visit Jig paid me a high compliment indeed. He gave me some artifacts he'd been keeping. A plaque with a Dauntless control stick handgrip and another one with a working WWII aircraft 8-day chronometer. They were real treasures and I was very moved by his generosity. He even signed a picture of himself for me.

"I heard Ginger whispering to Linda that she told Jig to give them to Daddy because she wanted them out of the closet."

Well, be that as it may, it was appreciated.

As I said I respected those people, not because they were famous, but because of what they had done. Walking on the Moon, flying pioneering NASA spacecraft, or fighting the war in the Pacific were worthy of respect.

John Finn was the oldest living Medal of Honor recipient and the only one left from the 1941 attack on Pearl Harbor. He received the citation for shooting down two Japanese aircraft with a water-cooled .50 caliber machine gun. Not an easy thing to do. He suffered almost 20 wounds from enemy strafing.

John was an acquaintance from my reenacting days and I renewed my friendship with the venerable old Navy Lieutenant after starting at the museum.

He was a wonderful old gent, living in Pine Valley in the east county. He loved to tell war stories, and his mind, despite just having celebrated his 100th birthday was sharp and witty.

🐕 "John was really fun. He was an old farm boy who knew a good dog when he saw one. And when he met me it was an instant friendship. John liked to play with me and feed me. Daddy said he was a war hero and a national treasure. But to me John Finn is my friend."

Well put, little buddy. The nation lost John in May 2010. Linda, Musket and I were at his memorial service. We'll miss him.

John Finn, Musket and Mark in 2010
Photo courtesy Linda Stull

I'm looking for a small-sized leather flight helmet, goggles and a red scarf. I think Musket would look great as a World War One flying ace.

Then I'll have his picture taken with our reproduction Fokker DR-1 Triplane in the colors of Manfred von Richthofen, the Red Baron.

And of course it will be called 'Musket vs. the Red Baron.'

"That might be cool. Since Daddy got to meet so many of his astronaut heroes maybe I could meet Snoopy! I've always wanted to ask him how he could sleep on that doghouse. Every time I try it I roll off."

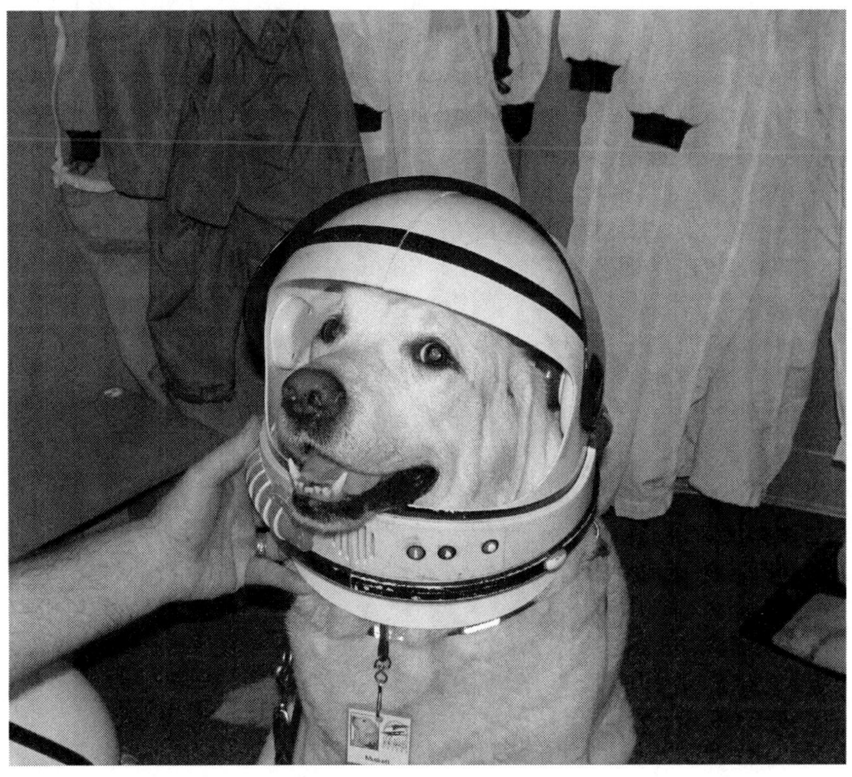

"Houston, I have to pee."
Photo courtesy Linda Stull

Straighten Up and Fly Write

When I was laid off from ISD in 2009 I began writing full time. I submitted stories that appeared in *Dog Fancy*, *San Diego Pets* and *Bark*. Most were about Musket and our work at the museum.

"Daddy wrote stories about me and suddenly I was a celebrity. Everybody knew who I was. It was hard guiding Daddy with people pointing at me."

With my contacts in aviation, and through the Distinguished Flying Cross Society I interviewed pilots, airmen and veterans. I wrote stories for *Flight Journal*, *EAA Warbirds*, and *The Hook*, the journal of Naval Aviation. In less than a year I'd written over a dozen articles and started getting calls from other magazines interested in my work.

I had finally found my niche.

Because of my writing I met dozens of wonderful and awe-inspiring people, who'd been involved in some of the most historic events in aviation and war. I wrote about the restoration of rare warbirds and the careers of Navy and Air Force veterans. Captain Wallace 'Griff' Griffin was another dive bomber pilot who became a local celebrity after my article about him in *Flight Journal* was published. Ed Davidson had flown missions as a B-17 pilot over Europe, and generously helped me find other veterans for articles. Another man who also became a good friend was Colonel Steve Pisanos, a fun and active 93-year old fighter pilot who'd been a double ace in the war. He wrote an autobiography entitled 'The Flying Greek.' He took a real shine to Musket and loved to play with him.

🐈 "Steve Pisanos. You'd never know the man was over ninety years old. He was in great shape. He said it was due to having olive oil with every meal."

Being a writer is fun, and I'm happy to be paid for it, but the perks are fantastic!

I was given free rides in a Commemorative Air Force (CAF) Douglas C-53D Skytrooper which had actually carried paratroopers over Normandy on D-Day, and a beautifully restored B-25 Mitchell medium bomber. Those were in gratitude for the good publicity my writing garnered for the organization. Musket didn't go with me on those flights because he would have been miserable with the noise. They weren't built for comfort.

🐈 "And no flight attendant to rub my belly and give me water. That's the only way to fly."

But the greatest gift I could receive took place on April 11, 2011 when I was offered a ride in a B-17 Flying Fortress. That had been on my Bucket List for years. And because I had written articles for EAA Warbirds, the owners of the plane, I got to go for free.

"I know Daddy was really happy to get the ride, but I didn't want to leave him. Linda held my leash while Daddy was taken out to this great big airplane. When he got inside it, Linda tried to lead me away. I didn't want to go. That was my daddy going away without me."

Linda told me Musket was very hard to move. His claw marks are still on the concrete tarmac.

"Yep, they are."

My ride was a truly wonderful and memorable experience. I know it might be hard for some readers who have no interest in old planes to understand, but I'll never forget the feeling of those four powerful Wright Cyclone engines permeating my bones and soul as we soared over the county. To be in one of the most famous aircraft of all time I was actually crying with the emotion.

"When Daddy came back, I dragged Linda out there to greet him. His face was all wet and I licked the tears off. I know he was just happy to see me."

I was invited to airshows all over southern California as a member of the press with a media pass, which gave me access (that word again) to the pilots and aircraft.

Musket accompanied me to the airshows, and handled it very well. I was pleased that I never had a negative reaction to approaching a pilot and introducing myself as an aviation writer. Though they might have been surprised at someone with a Guide dog or white cane writing articles about aircraft and history, they never showed it. In time my reputation preceded me and I became part of the club. Musket helped a great deal. He did his usual 'Hello' tail-wagging, which no one could resist.

During an interview he fell asleep in the sun, but when it became too hot, moved under the wing of an airplane. Often someone in the crowd noticed the sleeping Guide dog.

🐈 "Yeah, that was funny. They must have been thinking the pilot was blind. But then again, there is such a thing as 'flying blind,' isn't there?"

If he didn't want to leave the cool shade of the wing, often some kind volunteer would bring a golf cart around to give us a ride. He never minded that one bit.

🐈 "My chauffer. Take me to the treat chalet, please."

Along the way, Musket and I were asked to be on the radio.

Rich Kenney, a local airshow promoter, liked my voice and knowledge of aviation history, so he asked me to be a co-host on a local aviation talk show. I enjoyed it and felt very comfortable behind the microphone. It was called 'On Air Aviation' and the shows were all recorded and posted on the website.

🐈 "Daddy was on the radio. I snored. You could hear me clear as crystal."

Musket didn't get much involved in them but he was there, charming the staff and our guests, which included the famous actor Cliff Robertson.

How I met him involves another actor.

When Mom was staying at the nursing home in Vista I met a woman who'd been a child movie star in the 1930s. Marilyn Knowlden had been in dozens of great films, and starred with Fredric March in *Les Miserables* in 1935, and Norma Shearer in 1938's *Marie Antoinette*. She was one of the last living actors from Hollywood's Golden Age.

I convinced her to let me interview her for a story. It was published in *Classic Images* in 2010 and started a long and amazing series of events. Marilyn introduced me to her publisher, who accepted my proposal to write a book about aviation in the movies.

Read it again, it's still the same. A blind man writing about movies.

🐈 "Here's our secret. I watched the movies and he wrote what I told him."

No, let's be honest Musket. I started writing 'Flying on Film: A Century of Aviation in the Movies, 1912-2012,' a comprehensive history of aviation on film.

I scanned scores of books and articles into my computer, collected over 200 movies on video and DVD, and interviewed several authors.

Friends in the museum library, including Pam Gay, a sweet lady who doted on Musket also contributed to the project.

🐕 "Pam was a great lady. While Daddy was working in the library, she sneaked treats to me and made sure I had a comfy place to lie down. I liked her a lot."

I was able to talk to several movie celebrities, including Louis Gossett Jr., Sean Astin, David McCallum, Jack Larson, who'd been Jimmy Olsen in the TV 'Superman' series, and Cliff Robertson. All had been in aviation films and were very helpful. Robertson called me and we spoke several times on the phone. My veteran friends also contributed by helping me find men and women who'd been involved in the actual events depicted in the films.

I listened to the movies, most of which I'd many times over the years and knew by heart.

🐕 "I still think my way is better."

Busy Blind Guy

Along with radio, writing and airshows Musket and I worked together while I did a series of lectures for OASIS and other adult education programs in San Diego. That came about when Ellie Hodges had convinced me to try doing lectures. She said I had a great voice and would be really popular.

So I did, and over the last two years, I created a series of PowerPoint presentations about the *Titanic*, the *Hindenburg*, the Brooklyn Bridge, the Palomar Telescope and many other subjects. They have been very popular and I have at least 40-50 attendees. But I often wondered if they came to see me or Musket.

🐈 "Let's go with the latter. They came to see me. I walked among them while he was talking, sniffing and kissing their hands. Most of them were older people, lots of ladies. Daddy sometimes gave them treats to give me. I know he pretended to be annoyed when I wanted attention but was really proud of me."

Yes, that's true. Musket broke down the barrier that often existed between a speaker and an audience. He was very good at setting people at ease. All that I'd learned while doing outreaches for ISD and at Toastmasters came in handy when I talked for two hours about the Pearl Harbor attack or the Apollo Program.

🐈 "Daddy started a business called FUNspeakable to promote his entertaining speeches. He's getting it set up on the Internet. He's going to do a lot and I will be going to all of them. So if you are there, bring lots of treats."

As the reader might have guessed, I've been one busy blind guy. I may be spreading myself thin, but I'm having a good time. Writing, lecturing, radio shows, airshows, they're all ways to earn a living and do what I like best.

🐈 "And talk about me, right? What other reason could there be?"

CHAPTER ELEVEN

MUSKETMANIACS

What do Huckleberry Hound, Underdog, Pluto and Snoopy all have in common besides being fictional cartoons?

They are loved by millions of people. Musket is getting there fast.

This chapter is dedicated to the ladies whose hearts he has won.

Musket isn't a thoughtless Romeo. He loves people with sincerity. But his heart truly belongs to his mommy.

They all have something in common, besides their love of dogs and being nice. They're all Musketmaniacs.

I originally coined the term 'Puppywhipped' when Jane began to drop some of her original rules and give in to Musket's charm.

"You're puppywhipped," I laughed.

"Yes, I am," she agreed. "You got a problem with that?"

"Nope. Not me."

Just too cute to resist

🐕 "Mommy wasn't puppywhipped. I don't know what Daddy is talking about. Mommy, can you fluff my bed a bit? I can feel the floor. Thank you. Good Mommy. Now, what were you saying, Daddy?"

I recognized that term was a bit racy so in deference to politeness, started calling them Musketmaniacs.

With a few exceptions, Musket's most ardent admirers were women or girls.

Musket attracted women like Hugh Jackman in a thong.

I want to make one thing clear in this chapter, for the record.

When I was filling out the application for Guide Dogs, I included my preferences of breed, gender, disposition, and so on.

But one category is NOT included in the application. I want that understood.

There is no 'Chick Magnet' choice.

This started with Keith Tomlinson, one of Guide Dogs' field instructors. We first met him about a month after graduation, when he came to the house to see how we were getting along or if we needed any post-graduate training.

I told you they had their act together.

Anyway Keith, Jane and I were in the living room, chatting about Musket. Then Keith, who is as much a wise guy as I, commented on how good-looking Musket was.

"He's really got the look, doesn't he? Mark, you must have checked off the 'Chick Magnet' box on the application."

Jane said nothing but I knew she was giving me 'that look.' I could feel my skin beginning to blister.

There is no such thing on the application.

But there should be.

"Keith was one of my friends from Guide Dogs. He helped Daddy with anything he needed. But I noticed that when he came to visit Daddy at work or home, Daddy made sure I behaved. He didn't want to give the impression he wasn't doing a good job taking care of me. Right Daddy?"

Thanks a lot, stool pigeon.

Now that I've cleared that up, let's move on.

Musket was a lovely looking dog and it didn't take much for a woman to notice him. It was less common with men but did happen.

This book may have given the impression every single person who saw him was instantly smitten. Of course that wasn't true. Some people didn't notice him. Or they just weren't dog people. So he could be resisted.

In a way it was a good thing. If everybody we passed each day wanted to meet him we'd never get anywhere.

🐕 "What's wrong with those people? I must be losing my touch. Maybe I need a makeover."

This is a sampling of his victims . . . ah, sweethearts and buddies.

Sharon McCabe was one of Musket's first big fans. As a manager at ISD, she and I had become friends early on. When she learned I would be getting a Guide dog, she was very supportive.

And a little greedy. She became one of Musket's 'Aunts.'

Aunt was as close as Jane would allow. Jane could be possessive at times and had to approve of a new girlfriend for her baby.

But Sharon, a lovely older blonde with a sweet personality was just fine. Musket often accompanied me down the hall to Sharon's office and the first thing he did was stick his head in her trash can, looking for food. I discouraged that right away but he still tended to do it.

Sharon thought he was cute. She was often the first to offer to take Musket when we were going on a trip.

🐕 "He never gave me to Sharon. I knew he wouldn't because I would probably be spoiled beyond repair. Sharon had no willpower against my begging."

Another of Musket's groupies was Claire Stratton, one of my original counselors at ISD. She was one of the most ebullient and gregarious people I've ever met. She often called from her office and asked "Can I have Musket for a while?"

I usually agreed and in a moment Musket snapped alert, hearing Claire's high laugh from down the hall. "Musket, stay." His tail beat the side of my filing cabinet like Rosie the Riveter making a B-17. Nothing a ball-peen hammer and some Bondo won't fix.

I had to keep him under control because I didn't want him racing down the hall like a Tomcat off a carrier catapult.

He was a bit heedless of others at those times. When Claire came in all bets were off and he jumped on her like a deranged kangaroo.

Claire had a laugh somewhere between Witchiepoo from H.R. Pufnstuf and Tickle Me Elmo.

🐕 "That's about right. I could hear Aunt Claire from a long way off. I was always excited to see her."

Claire Stratton, one of Musket's sweethearts

She took Musket from office to office, spreading good will and canine kisses.

Claire gave him treats but I was firm about what she could and could not give him. Bananas were fine. Claire put a bit in her mouth and Musket took it from her.

Jean, the senior receptionist thought it was gross. That only encouraged Claire, who went out of her way to give Musket a banana slice in front of Jean. I think if Musket ever kissed Jean it would be like Lucy van Pelt used to do in *Peanuts*, where she ran around screaming 'Auugh! I've been kissed by a dog! Get some iodine! I've been kissed by a dog!"

"I thought it was funny. Claire and some of the other ladies at the office liked to get kisses from me in front of Lucy . . . I mean Jean."

I often found Musket being pampered, petted and even cuddled by those women. And he wasn't shy about it. In the middle of a work-related conversation if he thought he wasn't getting the attention he deserved, he flopped down, rolled on his side and lifted his arms.

🐕 "Rub my belly! C'mon, you know you want to."

There were several other card-carrying Musketmaniacs. Valerie, Monica, Jeri, Rachel (she preferred 'Raquel' as in Welch), Amy and Mary. They got Musket excited by just walking past my desk and blowing him a kiss. "Hi, Musket!"

Musketmaniacs Valerie Arita, Monica Barazza, Sharon McCabe

And a few, I won't name names, were relentless. They actually goaded him into becoming a tail-wagging, jumping deranged furball of joy. They know who they are, and I hope they can live with their shame.

"What was the harm in that? I made them happy. Sheesh Daddy, lighten up."

Annika Anderson was a frequent visitor to my office. Not to play with or even to feed Musket but to snuggle. Annika was a Korean girl adopted by American parents, hence her Scandinavian name. I won't deny I was thrilled when I heard the center had hired a girl named Annika Anderson. Ya sure, yumpin' yiminy.

But when I stuck my head into the office and saw what appeared to be a lovely Asian girl, I was confused.

She introduced herself and we quickly became friends.

So did Musket.

Annika fell in love with him right off. Soon she started coming to my door and asking to visit Musket.

"Sure," I'd say, not turning from my computer. "Help yourself."

Of course Musket needed little encouragement.

Annika came in and shut the door. I paid no attention because I knew what she was doing.

She got down on the floor next to Musket and snuggled with him. Spooning.

She loved his soft fur and warm belly. He calmed her when she'd had a stressful day.

I went right on working. There was no harm in it.

"I miss Annika. She went to another job. She was very special to me."

Other Fans

I've been going to audiologists since I began wearing hearing aids. My favorite was Dr. Judy Horning in Rancho Bernardo. She had been taking care of me for a decade.

She never charged me for adjustments, and at a time when money was tight arranged for donations of brand-new programmable hearing aids for me. They would have cost about $4,000.

Judy was a bright, effervescent, witty, (her own words but I agree) extremely capable woman in her sixties who really cared about her patients.

And she was also one of Musket's sweethearts. When we went to visit her office, Musket always pulled me up the stairs to get to Judy as fast as possible

🐕 "She was really nice and talked to me like a person, not a dog."

She once invited me to speak at a meeting of the Rancho Bernardo Lions Club. Of course I accepted. The Lions made a lot of donations and grants to help disabled people with education and personal goals. I often referred some of my consumers to the Lions Optometric Clinic, where a person needing glasses could receive low-cost care.

She introduced Musket and I to the members, all nice and socially involved seniors.

I spoke about life with a disability and what independence really means. Of course I knew Musket was a source of interest and told the members about Assistance dogs.

🐕 "They took pictures of me and Daddy and Judy together. I felt special, although I'm glad the lion never showed up."

Judy was on our Christmas mailing list so she received our newsletters. The first time we visited her after Christmas she raved about how clever the newsletter was and how smart Musket was to write it. She even read it to some of her patients and kept it after the holidays.

🐕 "Daddy told her he really wrote it. I don't think she believed him."

Musket was pretty much the only Guide dog at the airshows, and he attracted a lot of attention.

🐕 "I met some nice pilots. One lady named Grace McGuire had a big silver plane she named 'Muriel.' Grace loved me."

Grace McGuire owns the only surviving Lockheed 10-E Electra in the world. She recovered it from a scrap heap in Florida over a decade ago and has spent years and most of her money restoring it. The Electra is the same model that Amelia Earhart flew on her ill-fated flight around the world in 1937.

'Muriel' is a beautiful, polished treasure of a bygone era. I felt a true connection to the old plane and ran my fingertips along her smooth, gleaming riveted aluminum flanks. The same hands which had driven the rivets had constructed Amelia's plane.

Grace plans to fly 'Muriel' on a re-creation of the 1937 flight. I wish her good fortune and the wind beneath her wings.

Musket with his friend Muriel, a rare Lockheed 10-E Electra
Photo courtesy Linda Stull

🐕 "I liked to lie under 'Muriel's' wings. During the airshow, she asked Daddy if I needed anything. She was worried about my paws on the hot concrete and made sure he took care of me. She brought me treats and lots of ice-cold water."

For sure Grace was bitten hard by the Musket bug.

Not all Musketmaniacs were adults. A few were under the age of ten. At the museum there was a mother who brought her kids to a lot of the birthday parties we hosted in the Pavilion. And one cute little moppet fell for Musket's furry face right away.

"She liked to chase my tail. I wagged it while she tried to catch it. Sometimes I let her. She was very sweet. And every time she saw me she put her arms around my neck to give me a hug."

On the Giant Screen

ISD hired a consultant to find grants and funding sources. Jeanne Merrill, a short, blonde, vivacious and intelligent lady, like every woman in this chapter quickly fell under Musket's considerable charm. He liked her so much he steered me right into her office when we walked down the hall. He put his paws on her desk to give her a wet hello.

Jeanne and her husband Ted were very socially conscious people who donated money to charitable causes.

The Helen Woodward Animal Center in Escondido California was a non-profit organization dedicated to saving the lives of injured or sick animals and enriching the lives of people who could benefit from their love.

When Jeanne told me she and Ted won a drawing from their donation, I learned they were going to be recognized at Petco Park before a San Diego Padres baseball game. The Helen Woodward people were going to provide an Assistance dog to be with Jeanne and Ted for the announcement but as things turned out, when the day came there was no dog available.

"Oh but there was. Me. Jeanne asked Daddy if she could have me with her on the field for the presentation. Daddy said sure as long as he was nearby.

But it turned out different. We went to Petco Park. For some reason I like the name. We waited to be called, while the 'Pad Squad,' a bunch of really nice girls took good care of us.

Daddy had shown Jeanne how to lead me out to the field. But when the time came Daddy was told to go too.

And that's how in front of 30,000 baseball fans I was on TV and the giant screen. The public address introduced Jeanne and Ted, and then Daddy as working for ISD. And then they introduced me.

I got the most applause. 'Don't cry for me, San Diego . . ."

I later learned that one of the girls from the veterinarian's office was there that day and yelled out. "That's my friend Musket!"

The Merrills, Mark and Musket at Petco Park
Photo Courtesy San Diego Padres

It really happened. It may seem there is no way any single dog other than Lassie or Benji could garner so much attention and be the focus of so many remarkable encounters but every word of this is true. I cross my heart. I've never met a dog like him.

By the way, after the Petco Park event, Jeanne and Ted treated me to dinner at a trendy burger place. You know, the kind of restaurant where you can hear 1950s music, sit in 1950s furniture and enjoy 1950s food and drink at 2010 prices.

That's where Jeanne learned about Musket's French Fries for Protection Racket.

I told her not to give in. But she wimped out and paid up.

🐕 "Do I hafta get rough wid youse guys? Don't make me use my soulful eyes on you."

Service with a Smile

We had a nice dentist named Dr. Melinda Marino, who, unlike every dentist I've ever had, I really like.

Sort of.

Anyway, she too was a Musketmaniac. She proved this when Jane made an appointment for a cleaning and Dr. Marino said, "You can't come in unless you bring Musket."

🐕 "Aww, isn't that nice of her? Okay, Daddy, let's go to the dentist. I think you might need a checkup, hmmm?"

Molly, a beautiful blonde lady with the voice of an angel, was the manager at our bank. Molly came out of her office when we entered the bank and said hello to him. He never walked into that bank without steering me to Molly's office.

🐕 "Good golly, Miss Molly gave Daddy money and gave me treats."

'Good golly Miss Molly?' Oh, boy.

At malls or other places we shopped regularly, Musket was welcomed. In Grocery stores, the bank, restaurants, Starbucks, office supply, Kinko's, bookstores, his Musketmaniacs awaited his visits.

A favorite bistro near our house was Champagne Bakery, which served pastries, sandwiches, soups and the best baguettes in the world.

Jessica was the manager. She too met Musket for the first time over a counter, and recognized him from TV during the McDonalds incident. "I know you! I saw you on TV!"

We chatted about the story for a few minutes as I waited for my fresh baguette. Ever since then I asked for Jessica when I went to the bakery, even if I was merely passing by. I think Musket's greetings were the best gifts anyone could receive during a busy work day.

"Jessica had really good food there, but Daddy didn't let me have any. He thought it wasn't good for me. Shouldn't I be the judge of that? I am very particular about what I eat.

Excuse me, I see an old Cheese Puff on the sidewalk. Gotta run."

Toni and Rick Kraft had lived next door to Mom and Dad. She owned a terrific outdoor bistro in the Rancho Bernardo Winery called Café Merlot. I give it five stars for superb food, great service and staff with personality.

"Toni and Rick were two of my favorite people in Nanny's neighborhood. They were both really sweet to me. When Toni's dog Toby died I knew something was wrong and went right to Toni. I gave her lots of kisses and she cried. I think I made her feel better. I hope I did."

Ellie Hodges was one lovely lady, a true dog lover and a Musketmaniac. During the time Jane was caring for her parents, Ellie brought meals, desserts, spent time talking with them, just being helpful. She was also one of the biggest fans of my writing and was the catalyst for my lecturing.

Ellie took us to Café Merlot for lunch one day. We had a wonderful time with the waitresses fawning over my crazy dog.

Toni and Rick came out and chatted with us. After a truly succulent shrimp quesadilla, Toni treated us to some of the most sumptuous and sinful desserts I've ever had. I have a sweet tooth and it was overindulged to a fare-thee-well.

"Daddy didn't give me any because it had chocolate on it. But Mommy knew Daddy couldn't see, so she snuck a little of her peach cobbler dessert to me. That's why I love my mommy. She can be sneaky."

Women Without Willpower

At the Braille Institute in La Jolla everybody knew us. After the McDonalds incident they copied the newspaper article and enlarged it. They were posted in the cafeteria and reception area. Celebrity wasn't easy but we lived with it.

Ruth was seriously smitten. Musket couldn't walk past the front desk without Ruth going nuts. Bear in mind this was a woman who saw Guide dogs every day. She HAD to give Musket a treat, otherwise she had withdrawal symptoms. She couldn't help herself. She even took pictures of him with her cell phone.

"I know how Daddy felt about it, but we had to understand and help her cope with it."

Kathy, Tracy, and Louise were also smitten. Kathy was my first counselor and as sweet as any lady I've ever known. She greeted Musket in a very ladylike manner. "Hello how's Musket today?"

Tracy was a counselor and like me a very strong advocate for Independent Living. We collaborated on several projects. I truly liked and admired her. And she truly liked and admired Musket.

She tolerated me because I was his daddy.

Seriously, we got along great. I enjoyed talking with her even if most of the time she was kneeling by Musket, rubbing his belly.

"Kathy was pretty and sweet to me, but not as wild and crazy as Ruth. Tracy was cute and fun to play with. She was also kind of short so it was easy for me to kiss her."

Louise worked in the library. She got me all the audio books I ordered. I think I overworked her, but she liked me anyway. Musket always went right past the desk to her office and said hello. She was fun and always laughed at my humor.

🐕 "Louise thought I was the coolest dog in the world. I think she was a very smart lady. Like Ruth she too had a problem. Anyone who laughed at Daddy's jokes was in serious need of therapy."

Early in 2009 we met Sandra Hayhurst, who worked for the Arthritis Foundation in San Diego. We went to their offices one day for a meeting and Sandra came out, took one look at Musket and immediately fell under his spell. She asked if she could take him around to introduce to the rest of the staff. After ten minutes I wondered if she'd taken my dog for good.

Sandra was a fun, lovely intelligent woman in her (age withheld under threat of torture) who had two dogs of her own. But Musket became her favorite. Even when she called on a professional matter the first thing she asked was 'How's my Musket?"

🐕 "She had my picture on her desk. BETWEEN the photos of her dogs. She said she couldn't find one of just me, so Daddy was in it too."

The museum added to Musket's growing fame and fans. Linda Stull, who I've mentioned previously, was one, but we also shared a love of airplanes. Her father was a B-17 navigator during the war, and she loved the Flying Fortress.

And unlike most women (NOTE: This is NOT meant as a sexist generalization so put away the tar and feathers, ladies) she knew the difference between a P-51 Mustang and a Supermarine Spitfire.

And she loved Musket. When she came to the museum or airshow she made healthy doggy treats for him and could never resist his begging. But she was a warbird buff so I looked the other way.

🐕 "How's that for irony? A blind guy 'looking the other way?' Anyway Linda was really sweet and made treats for me. She once got some gravy on her elbow so every time I saw her I licked her elbow, just in case."

As if Musket didn't already have a large fan base, in July 2009 the *San Diego Union-Tribune* did an article about us. It centered on our work at the museum, featured on the front page of the local section.

There was even a video, posted on the paper's website. It showed Musket leading me around as I conducted a tour.

"I had on my cutest look. But seriously, I was proud of what we did together and I never did anything to shame my profession."

The article was a big hit with the museum and our friends. When Jane and I attended a volunteer appreciation banquet a week after the article came out, at least fifty people wanted to meet musket. "I read about him in the paper! He's really cute. Aw, look at those eyes!"

The phone calls and e-mails poured in. Every single one of them was for Musket.

"I made a lot of new friends after that. We met people on the bus and in stores who wanted to meet me. I felt like a celebrity. I knew Daddy was proud of me."

Doggy Dudes

Just to break the monotony I'll introduce some of Musket' guy friends.

Aaron Dawson was one of the team at ISD. A young guy, and nice as can be. I teased him about being very young, which is a trait common in old farts like me. He was crazy about Musket. When I was at my desk facing the computer, I sometimes heard a voice pitched so high only bats could hear it. That was Aaron's voice when he was talking to Musket.

"Musss-kie. How's my Mus-kie?" He didn't sound like that all the time. Just when he was awake.

If Aaron was over 25 it isn't by more than a couple of minutes. I had to be nice to Aaron. Jane adored him.

Anyway, he worked Musket into a frenzy of tail-wagging and jumping.

"Aaron," I said without turning. "What are you doing to my poor dog?"

"How did you know it was me?"

"Because all the women in the office have deeper voices. The treats are in the bowl."

"Aaron was cool. He liked to play with me and wasn't afraid to really roughhouse it. I had to be careful because I think I outweigh him. At least that's what Daddy said."

Dick Graham and I met when I caught him petting Musket at a bus stop. He was not exactly 'The Sneaker,' but just bent over and indulged himself.

I felt the quiver in the leash and said 'Please don't touch my dog."

Dick was immediately apologetic, unlike a lot of pooch petting poachers.

Right away I felt bad and said it was okay. I gave him the Nickel tour of Assistance dog etiquette and let him meet Musket properly.

Since that day Dick and I greeted each other and Musket was always happy to see another of his big buddies.

Dick was ex-navy and worked at the Naval Medical Center in the computer room.

We found a lot to talk about on the bus, and our conversations were always fun, entertaining and varied.

The only thing about Dick I found funny was he wasn't a 'doggie kiss' kind of guy.

"I liked Dick right away. He was a very nice and soft-spoken man. I miss seeing him because he retired last year."

When I was still into re-enacting, I was part of a Roman Legion. Yep. That's what I said. It wasn't as tricky as carrying a gun. Legio IX Hispana re-created a First-century legion as accurately as possible. They made their own armor and gear, and did parades, encampments and even appeared in History Channel documentaries.

Mario Padilla was the legion's *Optio*, or sergeant. When he was in his armor and helmet, carrying a sword and shield, it was easy to imagine how a Roman legionary would have looked. With curly black hair and dark eyes, chiseled features, he was fully six-foot tall, broad-shouldered and very masculine. I mean, even when he wore a skirt this guy was *butch*.

What the well-dressed blind Roman Legionary wears

Musket came with me to some of the trainings and slept while I learned to swing a sword and throw a spear.

The others learned to duck.

🐈 "I wasn't sleeping. I was keeping my eyes tightly closed.

I liked Mario. He was a big strapping man with a deep voice. When he came over to see Daddy I went right up to him. "How's Musket?' Mario was my friend."

Just in case you wondered, I had a roman name. it was Marcus Lucius Apollonius.

Musket's name in the legion was Ballista, a sort of Roman artillery.

At Halloween, I donned my Roman gear for parties at work.

Imagine a Roman legionary in armor and helmet, being led by a Guide dog.

Monica at the office thought I had sexy legs.

"Monica believed in the Easter Bunny too."

Lee Price was another work buddy of mine. He was in his early sixties, and as nice and generous as any guy can be.

When I say 'guy' I mean it. He was a serious girl charmer, but being a cute old man he could get away with it.

He'd survived a very bad stroke many years ago and eventually regained his mobility and speech.

Lee worked in our North County office and knew more about housing and community-based living than anybody.

He also knew more about beer than anybody.

A big Musket fan he often gave us rides home. He always said hello to his furry buddy before me.

"I liked Lee a lot. He was really cool and very funny. He looked like Santa Claus without the beard."

Lee's favorite hangout was Stone Brewery in Escondido. Stone was one of the most successful craft breweries in the country. The place had style. A terrific beer garden and restaurant serving really superb and unique meals washed down with their signature beer, Arrogant Bastard Ale.

Strong stuff. It made Budweiser seem like making love in a canoe.

"Making love in a canoe, Daddy?"

Yeah, F-ing close to water.

"Badabum!"

Okay that one might not make it past the editor.

Everybody at Stone knew Lee. I mean everybody. And when he brought us there, he was greeted by the owner and all the staff. He introduced me and then Musket, who of course was fawned over by the pretty waitresses.

Never any access problems at Stone. Check them out on the web sometime.

"I never had to ask for water or anything. The people at Stone knew just what I wanted. No, not beer."

There were many more Musketmaniacs, but I'd need another book for them all. I'll just close the chapter with this: I love dogs, and have met hundreds of friendly, cute, intelligent, loyal and special dogs.

Musket is only one of many. But no matter how hard I tried to convince myself or anyone else, it wasn't any use.

He had something. And if I could bottle and sell it on the internet I'd have more money than Bill Gates.

"I had lots of girlfriends and guy friends. Lots of dogs are friendly and cute. I don't know why Daddy thinks I'm special. He even goes out of his way to bring me to see my friends. Men and women, boys and girls, even babies smiled when they saw me.

I didn't get it but it was my other job to make them happy.

As long as I guided Daddy safely and gave Mommy a lot of love, I had more to spare for my Musketmaniacs."

CHAPTER TWELVE

WHERE IS SHE GOING WITH THAT THERMOMETER?

I never gave Musket any food which was bad for him. The food scraps might not be real dog food but were within reason. Really. I was very careful with his health.

As you know he begged a lot. If you haven't caught on yet, I suggest going back to Chapters One through Eleven. We'll wait for you.

Okay. Let's move on.

He thought anything someone put in their mouth was good for him. Of course it wasn't. Jane and I were pretty strict, despite our wimpy willpower when he started the 'Begging Pose.'

"Well, this doesn't sound good. I'm getting a bad feeling about this."

For instance, I love chocolate. A lot. I'm a chocoholic and proud of it. "Just give me the chocolate and no one will get hurt." Or "Step away from the chocolate and keep your hands where I can see them."

Get the idea?

Not even close. Let's say I was a scientist with the secret rocket formula and was captured by evil agents of an eastern country to be determined later.

They could torture me with beatings or the rack, or even with the threat of being locked in a closet with an insurance salesman. I wouldn't give them the formula.

A hot busty blonde wouldn't make me betray my country.

But just hold a bar of Scharffenberger Extra Rich Milk Chocolate in front of me, and . . .

"Do any of you guys have a pen?"

Musket can't have any. I don't give him chocolate, onions, raisins or other things I know to be bad for dogs. Onions can cause renal failure. I'm always learning what not to give him. We want our baby to be healthy and happy.

Like all carbon-based life forms, he's had some health problems. And this chapter is about them.

"I know Daddy tried to keep me healthy. I'm middle-aged as dogs go, no longer a puppy. I feel pretty good and have lots of energy, love to play and can keep working as long as he needs me.

Daddy put this chapter off until nearly the end because it's about going to the vet.

I did like the people at the clinic, most of the time. They said hello as soon as they saw me. Daddy had a regular routine. He was careful of my weight, even though I didn't get enough to eat, and weighed me whenever we were near the vet.

He took off my harness and told me to get on the scale.

I didn't need to be told.

A girl told him my weight and then I got a healthy treat. That's the routine.

The other times we've gone there I don't want to think about."

Carmel Mountain Ranch Veterinary Hospital was a short walk from the house. When I came home with Musket in 2002 one of the first things I did was to bring his medical history and vaccination records. I introduced them to their newest patient.

Guide Dogs gave me instructions on when and how often he should have his vaccinations, checkups and other regular treatments.

Guide Dogs provided an annual stipend for veterinary care, which paid for regular checkups and minor procedures like nail trimming and teeth cleaning.

If something more extensive was needed, the vet wrote a report and recommendation which was sent to the school's veterinary department for review. If the treatment was warranted in order to protect his life or assure his ability to work, it was paid for by Guide Dogs.

I won't pretend this wasn't an incredible arrangement. Veterinary care is expensive.

But since Guide dogs cost upwards of $50,000 to raise and train, the investment is important to give them as long and healthy a working life as possible.

The assistance from Guide Dogs was a great comfort to Jane and I over the years, as this chapter will illustrate.

And there were times we needed a lot of comfort. Times I don't ever want to relive. But this book is about our lives with Musket, in both sickness and health.

🐕 "I'm not farting rainbows about it either."

Musket soon felt comfortable with the good people at the vet's office. They took good care of my little buddy.

When an animal is sick, they can't tell their owner. It's up to the human to know something is wrong and take care of it. I'm sure being a parent of a small child is no different.

I felt a great deal of empathy for all animals in pain. When I heard about some creep abusing an animal or beating a horse I become almost incoherent with rage. Those people, and they don't deserve to be part of the human race, are the lowest of the low. Like men who abuse women they deserve NO compassion.

When Musket was attacked by that other dog I was not only in shock from the viciousness of the attack but a terrifying fear of his being badly injured and not able to help him.

I still have nightmares about it.

Musket sometimes seemed under the weather, slow, lethargic, and even drowsy. The first indication was when he wouldn't give Jane any kisses. I knew something was off with him. Feeling his nose was first, and it was often a good barometer of his health. Cold and wet, good, warm and dry, bad.

🐕 "I wondered why Mommy and Daddy always held my nose when I didn't feel good. I thought it was a 'make the hurt go away' switch."

Musket's tail also broadcasted his emotions; happy, sad, guilty, tired, nervous, excited or sick, and we used that as well.

His medical history said he had experienced occasional problems with his bowels. Diarrhea. In short, he got the runs.

And it happened about once a month on average. But his appetite, no matter how he felt never wavered. He could be running outside every five minutes to go, but he never left a bit of food in the bowl.

I knew if I ever found food in his bowl something serious was wrong.

So far it has yet to happen.

🐕 "Leftover food? In my bowl? Now? ExcusemeIgottagobye!"

A friend of Jane's who bred Irish Setters told us some dogs don't handle corn meal very well and a lot of dog foods used corn meal as fillers.

The next time we were at the pet store to buy a bag of Eukanuba, I asked Jane to read the ingredients.

There is was, bold as brass. Corn Meal.

That decided it for us. We asked her friend, an energetic lady named Vicki, what food she recommended. I also asked the good folks at our vet's office.

One of the brands they both agreed on was called Wellness. It was a bit more expensive, but that was of little concern. We began buying Wellness Reduced Fat.

🐕 "Reduced fat. Sigh. Why don't you just shoot me?"

And guess what? Musket's bowel problems cleared right up. He hasn't had more than two or three episodes in the last three years.

🐕 "Good thing, too. It hurt and I was always so tired."

Another common problem for Labradors was ear infections, because unlike dogs with erect ears like German Shepherds, Labrador ears tend to retain moisture. I cleaned his ears periodically.

"I said it before. I HATED it when he did that. Baby butt cleaners in my ears!"

His teeth were in great shape, because he was pretty vigorous about chewing bones. That's the very best thing for a dog's teeth.

And since I'm on the subject, I can't understand how they could chew solid bone and not have it hurt their teeth. Musket gnawed away so hard I often heard a loud 'snap' or 'crack!' But it didn't bother him at all.

"Okay, Daddy. Work with me here. Dogs are carnivorous. We're *supposed* to chew bones. Got that?"

I tried to brush his teeth regularly, but that crazy dog kept sticking his tongue out and licking the brush. There was never any paste left when I got to the teeth. I needed four hands. Two to hold his mouth open, one to hold his tongue and the other to brush.

"I liked the liver flavor the best, Daddy. Just squirt some on a plate. I promise I'll wipe it on my teeth."

Taking care of Musket's claws was made easy by him being a Guide dog. Unlike most domesticated dogs, he walked on concrete for long periods. That kept the claws trimmed close. But his dewclaws, the long curved sickle-like ones on his inner front paws got very nasty. They could make a Velociratpor jealous. So they were trimmed about once a year.

"I didn't mind because the whole time the girls were holding me and petting me and cooing at me. Ahhhhhh. I felt like a Roman emperor again."

That's Getting too Personal, Doc

He had a regular checkup every April. Musket always got excited when we arrived at the vet's office. He was probably thinking he would be weighed and get a treat.

But after the weighing, we sat down.
That's when he knew something else was coming.

🐕 "Yeah, and I knew I wasn't going to like it."

The examination rooms were about ten feet square. Not big enough for him to run away. The vet, a lovely woman with a gentle personality and soft voice named Dr. Gray, and her assistant got on the floor with Musket, while I kept him calm. They checked his ears, teeth, heart, lungs and eyes. In fact the eyes are kind of critical if you think about it. Dogs can get cataracts too. Musket's eyes have to be perfect for him to do his job.

Then came the most dreaded part of the examination.

🐕 "Where's she going with that thermometer?"

The first visit to the vet in 2002 went fine because he didn't know what was coming. He liked Dr. Gray. She caressed him while she did her exam. But when she raised his tail and slipped the thermometer in his butt, Musket gained a whole new opinion of her.

🐕 "Yeah! I knew she liked me but not in *that* way! I just wanted to be friends."

From then on Musket didn't trust her or the other vets. Jane was with me for the next visit, when we were still having trouble with his bowels.

She saw what Musket did when the nurse brought out the thermometer. She burst out laughing while trying to calm him at the same time.

He took one look at the evil-looking gleaming shaft in the nurse's hand, and seeing no way out of the room, backed into a corner.

I don't mean he just moved to the corner. He wedged his butt, tail and all in as tightly as if he were trying to stop a leak in the dyke.

And his eyes never left that thermometer.

🐕 "Just keep your hands where I can see them lady. My teeth are registered as lethal weapons. Don't make me use them."

'Butt' resistance was futile and with our comforting and petting Musket, they got his temperature.

He did it every time we went into the exam room. Musket was not only a fast learner he had a phenomenal memory.

But what's interesting was vaccination shots didn't bother him a bit. Didn't even flinch.

🐕 "Yeah, that's right. I didn't mind them. Daddy often said he wondered if I could feel pain. He sometimes stepped on my tail and all I ever gave him was a dirty look. I didn't yelp or cry. I guess I'm just a macho dog."

Twice over the years Musket's health really scared us. The first was in 2005 when the exam revealed a possible tumor.

🐕 "Guess where? In my butt! I think that thermometer did it!"

Dr. Gray told us she had 'a concern.'

A tiny chill touched me. Apparently she'd found a small mass, shaped like a mushroom, growing from the inside of his . . . there's no way to say this delicately, anus. And she was worried it might be cancerous.

The first hints of panic began to be felt in Jane and I. Dogs can get cancer just as humans can and in the case of an Assistance dog, and at best could force them to retire. And at worst . . .

My brother's dog Jeremiah had died of cancer just the year before.

We asked what could be done. Dr. Gray told us to take Musket to a specialty clinic in San Diego where they could not only identify the mass but also do surgery.

🐕 "I knew something was wrong. I could hear it in Mommy and Daddy's voices."

We made an appointment at the clinic and two different doctors made the same diagnosis. Perhaps not cancer, but it should be removed.

So with heavy hearts, we arranged to have Musket undergo surgery. Guide Dogs paid for the treatment.

For the very first time since meeting Musket on that Dog Day Afternoon in 2002, I was not going to have Musket near me that night. Jane was even more distraught. She feared for her baby's life.

The whole family, mine and Jane's circled around us, praying for their Musket to be okay. Everybody at work, on the bus, our neighbors, consoled us. It might seem like a lot for a dog, but that's the kind of love Musket brought out of people.

When we left Musket at the clinic that day, we were both shaking, worried and feared leaving him there. The last thing we saw was his bewildered and hurt look as a girl in white scrubs took him away.

That was the longest night of our lives. We sweated it out and worried. Our supporters called and asked for news.

"All that night I was in a big cage. The nurses were nice but I was scared and hurt. I didn't know why Mommy and Daddy gave me away to those people. I missed sleeping next to Mommy."

The next afternoon we went to pick him up. We were happy to be getting him back but still feared the worst.

A pretty nurse named Vanessa, who was apparently Musket's newest girlfriend, brought him out. When he saw us he went nuts. He jumped and whirled and tried to kiss us both at the same time. He seemed fine.

I thanked Vanessa, who said we could bring Musket back anytime. She really liked him. Remember this was a girl who took care of pets all day long.

The doctor took us into his office and dropped the bomb.

"I was so happy to see Mommy and Daddy. I kept trying to kiss them while they talked to the doctor who worked on me. He was nice but all I wanted to do was to go home and eat and lie down with Mommy."

"We can't find it," he said. "The mass is gone."

Jane and I were dumbfounded.

"What do you mean?" I asked.

He again said he didn't know where the possibly cancerous mass had gone but it was no longer in Musket.

"So that's it?"

"I think so. There's no more mass. We tried to find what was on the x-rays, but it's just not there. He's fine."

🐕 "I could have told him that before he went digging into my butt,"

Jane and I lost no time in bringing him home and calling all his friends to let them know he was okay. He was given a lot of special treatment for the next few days, sleeping on the bed with us, getting a bit more food and treats.

🐕 "That part was great. I think I would get a butt-scan every year just for that."

Night Fright

The second time Musket scared us was sudden and as shocking as the dog attack. The date was September 9, 2007, a Sunday evening. I'll never forget it. I was in my garage office writing when Jane called me on the phone from upstairs. Usually it was just "I think Musket needs to go. Can you let him out?"

But that night was different.

"Honey, I think something's wrong with Musket. He's very lethargic. He won't get up from his bed and when he was walking he bumped his head into the wall."

I didn't ask questions but raced up the stairs. Even blind I can move fast when I have to.

I called Musket to me and he came, but very slowly, as if he were drunk.

🐕 "I felt very strange and my bed was moving. I was getting scared until Daddy came up to help me. He called me and I tried to go to him but I don't know if I made it."

Then Musket started to shake in my hands. His body was shuddering in a way that frightened me. I tried to calm him, not knowing what was happening when he fell over on his side and began convulsing.

Jane screamed.

"Call 911!" I said.

I first opened Musket's mouth to find out if he was choking on something. When I thrust my fingers down his throat I found nothing, but his teeth gnashed on my hand. He was having some sort of seizure.

I was dimly aware of Jane on the phone asking for help. "My husband's Guide dog is having a seizure! Where can we take him?"

After about five minutes, the seizure ended and Musket stopped shuddering. He was breathing very heavily and Jane said his eyes were rolled up.

"We can take him to Emergency Pet Care in Poway," she said, going past me. I carried my Musket, limp as a wet rag, down the stairs. Jane stayed just ahead, guiding me. She ran into the garage and got the car running. I put him in the back seat and crawled in next to him.

We drove the dark streets with fear in our hearts.

"Daddy was holding me close and petting my head, but all I knew was that we were going somewhere at night. I could smell the fear in Mommy and Daddy and that scared me even more. I couldn't stop shaking."

The emergency clinic was about a ten minute drive and they were waiting for us. With Jane's guidance I carried Musket, who was awake but panting and shivering, inside.

We took him into an examination room. The on-duty doctor checked him over and found nothing seriously wrong.

He was still panting and very agitated. There was blood on my hand and in his mouth. He'd bitten his tongue.

"I woke up in a room with lots of lights and strange people. I was very scared, but Mommy was holding me really close and she was shaking even more than me. I tried to lick her hand but my mouth wouldn't work right."

We learned that dogs can have seizures, and they're often not serious unless frequent.

They gave him a shot and told us to take him home. "He'll sleep for a while, and when he wakes up he'll be dizzy and confused."

We were also to tell our vet if any other seizures occurred.

The shot made Musket one woozy puppy. He couldn't stand up and his eyes rolled.

It was almost funny. Almost.

Carrying him back out to the car, I heard Jane thanking the staff of the all-night clinic.

On the way home I rode in the front with Jane, holding her hand while she drove.

The next day Musket was almost his old self again. He'd been through a bad night.

"The next day I felt weak and my back legs wouldn't do what I wanted. I think they put a thermometer in my butt when I was asleep."

I called Keith and the vets at Guide Dogs to tell them what happened. As long as the seizure did not return, or no more than once a year, it wasn't anything to worry about. If they came as often as twice a year, medications could be prescribed to control them.

The cuts and scratches on my hand healed in a couple of weeks. But the wounds on our feeling of security would never heal.

It had been a horrible scare and not one we ever wanted to repeat.

Since that night he hasn't had any seizures. Knock on wood. We've been very alert for any signs of them. My main worry was that one might happen when we were out working and not near any help. But that's why I have a cell phone now.

Groggy Doggy

This chapter was first written only a week after Musket underwent some surgery.

Like most Labs he developed fatty cysts on his flanks and belly. Most of them were less than an inch in size and of little concern, but he had one on his left side behind the elbow which had grown to alarming size in a year.

It wasn't life-threatening, but it could have become a real problem. It was also right under where the harness belly strap rested and might have caused pain later on.

So the doctor, Guide Dogs, Jane and I agreed it should be removed.

🐕 "Removed? Remove what? They already took my nuts. What more do they want?"

I was less concerned with the outcome of the procedure than I was with the first hour of the day.

He expected to get fed right after I let him out.

But he couldn't be fed the day of the surgery.

🐕 "Shudder. I still shake when he says that."

I didn't want to see the expression on his face. Well I couldn't anyway but you know what I mean.

I fed him at dinnertime the night before so he wouldn't go more than a day without food. He wolfed it down right away.

In the morning I let Musket out as usual but not, as per usual, (is that proper grammar)

I Did Not Feed Him.

🐕 "Oh, that was hard to take. How could he do that to his loving, devoted, starving little doggy?"

Jane and I gave him a lot of attention and extra loving so he'd know he wasn't being punished or something was wrong.

🐕 "Yeah. How did that carefully thought-out strategy work for you? I got a major Press Release. It didn't work. All I saw was an empty food bowl. He had to feed me. It's in the agreement with the school. I was going to call Keith and tell him Daddy was neglecting me."

I got my cane and we left. I think he sensed something was up but not sure what. Jane brought Musket up to her and gave him kisses.

"Mommy loves you. I want you to be a good boy and make me proud. You'll be okay. Mommy will pick you up later."

🐕 "That did it. I knew something bad was going to happen. Mommy never said that before."

Jane headed over to her parents and I took my little worrywart into the vet. And right away his whole attitude changed. Melissa, one of his favorite nurses, smiled when we came in.

Did he start whining? Did he try to hide in a corner? Did he pull frantically at the leash begging to get away?

No, he went to the counter and gave Melissa The Look.

🐕 "Well she always gave me a treat. And since Daddy didn't love me anymore . . ."

Beggar boy never took his eyes off the bowl on the counter even when Melissa went over the procedures and paperwork with me. The only words I heard her say were 'possible anesthetic complications.'

Suddenly I was more nervous than Musket.

As I stood to leave, I pulled him to me and said, "Musket, Daddy loves you. You'll be fine and we'll pick you up later. Can I have a kiss?"

He never took his eyes off the bowl.

🐕 "Oh NOW you're paying attention to me. Too late. Melissa will feed me. You're leaving? Okay, bye. Now Melissa where were we?"

I walked home using the cane, which was no problem in daylight. But that was one long slow day.

🐕 "It wasn't slow where I was. They took me to yet another cage, and gave me a shot. A lot of people were looking at me and talking. I heard other dogs barking. Then Melissa patted me. I got really sleepy and . . ."

Jane picked him up from the vet on her way home.

She almost cried when she saw her baby with a big bandage wrapped around his chest. He didn't respond to her at all.

"He's going to be very lethargic and groggy for at least a day," the nurse told Jane. "He can have half his food if he wants but he'll probably just sleep."

"Oh you can bet on it . . ."

The nurse also told Jane that Musket whined most of the afternoon, and of course the staff were fawning over him. Musket garnered all the attention he could get, doped-up or not.

"I just wanted them to feel needed."

The good news was the mass they'd removed was definitely fatty tissue. Not cancerous. Dr. Gray said it was like a breast implant. Just one more and they'd be perfect for a pair of C cups.

Note: that was her joke, not mine.

"Well don't look at me for the second one, lady."

Jane tried to get some reaction from him but he just stood there, swaying as if in a stiff wind. They had to help him into the car.

"They did? I don't remember that. I was happy to see Mommy, but I was so sleepy and my butt wasn't listening to me. My tongue was asleep too."

When she drove into the garage I was happy my little buddy was home.

"Can you help get him out?" she asked me. "He's not really awake."

She wasn't kidding. I had to pick him up very gently and carry him into the house.

"Why is the world moving so much?"

The throw rug by the front door was the best place and we could be near him while we had dinner.

In all the years we've had Musket it was the first time he didn't sit by the table watching the tennis match.

Dr. Gray had assured us he'd be his old self in a day or so.

🐕 "I could hear them eating and I smelled the chicken pot pies. But I couldn't move. My side hurt and all I wanted to do was sleep.

Daddy was gonna owe me big."

The next 24 hours were different to say the least. I carried Musket up the stairs. Thank God I'd stuck to my weight training.

Jane put a thick towel on his bed and with some difficulty we got him into it, making sure the bandaged area was clear.

Sleep came hard for us that night.

But not for Musket. He was out cold. He was just going to have to sleep off all the happy juice they'd given him. He was one groggy doggy.

After seeing the vet

"The room kept spinning and I wanted it to stop."

At around eleven at night he started whining and Jane woke me.

"He's crying," she told me in a worried voice.

No arguments from me. "Okay, let's find out what he wants." Kneeling next to him I felt his body. He wasn't trembling or breathing hard. Ever since the seizure I was very sensitive to any odd signs.

"I wanted to go pee, and Daddy finally figured it out."

He was slow and wobbly going down the stairs, but he managed it. I went outside with him. He hadn't had any water or food for a full day so I was surprised he had to go.

But finally Mr. Wobbly came in. "Want something to drink, little buddy?"

"Hello? Anybody home? It's been a whole day."

I filled his bowl with fresh water and he went at it. He drank

And drank.

And drank.

I thought he might actually have been able to drink one of those vats the waitresses always gave him.

"I had to drink a lot before any made it into my stomach. My mouth was so dry the first quart didn't make it past my tongue."

Jane told me that after anesthesia patients were often very thirsty and I guess that went for dogs as well as people.

"What was your first clue?"

I helped him upstairs again and with little coaxing he was in his bed sleeping again. I could swear I heard sloshing noises.

"Nighty-night, Mommzzzzzz."

The next morning he was a little more awake, but still droopy. I fed him more than usual and he ate it but not with his normal vigor.

He wasn't yet his old self and Jane didn't expect any kisses. For all we knew he was still upset at being left at the vet all day.

🐕 "Yeah, I'd go with that, Einstein."

Jane drove over to her parents while I did the dishes and made the bed. Musket was never far from me in case he needed anything.

At noon I was letting him out to pee, when Jane drove in. Musket's tail was wagging as he went right to her and she bent down.

"Mommy get kisses?"

She sure did. That was the best thing we could have seen.

Musket was back.

🐕 "Hi Mommy! Did you miss me?"

He wouldn't have to wear the Elizabethan collar, but he would wear one of my T-shirts to protect his side.

🐕 "I've seen dogs wearing those ridiculous things and always felt sorry for them. Surely no one would to that to me."

Even though he was healing well, there would be no belly rubs for a while.

🐕 "Whatchu talkin' 'bout, Daddy? No belly rubs? Dang. It kept getting worse all the time."

Oh sure. I didn't hear him complaining about being carried upstairs, being given extra treats or lots of tender loving care.

🐕 "Oh, well . . . I've been sick. Cough, cough."

We took him over to Jane's parents. Of course Mom asked Musket how he was feeling and Dad, who was in the advanced stages of Alzheimer's, was puzzled about the shirt and why he couldn't give

Musket any belly rubs. But otherwise it was business as usual, a lot of attention and spoiling.

🐈 "I gave them both kisses but Daddy held me to make sure I didn't hurt myself."

He didn't go back to work for another week. I took that week off work to stay with him. After that Jane brought Musket with her to Nanny and Pop-pop's every day.

I used the old standby, my trusty white cane. Thanks to Miss Virginia's training I was fine.

But I'm not going to lie. I missed having him with me.

Musket's friends sent cards and letters to their favorite Guide dog.

'Get Well Musket' was on every one of the notes he received from his fans.

Jane had to read them because Musket was too busy being treated like royalty.

🐈 "Read the one from Sharon again, Mommy."

He grew stronger and more active. The area where the cyst had been began to fill with fluid. He didn't try to scratch or get at the scar but we were alert for it. When he was with me I kept my hearing aids cranked up as high as possible to hear the telltale jingle of his tags.

🐈 "Every time I tried to scratch Daddy hovered over me like a deranged paramedic.

'No, Musket, no.'

Okay Dr. Kildare, chill out. I wasn't going to touch it. When Daddy turned up his hearing aids he heard better than a bat."

I put him out on the balcony in the sun so the heat would help him heal. He was wearing an old black t-shirt and the fabric absorbed the sun's rays. He was in sun worshipper heaven.

🐈 "Kiss me, Mr. Sun."

He went with me to the museum for the Apollo 8 Anniversary celebration. Jane had to take Dad to the doctor, so Musket had to be with me. But she dropped us off so he didn't have to ride the bus. He wore a red t-shirt with 'Who's your Santa?' on it. His friends were happy to see Musket and of course he made new friends among the astronauts.

When he was able to wear the harness again I bought a thick sheepskin sleeve for the belly strap to protect the surgical site. He settled right back into his routine, while the fluid slowly drained off. Soon there was nothing to indicate he'd had any surgery at all.

A couple of years ago he did have to wear the Elizabethan collar. Another cyst grew on his left rear leg and it required more surgery. Twice, in fact, because he was chewing at the stitches. Dr. Gray needed to go back and re-open the incision and put in stronger sutures. To keep him from touching them we finally accepted the collar.

"I was miserable. That thing was so big I had trouble getting through doors and even tripped on it. I couldn't drink water unless Daddy held the bowl up for me. A whole week. I learned my lesson and never touched my stitches. Snort."

Jane and I knew he hated it but he did obey, even when I held it out for him to put his head in. But it was hardest not giggling when we heard him bump a doorway or table leg. Payback time.

Most recently he started growing several small warts on his face, back and legs. They weren't more than a nuisance, and some were left alone. But others were removed if they might have caused problems later on.

Yes, we loved him, warts and all.

"So why do you keep trying to remove them?"

All the medical issues Musket had made me think about how long he would be able to work for me. He has been very lucky. Some dogs I know have been seriously injured or suffered cancer, even heart problems.

No one wants to have a sick pet or Assistance animal and we're very alert for any signs of illness. But when the crisis was over and life picked up again, there was that tiny voice in my head asking the critical question.

'Should I shave my head before I go bald?'

No, not that one!

What will the future bring? The past has given Jane, me and all who know us a wonderful and memorable time with Musket. I wish it would last forever.

🐈 "You mean it won't?"

CHAPTER THIRTEEN

THE 401K-9 PLAN

An Assistance dog's lifetime can be more than a dozen years but its working life is often much shorter.

Labrador and Golden retrievers have become the *sine qua non* of Guide dogs. A Guide dog had to be at least 60 pounds in order to be strong enough to stop its full-grown adult handler in an emergency.

That's why you never see guide Chihuahuas. They'd have to be like a sled dog six-pack.

🐕 "I'd love to see that."

The other factors in favor of retrievers was their prospective working life, generally fewer health problems, and more gentle disposition than German Shepherds.

So how long would a Labrador be able to live and work? They're all different. Some had extraordinarily long lives, and could work many years beyond the norm.

I know of one Lab now working at the age of 13. He's been happily guiding his handler for over a decade.

🐕 "His poor aching paws."

But the average working life was about eight to nine years. And that means Musket has long since passed the halfway mark in his professional career.

🐕 "Hmmm. Maybe I better start talking to Daddy about that 401k-9 plan."

Everything has its Golden Age. The Golden Age of Flight, the Golden Age of Rock 'n' Roll, the Golden Age of Indoor Plumbing.

Oops.

🐕 "Caught you napping on that one, didn't he?"

Jane and I are in the Golden Age of Musket. He's still healthy, happy and spirited, and has only lost a little of his puppyish pep.

I'm sure he doesn't want to retire.

🐕 "Let's see. Hmmm. A nice retirement doghouse in Malibu might be nice. But I think Mommy would like a cabin in the Cascade Mountains. Oh, sorry Daddy. What were you saying?"

Ahem. Try not to hurt yourself getting into the Social Security line, old boy.

I don't know how long he'll be able to work. So far he's excellent. And but for his annoying trait of not picking up his toys he's still trainable.

🐕 "Why should I pick them up? That's why I keep him around."

But a day will come when I'll notice a slowing down, a reluctance to move.

I don't mean moving his furry butt when I'm trying to get past him, but when he hears the word 'Forward' and shows no enthusiasm. I may try the old 'carrot and stick' approach first. I'll tie a strip of chicken jerky on a stick extending from his harness.

🐕 "Hmm. I might give myself away if I go for it. Better to play the 'tired old dog role.'"

My first reaction will be to take him to the vet and see if he's okay, not hurting or having foot problems.

🐕 "Again with that howitzer of a thermometer! Okay I'll do it. I'm reaching for the stick, Daddy."

But if the vet tells me he's just showing his age, then I'll have to start making some hard decisions.

Guide Dogs for the Blind generally retains ownership of their graduate dogs. The policy was used in case the handler was not taking care of or was abusing the dog. The school could take the dog back.

🐕 "Does holding me while I get my temperature taken count as abuse?"

But one year after Musket came home with us, Jane and I applied for full ownership. It was mostly a paperwork matter, because he still received the veterinary stipend and full post-graduate services. But Jane and I wanted Musket to be totally ours.

When a Guide or Assistance dog retired, often the handler gave the dog back to the school so it would be available for adoption. The puppy raiser usually got first chance, but often a family who applied to the school to adopt a retired dog would take them.

Why give the dog up in the first place? Well they are pretty large dogs. And having two of them in an apartment might be difficult.

And of course there was the matter of a new dog in the house.

🐕 "Huh? What 'new dog?'"

Settle down, little buddy. Let me finish. Giving Musket up was never an option. We have room for more than one dog. And Musket is ours.

🐕 "Don't change the subject. What 'new dog?'"

Back to San Rafael

When I feel Musket may be slowing down to the point of not being able to work effectively, then it'll be time to call Keith Tomlinson. After getting a promise to drop the 'chick magnet' joke, I'll ask him to come and see what he thinks.

We'll walk with Musket for a little while. Possibly it's an odd behavior and he only needs a bit of reinforcement training.

But the day will come when Keith will tell me Musket should retire.

"Wait! Can we talk about this?"

It's not the end of the world, little buddy. Cheer up. You won't have to work anymore.

"But what will I do? It's all I know. It's not like I have a golden parachute!

What am I supposed to do, start a rock band? Go to law school? Work at McDonalds?"

Guide Dogs provides advice on the important issue of the transition from working to retired dog.

"Hmm. Wait a moment. That last one sounded okay. Working at McDonalds. I mean, they do sort of owe me . . ."

Not having gone through it and not knowing of any Guide dog handlers who have kept their first dog, I'm not sure what to expect.

But I can hazard a guess.

I'll apply to Guide Dogs for a new dog. And if my application is reviewed and they've forgotten my bad jokes, then we'll set a date for returning to San Rafael.

There will come a day when Musket won't wear the harness any more. It will be hung up, a tribute to his dedication and hard work, much as a medal for heroism would be for a veteran.

"Maybe my tan lines will finally fade."

As a re-train, I'll only be gone for three weeks, since the early skills and Juno training aren't needed.

Jane will have Musket at home with her. As a retired dog he won't have the same access rights he did when with me. But we'll have to accept that. It's not only fair to other dog handlers, it's the law.

His California Assistance Dog I.D. tag will be turned in.

This is getting harder to write than I thought. Let me wipe my eyes.

🐕 "I'm the one retiring and he's bawling!"

Graduation will be as emotional as the first time. Jane will be there with Musket, but her parents won't be there. This time Musket will be on the outer side of the patio railing.

When I step up to the microphone two things will happen.

I will not repeat the shameful non-performance of my first graduation. I already know what I will say.

The second thing? Musket will see me with another Guide dog.

🐕 "Hey Mommy, who's that strange dog on the patio with my daddy? Why is he wearing my harness?"

If you would like to know what I'll say, you're welcome to attend the graduation.

Or you can read on. It's cheaper and you won't need as many Kleenex.

After my new dog is presented to me (gender, breed and name to be determined later) I will accept him/her with a smile and probably a few tears.

"Thank you. The first time I stood here in 2002 I was so overcome with emotion I couldn't speak. To those who know me well it was like watching a modest Charlie Sheen.

What I had wanted to say then and will say today is thank you. Thank you all the team at Guide Dogs for giving so much of your time, effort and devotion to these wonderful and amazing animals. Thank you for giving me not one, but two beautiful guides to watch and protect me.

My first dog, Musket is here with my wife Jane. He's looking at me . . . no, he's sleeping. But if he were looking at me he'd be thinking, 'who's that dog with Daddy?"

Musket is retired now and can rest on his well-earned laurels. He's been the most loving, devoted and interesting animal I've ever known. Even though he won't be my guide he'll always be my fuzzy butt.

And for this new companion, this new 'little buddy' I have only this to say. When we get home you're going to have to endure Musket's confusion about not being the guide. But he'll get over it. Just remember this. Don't listen to a word he says!"

"Dang. I was hoping he wouldn't say that. Good speech Daddy, but can you drop the 'fuzzy butt' part? It's a little embarrassing."

Kanine Kudos

As the years go on, Musket will continue to slow down. And time will take its toll on his body and abilities, but his heart, his beautiful soul will always be strong and alive. I can't begin to understand how remarkable he really is. Everybody I know with a Guide dog believes theirs is the best. But even seasoned Guide dog handlers agree Musket is really something special.

I know the new dog will be well-trained, obedient, loyal, loving and hardworking. He or she will have their own special personality.

But they won't be another Musket. The hardest thing for me will be remembering that. The new dog deserves to be loved and accepted for their own abilities and gifts, not compared to its predecessor.

Musket is one helluva hard act to follow.

"Well come on, there just isn't any comparison, is there?"

With Musket I was able to go places, experience things, meet people and grow more than I ever could have done with a cane or even a sighted guide. In fact I'll say without reservation I couldn't have had such a wonderful life even if I wasn't blind.

Musket could never be called shy. Just being himself has brought so many rewards to our lives they won't fit in any single book.

“So what’s next? *Confessions Two? The Return of Musket? Musket: The Next Generation?* How about something New Age, like *Musket: The Retro Years*?”

Daddy Kiss

He’s well known now, and a little conceited, but if this book is the success I hope it will be, Musket will be darn near insufferable. Not as bad as Charlie Sheen but close.

We may learn what Paparazzi are really like.

🐕 "Okay boys, over here. Make sure you get my good side. Daddy, can you move over just a bit? You're blocking my light."

God help us.

The people he loves and are loved by will always remember his kisses, his beautiful face and playful spirit.

Jane and I will love him forever. He's our baby and the center of our lives. More than a working dog or even a pet, he's a friend, a comic, a beggar, a tease, a protector, a favored grandchild, a healer, a spoiled kid, a TV star, an ambassador, a friend to astronauts and veterans, a chick magnet, a heart-breaker and a scene stealer.

He's also my little buddy.

I had to go blind in order to get Musket.

It was well worth it.

It was a very good day when God gave Musket to the world.

🐕 "Sniff. Thank you Daddy. I love you too. Can I have a treat now?"

CPSIA information can be obtained at www.ICGtesting.com
Printed in the USA
LVOW031946301211

261841LV00002B/1/P